The First Book of

PC Paintbrush IV

The First Book of

PC Paintbrush IV

Deke McClelland

FIRST EDITION
FIRST PRINTING—1990

International Standard Book Number: 0-672-27324-1
Library of Congress Catalog Card Number: 90-62052

Acquisitions Editor: *Scott Arant*
Manuscript Editor: *Justine Couts*
Production Coordinator: *Steve Noe*
Cover Artist: *Held & Diedrich Design*
Illustrator: *Don Clemons*
Production: *Wm. D. Basham, Claudia Bell, Jill D. Bomaster, Brad Chinn, Sally Copenhaver, Travia Davis, Marj Hopper, Tami Hughes, Jennifer Matthews, Joe Ramon, Dennis Sheehan, Bruce Steed, Mary Beth Wakefield*
Indexer: *Joelynn Gifford*
Technical Reviewer: *C. Herbert Feltner*

Printed in the United States of America

Contents

6 *Adding Text, 169*

7 *Special Effects, 203*

8 *Printing a Painting, 237*

Introduction

When you think of graphics software for the PC, chances are that PC Paintbrush is the first name that comes to mind. Released in 1983, PC Paintbrush (version 1.0) was not only the first PC painting program but also the first PC software to run in color.

In the years since, PC Paintbrush has gained wide acceptance, its user base of 1.5 million installations making it one of the most popular and respected graphics programs in use on any computer. The enormous sales of the program are due in large part to the bundling of PC Paintbrush with various peripheral devices, such as the original Microsoft mouse, now a standard for PC pointing devices, and Techmar's 16-color graphics adapter board.

The acceptance of PC Paintbrush is now universal. Its native PCX file format is supported by almost every desktop publishing program running on the PC, including such luminaries as Aldus PageMaker, Ventura Publisher, and WordPerfect. Other graphics programs also read the PCX file format, including AutoCAD, Harvard Graphics, Corel Draw, Micrografx Designer, Adobe Illustrator, and many others too numerous to mention.

Since version 1.0, each upgrade of PC Paintbrush has delivered additional refinements and features. But no upgrades have proven so dramatic as PC Paintbrush IV and PC Paintbrush IV Plus, both of which offer more powerful commands, an enhanced drawing environment, a diverse color palette that can be highly customized, and expanded photo-retouching capabilities. As we embark upon the second full decade of personal computers, no other painting program packs supreme graphics control with such strong potential. PC Paintbrush was a trail-blazer in 1983; version IV will carry you well into the bit-mapped future.

Who This Book Is For

PC Paintbrush is a simple program to use. Most people can create basic drawings after working in the program two or three times. The user interface is intuitive, designed to mimic the pencil and paper environment familiar to most of us since grade school. Even if you haven't drawn in years, you'll find that using PC Paintbrush to draw is like getting back on a bike—it's one of those skills you simply never forget.

But even advanced technology cannot turn doodling into commercially viable artwork. If you want to create quality type and graphics for either printed or presentational material, you must know more than how to draw a squiggly line. In this book, we walk you through PC Paintbrush's extensive capabilities, demonstrating ways you can create high-quality artwork and save time in the process.

Only rudimentary computer knowledge is required. If you know little more than how to turn on your PC and load DOS, you will find this book easy to follow. We explain PC Paintbrush in a straightforward and concise manner so that you can become a proficient computer artist as quickly as possible and don't get bogged down in the unnecessary detail so often confusing to beginners.

We cover two similar ZSoft products in this book: PC Paintbrush IV and PC Paintbrush IV Plus. If you use other ZSoft products such as PC Paintbrush Plus for Windows, Publisher's Paintbrush, or an older version of PC Paintbrush, you will still find this book useful. Because special icons point out the new features available in PC Paintbrush IV, it's a simple matter to skip over these features and continue on to the information pertinent to your program.

Conventions

We've employed the following conventions in this book to make it easier for you to understand PC Paintbrush and to use this book as a handy reference guide:

Q This icon indicates *Quick Steps*, short and easy-to-follow instructions that explain step-by-step how to perform common tasks—like starting PC Paintbrush or backing up PC Paintbrush files to disk. You can find Quick Steps either by scanning the text for the Quick Steps icon or by referring to the alphabetical list of Quick Steps and their page numbers on the inside front cover.

4 This icon points out the new features that are available in PC Paintbrush IV. If you are familiar with earlier versions of PC Paintbrush, you can become acquainted quickly with version IV's expanded capabilities by browsing through each chapter for the sections marked by this icon.

+ This icon indicates features available exclusively to users of PC Paintbrush IV *Plus*. For the most part, these are halftoning and special-effects features. Users of PC Paintbrush IV can skip these paragraphs.

- Chapter introductions and summaries help you quickly identify the major topics covered in a chapter.
- Notes, tips and cautions are boxed to attract your attention.

Acknowledgements

My thanks to the following people for their help in making this book possible:

Scott Arant
Chelsea
Justine Couts

Dan Craiguloff
Charles, Vickie, and Catherine Pheasant
Rachel Rogers
Tim Rohrer
Carol Steier
Juan Thompson
Kathi Townes
and Elizabeth Pheasant

Trademarks

All terms in this book that are known to be trademarks or service marks are listed below. In addition, terms suspected of being trademarks or service marks have been appropriately capitalized. Neither the author nor Howard W. Sams & Company can attest to the accuracy of this information. Use of a term in this book should not be regarded as affecting the validity of any trademark or service mark.

Adobe Illustrator and PostScript are registered trademarks of Adobe Systems, Inc.

Aldus and PageMaker are registered trademarks of Aldus Corporation.

Apple, LaserWriter, and Macintosh are registered trademarks of Apple Computer, Inc.

AutoCAD is a registered trademark of Autodesk, Inc.

Corel Draw is a trademark of Corel Systems Corporation.

Epson is a registered trademark of Epson America Corporation.

HP and LaserJet are registered trademarks of Hewlett-Packard Company.

IBM is a registered trademark of International Business Machines Corporation.

MacPaint is a registered trademark of Claris Corporation.

Micrografx is a registered trademark and Micrografx Designer is a trademark of Micrografx, Inc.

Microsoft and MS-DOS are registered trademarks of Microsoft Corporation.

Xerox, Diablo, and Ventura Publisher are registered trademarks of Xerox Corporation.

ZSoft and PC Paintbrush are registered trademarks and PC Paintbrush IV, PC Paintbrush Plus, PC Paintbrush IV Plus, and Publisher's Paintbrush are trademarks of ZSoft Corporation.

Chapter 1

Getting Started

What You Will Learn

1

- *Installing Paintbrush on your computer*
- *Starting the program from a hard drive or floppy disks*
- *Using the mouse and menus*
- *Getting help*
- *Quitting Paintbrush*

This chapter focuses on getting Paintbrush up and running on your computer and becoming acquainted with its user interface. You will learn how to use the mouse to access menu commands, how to get help, and how to quit Paintbrush and return to DOS. If you are new to Paintbrush or personal computers in general, you will find this information essential to understanding future chapters.

Installing and Starting PC Paintbrush

Before you can use Paintbrush for the first time, you must *install* the program on your computer's hard drive, or if you don't have a hard drive, on two 720K or higher-density floppy disks.

If you know that Paintbrush has *not* been installed on your computer, skip to the section *Installing PC Paintbrush.*

If you or someone else have already installed Paintbrush on your computer, skip to the section *Starting PC Paintbrush* to begin using the program.

If aren't sure whether or not Paintbrush is installed, follow the steps in the *Starting PC Paintbrush* section. If Paintbrush does not start successfully, go back to the *Installing PC Paintbrush* section and install the program.

Installing PC Paintbrush

To use Paintbrush, you need an EGA or VGA display adapter, a mouse or other pointing device, a hard drive or two 720K floppy drives, and DOS 3.0 or higher. You will also need to know the models of your monitor, pointing device, and other equipment in order to answer the questions asked by Paintbrush during the installation procedure. If you don't know this information, refer to the manuals that came with your equipment. Make sure all necessary peripherals, such as your mouse or printer, are hooked up to your computer and installed properly on either your hard drive or floppy Startup disk. If you are going to install Paintbrush on floppy disks, you will also need two formatted floppy disks.

Q Installing PC Paintbrush

1. If you have not done so already, turn on your computer.	If you start your computer with DOS installed on a hard drive, the standard `c>` prompt appears on screen. If you start your computer with DOS on a floppy disk, your prompt reads `a>`.
2. To install Paintbrush on a hard drive, insert the original (better yet, a copy of the original) Paintbrush Setup disk in drive A. Type `a:` at the DOS prompt and press Enter.	Changes the current drive to drive A.

If you don't have a hard drive, remove the DOS Startup disk from drive A, then insert the Paintbrush Setup disk in drive A.

3. Type pbsetup at the DOS a> prompt and press Enter. — Runs the Paintbrush Setup program. A series of instructions appear on screen and you are asked to identify the display adapter, pointing device, and printer you are using. You are also instructed to swap disks periodically.

4. Follow all instructions and answer questions in the order they appear. — Installs Paintbrush on a hard drive or on two 720K floppy disks (referred to as "Run Disks" A and B). Returns you to the DOS prompt when you finish.

5. Type paint and press Enter. — Starts Paintbrush. □

> **Note:** If you installed Paintbrush on floppy disks, you will need to copy the font and picture files manually from the Paintbrush Setup disk to your disk if you want to access them. The Setup program does not copy these for you automatically.

Starting PC Paintbrush

The way you start Paintbrush depends on whether you've installed the program on a hard drive or on floppy disks.

Q Starting PC Paintbrush from a Hard Drive

1. If you have not done so already, turn on your computer. — If DOS is installed on the C drive, the standard c> prompt appears on screen.

2. Type cd\pbrush at the DOS prompt and press Enter. (If you specified a different — Changes the current directory to the Paintbrush directory Pbrush or to the directory

	directory name when you installed Paintbrush, type that name instead after cd\.)	where you installed Paintbrush.
3.	Type paint and press Enter.	Starts Paintbrush. ☐

Q Starting PC Paintbrush from a Floppy Drive

1.	If you have not done so already, turn on your computer with the DOS Startup disk in drive A.	The a> prompt appears on screen.
2.	Remove the Startup disk from Drive A. Insert Run Disks A and B, created during the Paintbrush installation procedure, into drives A and B. Do not try to run Paintbrush off the Setup disk.	
3.	Type paint and press Enter.	Starts Paintbrush. ☐

Did It Work?

If you installed and started Paintbrush successfully, an hourglass will appear on the screen with the message "Loading-Please wait...." Moments later, the screen will display the Paintbrush *desktop* shown in Figure 1.1. (If you're using Paintbrush Plus, the *dialog box* in the center of the screen will look slightly different.) Press Escape twice to remove from the screen, or *hide*, the dialog boxes that Paintbrush automatically displays when you first start the program. Your screen should look like the screen shown in Figure 1.2. Then proceed to the *Using The Mouse* section which follows.

If, after you type paint and press Enter, a message reading Bad command or file name appears instead of the Paintbrush desktop, the PAINT.BAT file is missing from the current directory. You are either in the wrong directory or the program has not been installed correctly.

Other error messages are also possible. For example, Paintbrush may not be able to find your mouse *driver*, the program file which operates the mouse, or you may have specified the

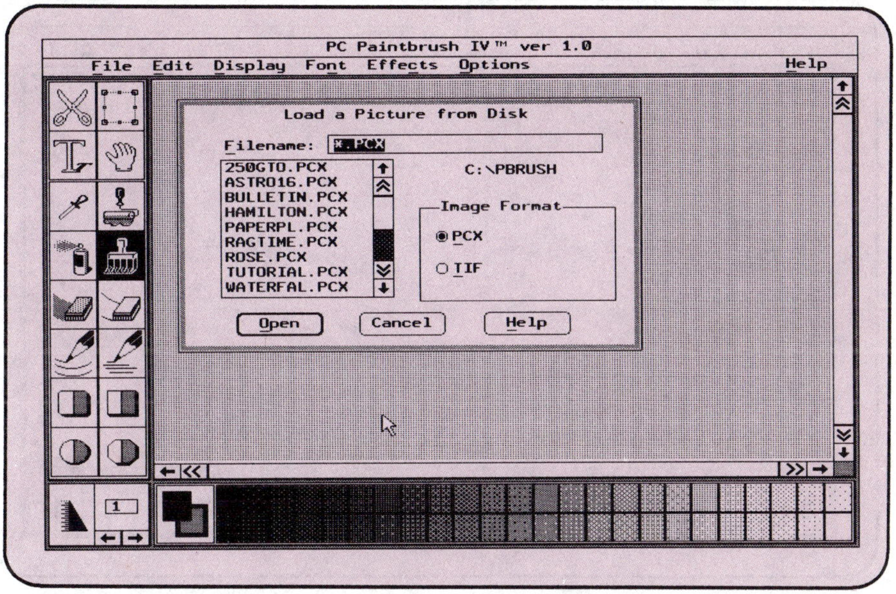

Figure 1.1 The PC Paintbrush desktop which appears when you start the program gives you the option to load an existing painting.

wrong monitor during the installation procedure, in which case the program may lock up when you first run it. Fortunately, Paintbrush allows you to change the mouse, monitor, or printer settings at any time simply by rerunning the PbSetup program from the directory on your hard drive that contains Paintbrush or from your copy of the Paintbrush Setup disk.

If error messages appear indicating either insufficient memory or other memory problems, rerun the PbSetup program and select the answer "None" when asked for your printer model. Paintbrush will then require less memory to run because it will use a smaller version of its memory-resident Frieze program, called "TinyFrieze," which is discussed in Chapter 9.

Memory problems are common if you try to use Paintbrush IV with DOS 4.0 or higher. In this case, ZSoft recommends that you deactivate any shells or memory-resident utilities in your CONFIG.SYS and AUTOEXEC.BAT files. If despite your efforts, Paintbrush still does not start or operate satisfactorily, call ZSoft Technical Support at (404) 428-0008, extension 371. If you have a modem, you can call the Technical Support bulletin board at

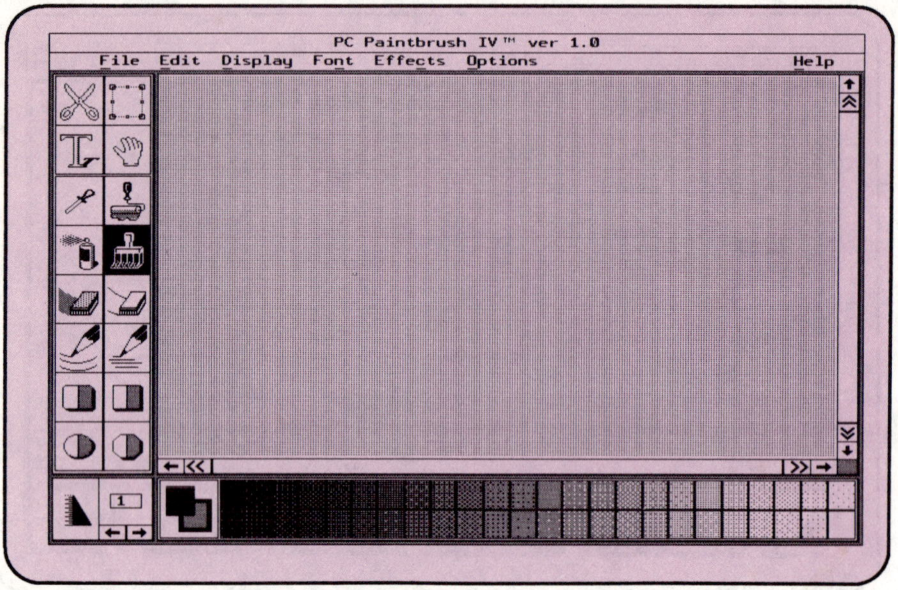

Figure 1.2 The PC Paintbrush desktop after you press Escape twice to hide the dialog boxes.

(404) 427-1045. Technical Support hours are 10 A.M. to 6 P.M. Eastern Time, weekdays only, the equivalent of 7 A.M. to 3 P.M. Pacific Time. Get your calls in early if you live on the West Coast.

> **Tip:** If you purchase Paintbrush IV Plus, you'll have fewer memory problems.

Using the Mouse

Throughout this book, the term *mouse* is used to denote any mouse-compatible pointing device, including drawing roller balls, tablets, light pens, and joy sticks.

If you already know how to use a mouse to perform such operations as *clicking*, *double-clicking*, and *dragging*, skip to the *Using Menus* section. Otherwise, read on.

Mouse Operations

Your mouse will have either two or three buttons. If it is a three-button mouse, the center button will be inoperative inside Paintbrush. Only the left and right buttons can be used to access Paintbrush's many tools and commands.

If you have never used a mouse, you may want to consult the documentation that came with the mouse for specific operating instructions. Get a feel for the mouse by moving it around. Position the mouse in relation to your computer so that the mouse is easily accessible. Since some Paintbrush functions don't require a mouse, you will be switching your right or left hand (depending on whether you position the mouse to the right or left of the keyboard) between the keyboard and the mouse on a regular basis. For efficiency's sake, place the mouse within easy reach so you don't have to grope around for it.

Now press the left mouse button and immediately release it. This quick pressing motion is called *clicking*. If you press the right mouse button and quickly release it, you are *right-clicking*. Other clicking variations are possible. If you press and release the left mouse button twice in rapid succession, you are *double-clicking*. You can also press a key while clicking with the mouse. For example, if you press the Shift key, click the left mouse button, and then release the Shift key, you are *Shift-clicking*. All clicking variations are performed while the mouse is stationary.

In addition, there are two fundamental mouse movements. *Moving* the mouse means to move it without pressing any button, and *dragging* the mouse means to press the left mouse button, move your mouse, and then release the button. Performed infrequently, right-dragging means to hold down the right mouse button while moving the mouse.

If the mouse does not seem to be operating correctly from the outset, it may not be installed correctly. If the mouse stops working after you've used it for a while, it more likely needs cleaning or servicing. In either case, refer to the documentation included with the mouse or call the dealer from whom the mouse was purchased.

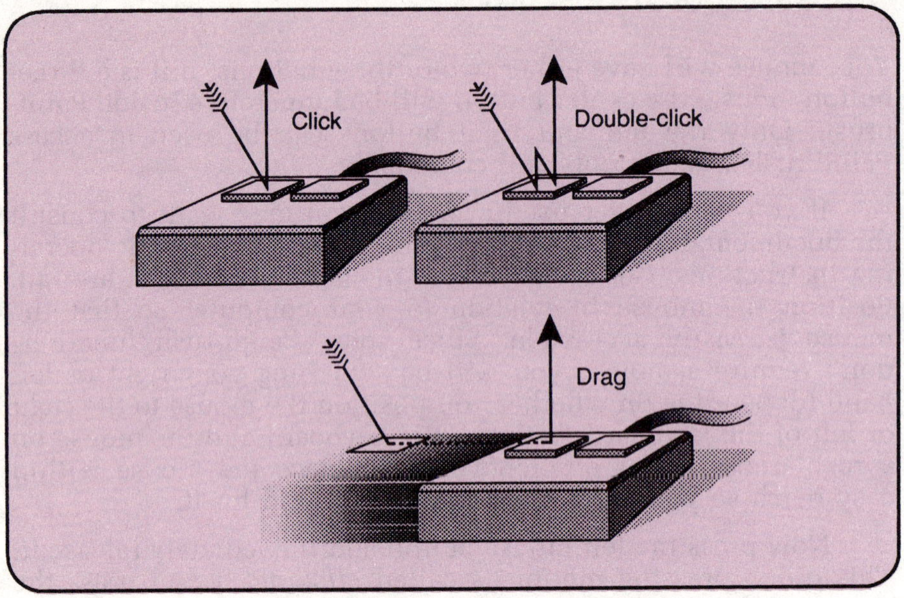

Figure 1.3 Several mouse operations.

The Cursor

On the Paintbrush desktop, a marker called the *cursor* tracks the movement of the mouse. The cursor appears as a dot inside the large gray area in the center of the desktop; if you move the cursor outside this area by moving the mouse, the dot becomes an arrow.

The cursor is the most important element in Paintbrush. Depending on its position, it allows you to draw, choose commands, select options, or click on buttons—in short, the cursor is your visual guide to all actions that you perform with the mouse.

In the sections which follow, you will position the cursor then perform other mouse operations to choose commands, get help, and quit Paintbrush.

Using Menus

When you start Paintbrush, a *caption bar* which reads `PC Paintbrush IV ver 1.0` or `PC Paintbrush IV Plus ver 1.0` appears across the top of the Paintbrush desktop. Under the caption bar is a *menu bar* containing the names of the seven Paintbrush menus: File, Edit, Display, Font, Effects, Options, and Help. Each menu offers a different set of *commands* which control different aspects of a painting.

4 You can view a menu by clicking with the cursor positioned on the menu name or by pressing the Alt key together with the key corresponding to the underlined letter in the menu name. For example, if you press the Alt key and the F keys simultaneously, the File menu will display, as shown in Figure 1.4. The File menu will be slightly different if you have Paintbrush Plus.

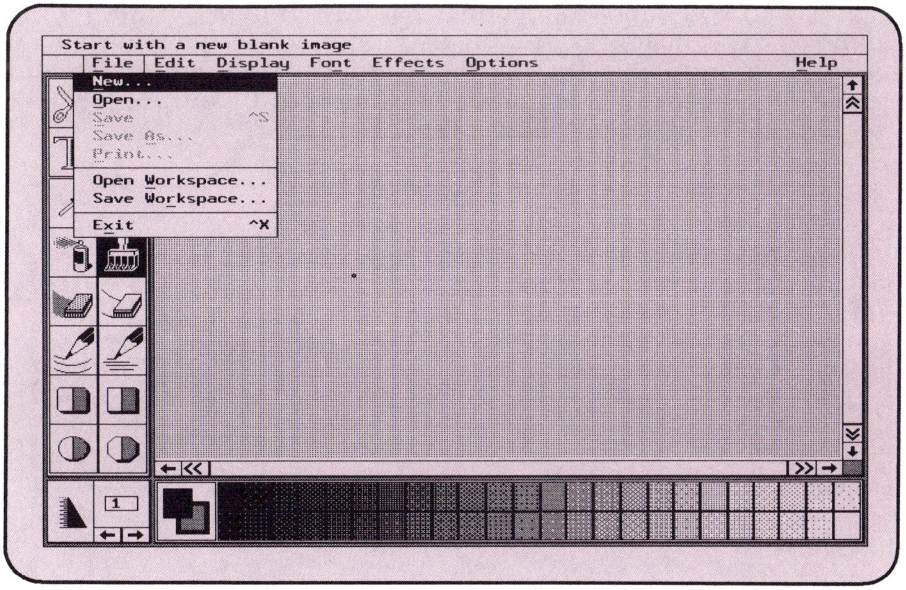

Figure 1.4 Display the File menu by clicking on the File menu name or by pressing Alt-F.

Each command in a menu performs the specific function indicated by its name. To *choose* a command, click on its name after you display the appropriate menu. Or you can type the key corresponding to the underlined letter in the menu name. For example, since the letter "O" in the Open command is underlined, you can press the O key to choose the Open command. You cannot choose menu commands which are *dimmed*. For example, in Figure 1.4, the Save command appears dimmed, indicating that it can't be used at this time.

> **Tip:** You can activate any menu, command, or option from the keyboard simply by pressing the Alt key, typing the appropriate underlined character, then releasing the Alt key. In the case of all commands and many options, you don't even have to press the Alt key, but it won't hurt if you do.

If you want to hide the menu currently displayed, move the cursor off the menu and click elsewhere on the desktop or simply press Escape.

When you choose a command followed by an ellipsis (...), a *dialog box* appears, as shown in Figure 1.5, requesting you to provide Paintbrush with additional information before the command is performed. Commands not followed by ellipses are performed as soon as you choose them.

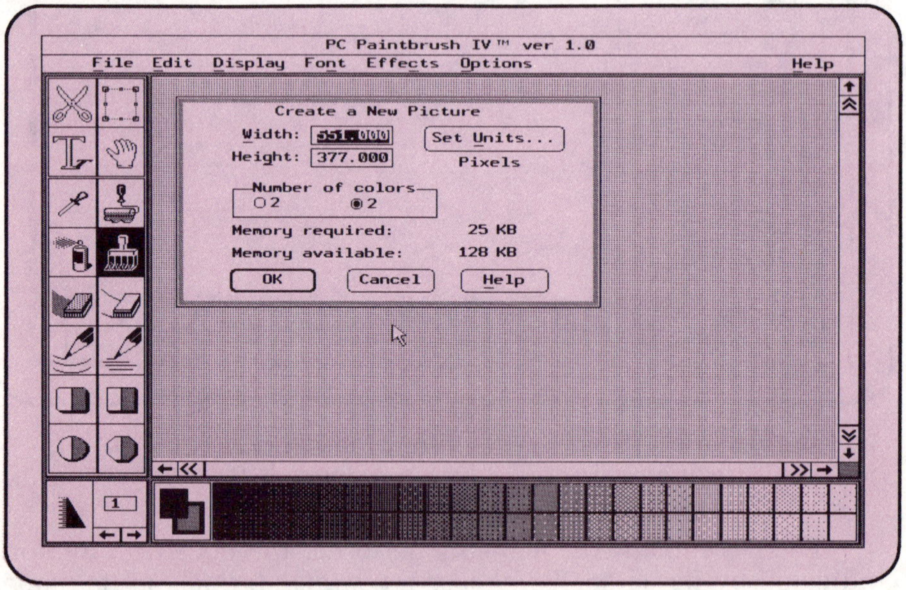

Figure 1.5 The dialog box that displays when you choose the New... command.

Notice in Figure 1.4 that letters preceded by carets (^) appear to the right of some command names. The caret symbol represents the Control key. You can access commands designated in this manner without having to first display their menus by pressing the Control key together with the key corresponding to the letter after the caret. For example, if the Save command were active, you could choose the Save command without first displaying its menu by pressing Control-S. Control-key combinations are called *keyboard equivalents*. Refer to the inside back cover for a complete list of keyboard equivalents.

Getting Help

4 If you ever become hopelessly confused using Paintbrush or merely have a question about a tool or command, you can avail yourself of on-line help, most of it new to version IV. Chances are, the program has many of the answers you're looking for.

The Caption Bar

The caption bar across the top of the screen is a ready source of information. For example, press Alt-F or click on the File menu name to display the File menu. The New... command will appear *highlighted*; that is, white against a black background. Notice that the text in the caption bar has changed from the name of the program (`PC Paintbrush`, etc.) to `Start with a new blank image`, which describes the function of the New... command. Press the Down Arrow key to highlight the next command, Open.... Now the caption bar reads `Get a new image from disk`.

Press Escape to hide the menu. Now position the cursor over the Scissors tool located to the left just below the File menu. The text in the caption bar reads `Cut, copy, or change a non-rectangular area of the screen`, which summarizes the functions of the Scissors tool. The caption bar also provides abbreviated information on the other elements of the Paintbrush desktop.

This kind of help is called *context-sensitive help* because the help messages appearing on screen change to reflect your current

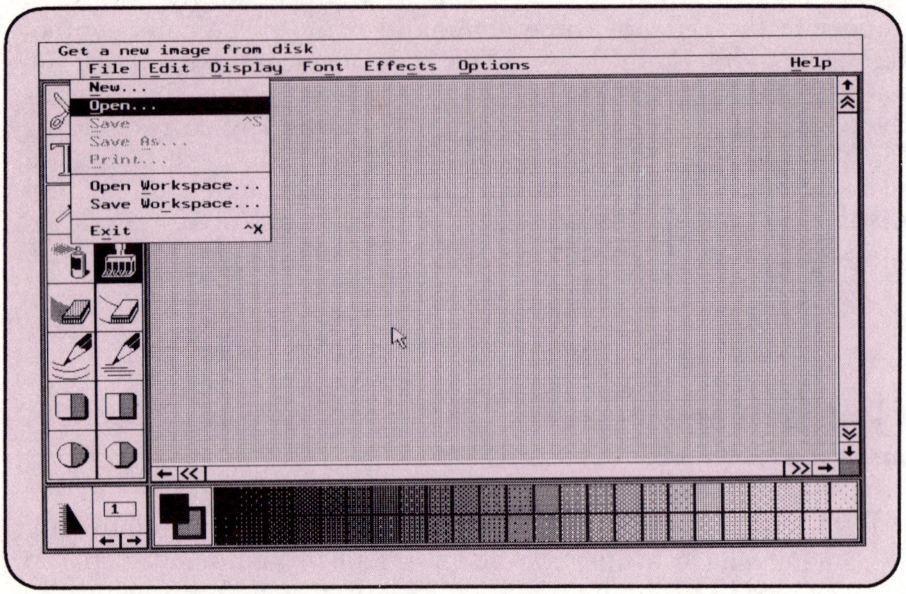

Figure 1.6 The caption bar explains the purpose of the highlighted command.

location inside the Paintbrush program. Depending on your computer system, the context-sensitive help feature can slow Paintbrush down, such that menus are slower to display and so on. If you get tired of seeing the caption bar change as you choose commands and select tools, you can turn this feature off by choosing the Context-Sensitive Help command from the Help menu, which is discussed in the *Other Help Commands* section.

Tool Help

Paintbrush also provides a method for finding out more detailed information about a tool than is shown in the caption bar. For example, right-click the Scissors tool to display the Paintbrush IV Help System dialog box, shown in Figure 1.7. The large *scrolling text field* inside the dialog box contains a description of how the tool works and what it does. To display additional information about the Scissors tool, click the down arrow icon on the *scroll bar* to the right of the field to scroll down one line of type. Or click the down double-arrow icon to scroll an entire page.

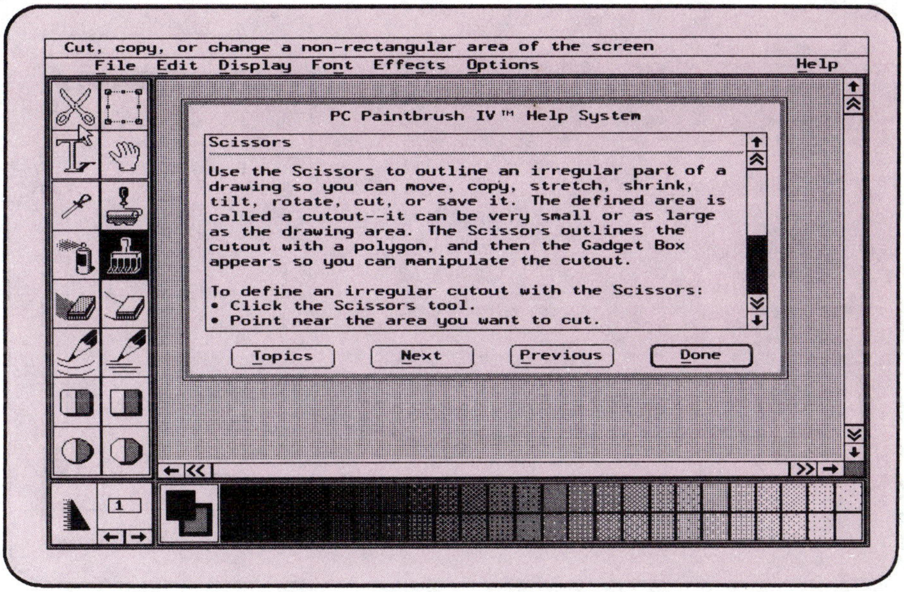

Figure 1.7 The Help System dialog box for the Scissors tool.

To display information about a different tool, click the Next button inside the dialog box or press the N key. The scrolling text field now displays information about the Gadget Box tool, the tool to the right of the Scissors tool in the toolbox.

To redisplay the information about the Scissors tool, click the Previous button or press the P key. Or click the Next button again to display information about the Text tool, the tool immediately below the Scissors tool.

Click the Topics button to display the Help Index, discussed in the section which follows. Click the Done button to hide the Help System dialog box and return to the desktop.

The Help Index

You can also access the Help System and Help Index dialog boxes, as well as alter certain help settings, by choosing commands from the Help menu, shown in Figure 1.8. Press Alt-H or click on the menu name to display the Help menu.

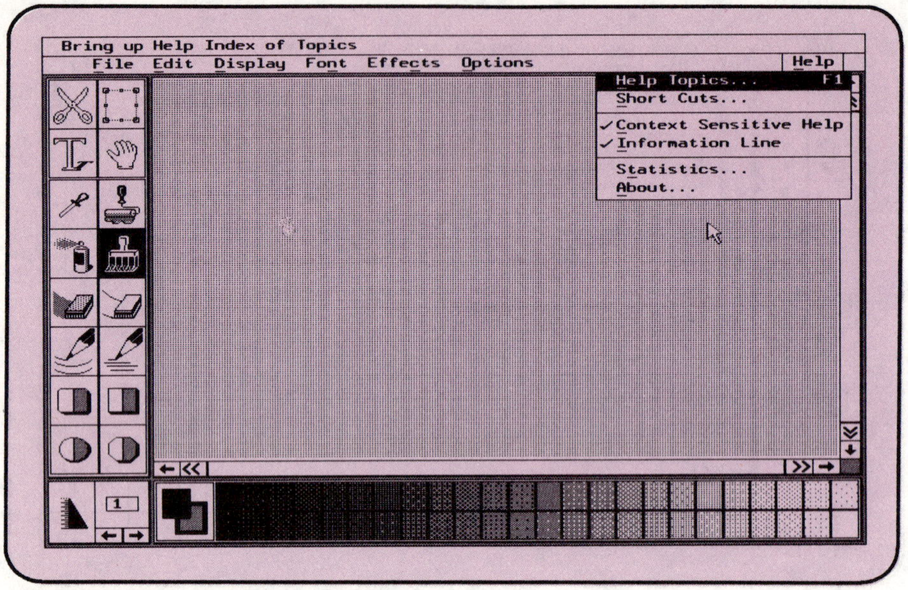

Figure 1.8 The Help menu.

Choose the Help Topics command (from the Help menu) or press the F1 key (from the desktop) to display the Help Index shown in Figure 1.9. A scrollable text field displays a partial list of the many help topics, which include tools, menus, and general information such as using the mouse or getting technical support.

Q Using the Help Index

1. Click on the scroll bar arrows on the right side of the text field or drag in the scroll bar. — Scrolls the list of topics up or down.
2. Click on a topic that interests you. (Or double-click a topic.) — Highlights the topic selected. (First click highlights topic; second click displays help information.)
3. Select the View button by clicking on it, by pressing the V key, or by pressing Enter. — The Help System dialog box displays information about the selected topic.

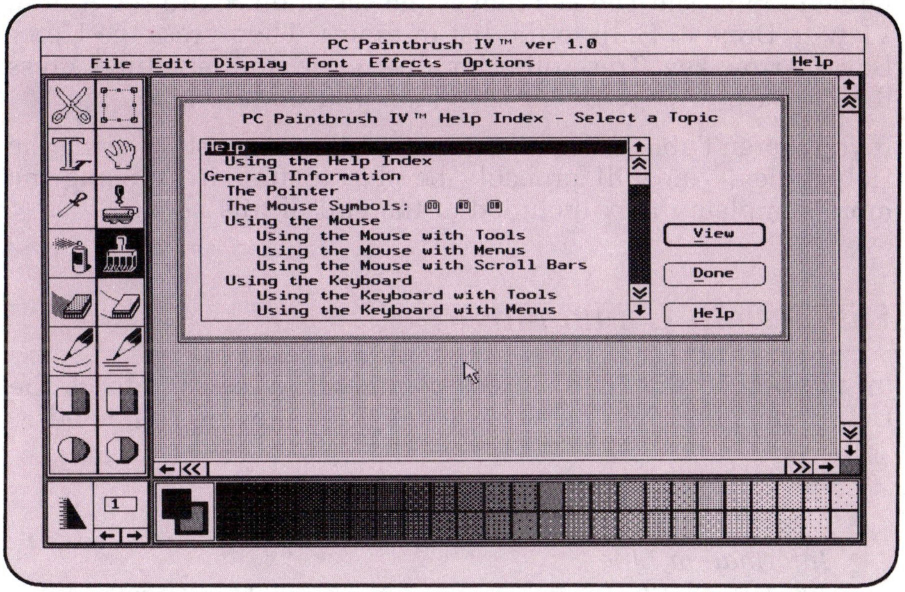

Figure 1.9 The Help Index dialog box.

4.	Click or drag the scroll bar.	Scrolls the information about the topic up or down.
5.	Select the Next or Previous button.	Displays information about the next or previous help topics in the Help Index.
6.	Select the Topics button.	Removes the Help System dialog box and redisplays the Help Index. (Useful if you didn't find the information you were looking for in this topic and want to review the list of other topics.)
7.	Select the Done button from the Help Index or Help System dialog box or press Escape.	Returns you to the Paintbrush desktop. ☐

✚ Paintbrush Plus offers a fast method to scroll up and down the Help Index without moving the cursor. First press the Tab key until an underline appears beneath the currently highlighted topic. The Tab key moves the selection round robin from View to Done to Help to the list of topics. Then press the Up or Down Arrow key. To scroll up or down five lines at a time, press the Page Up or Page Down keys after you underline a topic.

If you weren't able to find the answer to your question using the Help Index, you will probably be able to find it by using the more complete index included at the end of this book.

Other Help Commands

In addition to the Help Topics command, which produces the Help Index, the Help menu provides the following commands:

- *Short Cuts...*
- *Context Sensitive Help*
- *Information Line*
- *Statistics...*
- *About...*

The *Short Cuts...* command displays the Help System dialog box, shown in Figure 1.10, which contains information about keyboard equivalents (discussed in this chapter in the *Using Menus* section). If the Help menu is displayed you can choose the Short Cuts... command by clicking on the command name or by pressing the S key. If the Help Index is on screen, you can display the dialog box by double-clicking the Short Cuts topic. If you are elsewhere in the desktop, you can select Short Cuts by pressing Alt-H followed by the S key.

If a check mark precedes the *Context Sensitive Help* command, choosing it (from the Help menu) or pressing Alt-H followed by the C key (from the desktop) turns off the context-sensitive help information that appears in the caption bar when you move the cursor over tools or highlight commands. If no check mark precedes this command, choosing it turns on the context-sensitive help information.

If a check mark precedes the *Information Line* command, choosing it (from the Help menu) or pressing Alt-H followed by the I key (from the desktop) turns off the *information line* that appears in the caption bar when you move the cursor in the drawing window. If no check mark precedes this command,

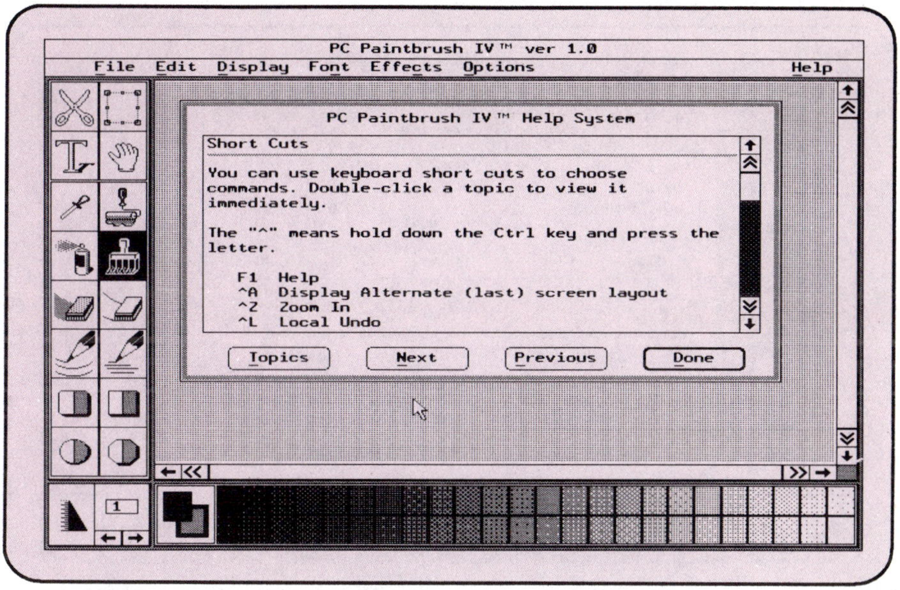

Figure 1.10 The Help System dialog box for keyboard equivalents.

choosing it turns on the information line. To learn more about the information line, refer to the next chapter.

Choosing the *Statistics...* command (from the Help menu) or pressing Alt-H followed by the T key (from the desktop) displays the Current Operating Statistics dialog box, shown in either Figure 1.11 or Figure 1.12, depending on whether you're using Paintbrush or Paintbrush Plus. This dialog box displays how Paintbrush is configured for your computer, including the monitor and printer options you specified in the installation procedure. It also shows the amount of memory available. You cannot change any of the settings in this dialog box.

Choosing the *About...* command (from the Help menu) or pressing Alt-H followed by the A key (from the desktop) displays a dialog box listing copyright and version information for your Paintbrush program, as shown in Figure 1.13.

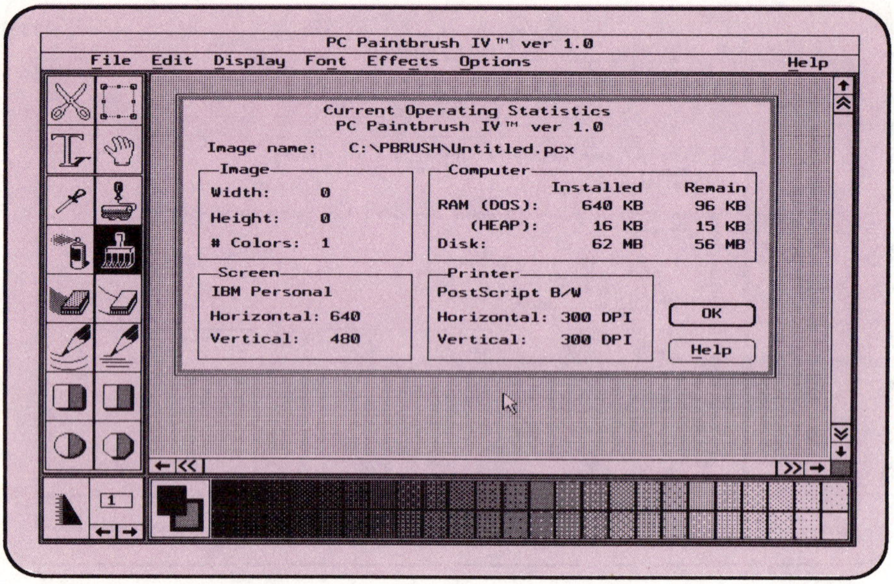

18

Figure 1.11 The Current Operating Statistics dialog box as it appears in PC Paintbrush IV.

Quitting PC Paintbrush

If you want to use a different program than Paintbrush, or if you want to stop working on your computer altogether, you must first *quit* the Paintbrush program. This will return you to DOS. You can quit Paintbrush using either the mouse or the keyboard. The keyboard route is faster, but you may want to use the mouse until you are more familiar with Paintbrush. Both methods of quitting the program are described in the following Quick Steps. The fastest method for quitting Paintbrush, which uses the keyboard, is described in the *Quick Quit* section following the Quick Steps.

Q Quitting PC Paintbrush Using the Mouse

1. Click on the File menu name in the menu bar.	The File menu displays.

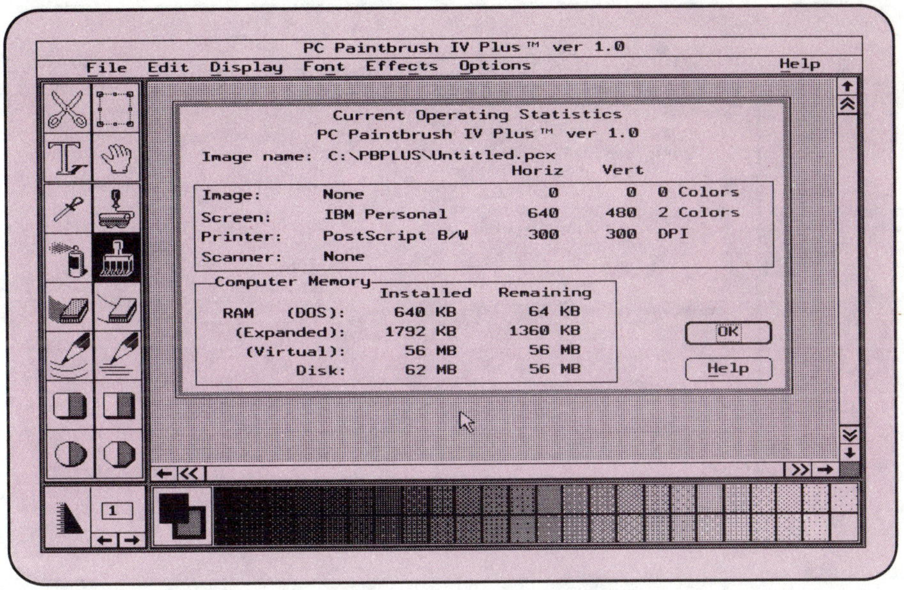

Figure 1.12 The Current Operating Statistics dialog box as it appears in PC Paintbrush IV Plus.

2. Move the cursor down the command list and click on the Exit command.

   Returns you to DOS. If you created a new painting or made changes to an existing painting, the alert box shown in Figure 1.14 appears, asking if you want to save your changes.

3. Click the Yes, No, or Cancel button in response to the alert box.

   Clicking Yes displays the Save dialog box so that you can save your changes. Clicking No tells Paintbrush not to save the new painting or changes made to an existing painting. Clicking Cancel cancels the quit operation and redisplays the Paintbrush desktop. □

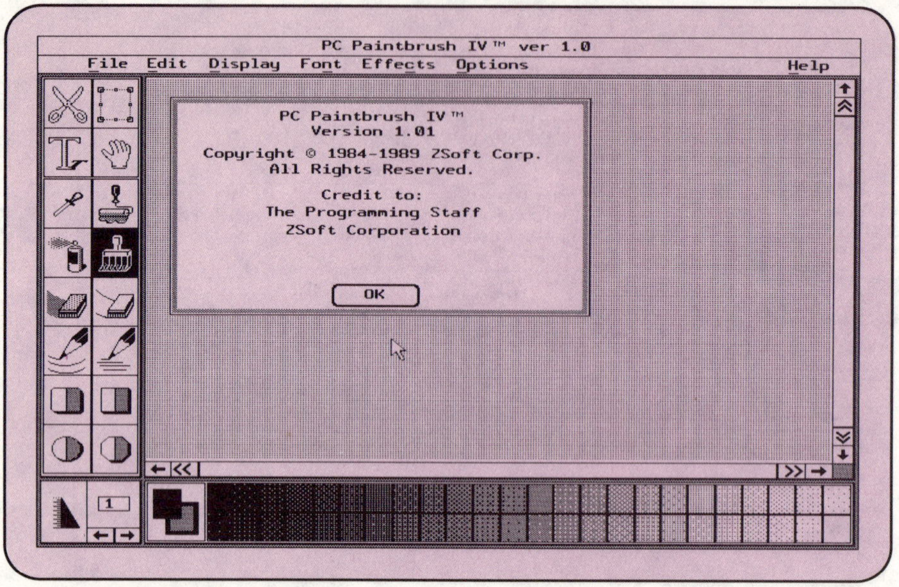

Figure 1.13 The About PC Paintbrush IV dialog box.

Q Quitting PC Paintbrush from the Keyboard

1. Press Alt-F to display the File menu.
2. Press the X key to choose the Exit command.

   Returns you to DOS. If you created a new painting or made changes to an existing painting, the alert box shown in Figure 1.14 appears, asking if you want to save your changes.
3. Press the Y key, the N key, the C key or Escape in response to the alert box. In Paintbrush Plus, you can also press the Tab key to move a dotted rectangular *marquee* from one button to the next. When the marquee sits on the button of your choice, press the Spacebar to select it.

   The Y key displays the Save dialog box so that you can save your painting. The N key selects the No button and tells Paintbrush not to save your painting. The C key or Escape cancels the quit operation and redisplays the desktop.

□

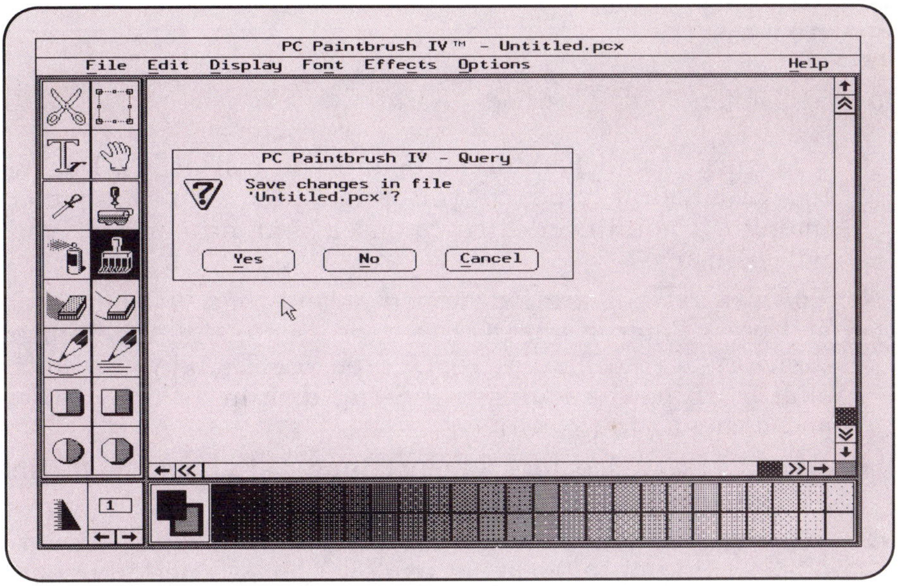

Figure 1.14 This alert box may appear after you choose the Exit command.

Quick Quit

The fastest way out of Paintbrush is to press Control-X, the keyboard equivalent for the Exit command, which will return you promptly to DOS. If you created a new painting or made any changes to an existing painting, the alert box shown in Figure 1.14 appears first, asking if you want to save your changes. Press the N key to select the No button, assuming, of course, that you don't want to save your changes. Or if you've been working ahead and have already created a masterpiece, good for you! Press the Y key and skip to the *Saving a Painting* section of Chapter 2 to learn how to save your artwork using the Save dialog box. Or press the C key or Escape to cancel the quit operation and return to the desktop.

> **Tip:** Pressing Escape always selects the Cancel button.

Summary

In this chapter, you've learned:

- You must install Paintbrush before you can use it. During the installation process, you select the display adapter (monitor), pointing device (mouse), and printer that you will be using.
- You can reconfigure Paintbrush at any time. Type `pbsetup` and press Enter at the DOS prompt from inside the Pbrush directory of your hard drive. Or type `pbsetup` and press Enter after inserting the Paintbrush Setup disk in a floppy drive and changing to that drive.
- You can save memory by installing Paintbrush with no printer selected.

- You need a mouse to use Paintbrush. The *Mouse Operations* section of this chapter explains how to perform common mouse operations like clicking, right-clicking, dragging, and so on.
- You can display a menu, choose a command, or select an option by pressing the Alt key simultaneously with the key corresponding to the underlined letter in the menu, command, or option name.
- The caption bar displays context-sensitive help for tools and commands.
- You can display the Help Index by pressing the F1 key.
- The fastest way to quit Paintbrush is to press Control-X followed by the N key.

Chapter 2

The PC Paintbrush Environment

What You Will Learn

- ▶ *Opening, creating, and saving paintings*
- ▶ *Converting paintings to the current palette*
- ▶ *Elements of the desktop*
- ▶ *Changing the screen layout*
- ▶ *Magnifying or reducing the view size of a painting*
- ▶ *Undoing mistakes*

This chapter gives you the opportunity to experiment with some of the basic features in Paintbrush. You will learn how to utilize the painting environment and acquire some time-saving techniques as well. If you quit Paintbrush as recommended at the end of Chapter 1, you will need to start the program again before you can proceed with the experiments in this chapter.

Opening a Painting

Every time you start Paintbrush, the Load a Picture from Disk dialog box appears, offering you the option to open (load) an existing painting. If you use Paintbrush, the dialog box looks like the one shown in Figure 2.1; if you use Paintbrush Plus, the dialog box differs slightly, as shown in Figure 2.2.

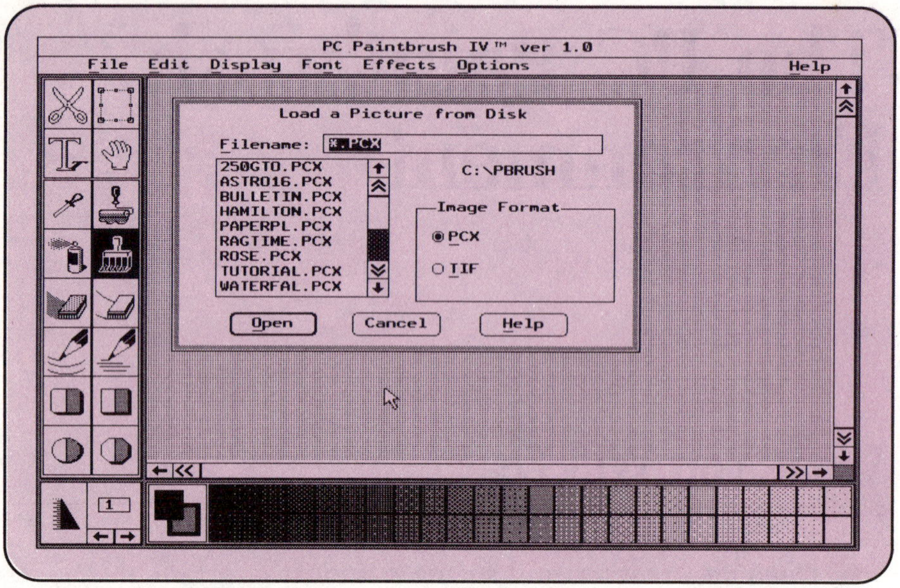

Figure 2.1 The Load Picture from Disk dialog box as it appears in PC Paintbrush.

The Load a Picture from Disk dialog box displays a list of paintings to choose from in a scrolling field (named Filename in Paintbrush and Files in Paintbrush Plus). The list of paintings will vary depending on the directory you are in and the Image Format selected. The two Paintbrush Image Formats—PCX and TIF—are discussed in the *Saving a Painting* section later in this chapter. In Figure 2.1, PCX files from the Pbrush directory are displayed. If you want to choose from paintings in the TIF format, you simply select the TIF button.

You can also change the contents of the list by changing to a different drive or directory. In Paintbrush, first scroll to the bottom of the Filename field. Then double-click the {..} file name to move back to the drive or directory in which the current directory resides. Double-click a drive name such as {-A-} to change drives. Double-click a directory name such as {DOS} to move into that directory. Or press Alt-F if you want to enter a path (drive and/or a directory) into the Filename option box.

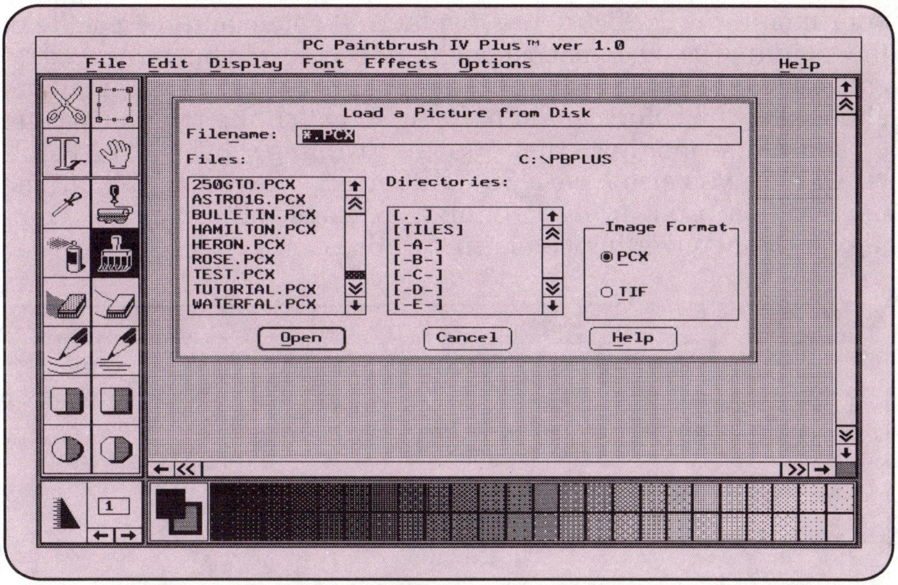

Figure 2.2 The Load Picture from Disk dialog box as it appears in PC Paintbrush Plus.

In Paintbrush Plus, if the file you want to open does not appear in the Files field, use the options in the scrolling Directories field. Double-click the {..} file name to move back to the drive or directory in which the current directory resides. Double-click
a drive name, such as {-A-}, to change drives. Double-click a directory name, such as {DOS}, to move into that directory. Press Alt-N if you want to type a path (drive and/or directory) into the File<u>n</u>ame option box. After you select a painting to open and press Enter, the painting will appear in the drawing window, unless another painting is already open or the painting contains more colors or fewer colors than your monitor is configured to display.

If another painting is currently displayed in the drawing window and if you made any changes to it, an alert box will appear, asking if you want to load the new painting without saving the current one. To discard the changes to the current painting and open the new painting, press the Y key. To continue working in the current painting, press the N key to cancel the Open... command.

A second alert box, shown in Figures 2.3 and 2.4, will appear before the painting opens if the painting contains more colors or fewer colors than your monitor is set up to display. For example, if your monitor is configured to display 256 colors and the palette of the painting being opened contains 16 colors, you will need to *convert* the painting using the options in the alert box. You can either alter the colors in the painting to match the monitor palette or adjust the monitor palette to the painting's palette. In Paintbrush Plus, you also have a Set Halftones... conversion option. The next section, *Converting Paintings*, explains the sometimes complex task of converting colors in paintings.

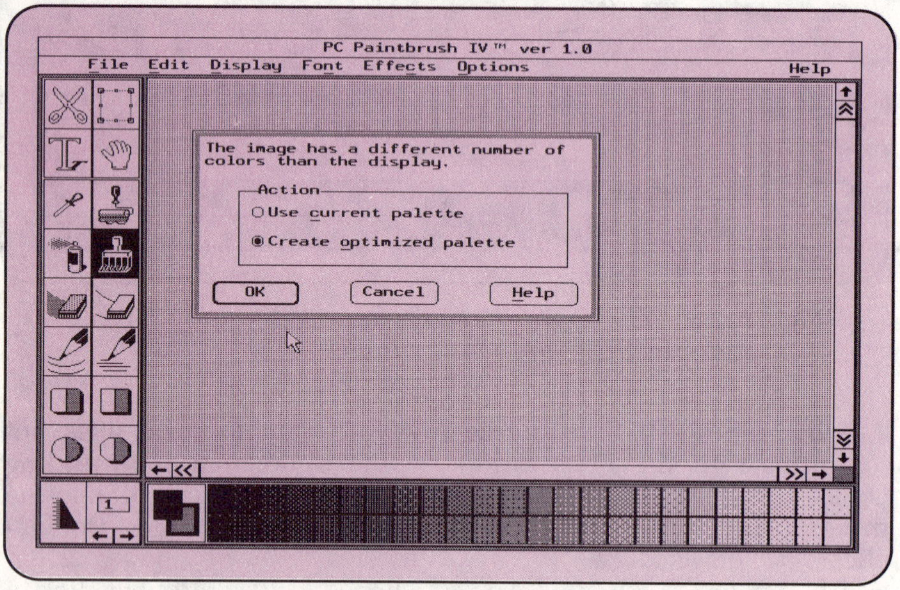

Figure 2.3 The PC Paintbrush alert box that allows you to convert a painting to the current palette.

After you select the conversion options and press Enter, the cursor will change to an hourglass and a progress message will appear in the caption bar. A few moments later, for better or worse, the converted painting will appear in the drawing window.

The following Quick Steps outline the procedures for opening a painting. Refer to the Quick Steps that apply to your version of the program.

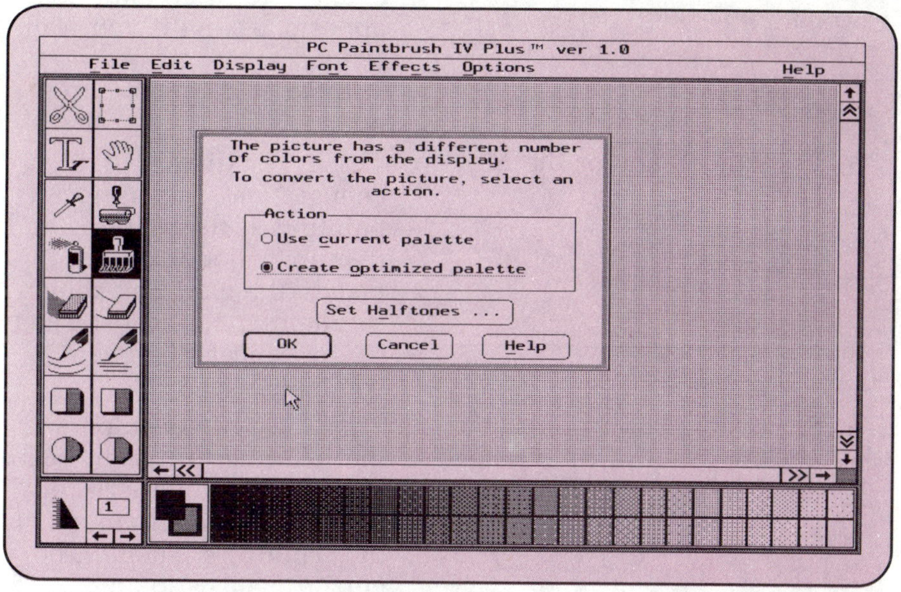

Figure 2.4 The PC Paintbrush Plus alert box that allows you to convert a painting to the current palette and determine the halftoning technique.

Q Opening a Painting in PC Paintbrush

1. Choose the Open... command from the File menu or press Alt-F followed by the O key.
   The Load a Picture from Disk dialog box displays.
2. Select the correct Image Format option. Press Alt-P or click on PCX to display PCX paintings, press Alt-T or click on TIF to display TIF paintings.
   Paintings saved in the selected image format appear in the scrolling Filename field.
3. Select a painting from the scrolling Filename field.
   Highlights the selected file name.
4. Press Enter to open the highlighted file name.
   Displays the selected painting in the drawing window. If another painting is open and if you made

	changes to it, an alert box appears, asking if you want to load a new painting without saving the current one.
5. Press the Y key or the N key.	The Y key discards the changes and opens the painting. If the painting and monitor palettes do not match, the alert box shown in Figure 2.3 appears. The N key cancels the Open... command.
6. Select an Action option by clicking on it or by typing the C key or the O key.	The C key alters colors in the painting to match your palette. The O key tries to adjust your palette to match the painting's palette. The cursor changes to an hourglass and a progress message appears in the caption bar. A few moments later, the converted painting appears in the drawing window. □

Paintbrush Plus offers additional file-opening features, including separate scrolling fields for files and directories and special halftoning controls.

Q Opening a Painting in PC Paintbrush Plus

1. Choose the Open... command from the File menu or press Alt-F followed by the O key.	The Load a Picture from Disk dialog box displays.
2. Select the correct Image Format option. Press Alt-P or click on PCX to display PCX paintings, press Alt-T or click on TIF to display TIF paintings.	Paintings saved in the selected image format appear in the scrolling Files field.
3. Select a painting from the scrolling Files field.	Highlights the selected file name.

4. Press Enter to open the highlighted file name.	Displays the selected painting in the drawing window. If another painting is open and if you made changes to it, an alert box appears, asking if you want to load a new painting without saving the current one.
5. Press the Y key or the N key.	The Y key discards the changes and opens the new painting. If the painting and monitor palettes do not match, the dialog box shown in Figure 2.4 appears. The N key cancels the Open... command.
6. Select an Action option by clicking on it or by typing the C key or the O key. Press the A key to select Halftone Options. Press Enter twice.	The C key alters colors in the painting to match your palette. The O key adjusts your palette to match the painting's palette. The A key displays the Halftone Options dialog box. The cursor changes to an hourglass and a progress message appears in the caption bar. Then a halftoning progress message appears. Moments later, the converted painting appears in the drawing window. □

As the Quick Steps show, opening a painting in Paintbrush is a fairly straightforward process, except when the palette of the painting is different from the palette of your monitor. If you will only be opening files that contain the same number of colors that your monitor is configured to display, you will not need to read the *Converting Paintings* section and can skip ahead to *The PC Paintbrush Desktop* section.

Converting Paintings

During the installation procedure, you can configure your monitor to display 2, 4, 8, 16, or 256 colors. Likewise, a painting created in Paintbrush can include 2, 4, 8, 16, or 256 colors. But what happens if your monitor is set up to display 16 colors and you try to open a painting that contains 256 colors? The painting has to be converted before it can be displayed.

4 Both Paintbrush and Paintbrush Plus allow you to convert paintings when you open them. However, the two programs offer slightly different methods for doing so.

If you are opening a black and white drawing on a color system, both versions of Paintbrush will present you with two options, as shown in Figure 2.5. If you select the first option, Keep as b/w, the painting will be loaded with the standard black and white palette, which prevents you from adding color to the file but also keeps the file from consuming the additional disk space required by colored files. If you select the Convert to color option, the painting will remain black and white but will retain the standard color palette; as a consequence, your file will become larger and consume more disk space when you save it.

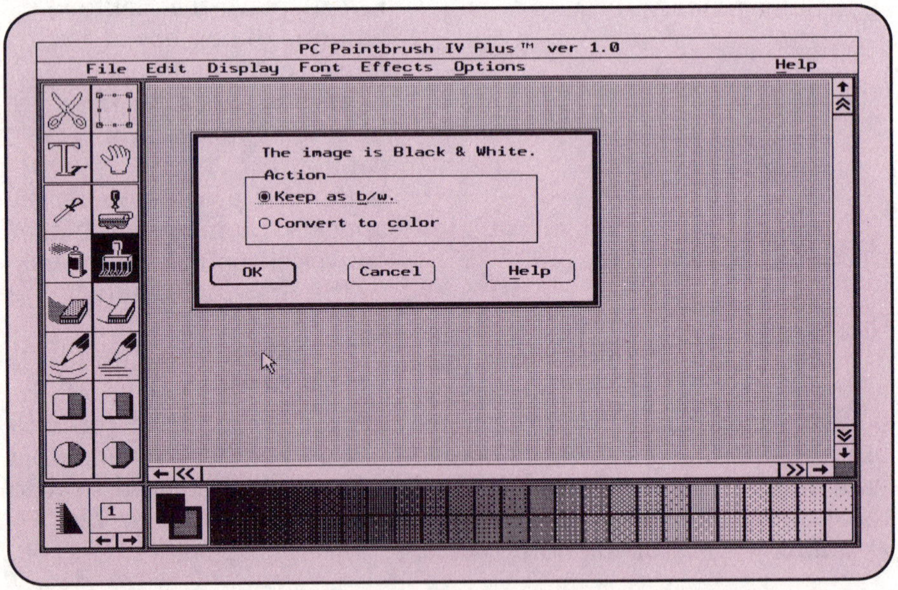

Figure 2.5 Select one of two options to open a black and white painting.

Both programs also provide two options for matching color paintings incompatible with the colors of your palette. The dialog boxes that display these options are shown in Figures 2.3 and 2.4. The first option, Use current palette, instructs Paintbrush to alter colors in the painting to match the colors in your color palette. If you select the second option, Create optimized palette, Paintbrush tries to adjust your palette to more accurately match the painting. Unfortunately, unless the painting contains *fewer* colors than your color palette, the Create optimized palette option will produce no effect, which limits this option's usefulness considerably. As a result, you can only select the Use Current palette option when converting, for example, a 256-color file on a 16-color system.

Controlling Halftones

+ Paintbrush Plus offers an additional color conversion option that makes all the difference in the world. Selecting the Set Halftone... button displays the Halftone Options dialog box shown in Figure 2.6.

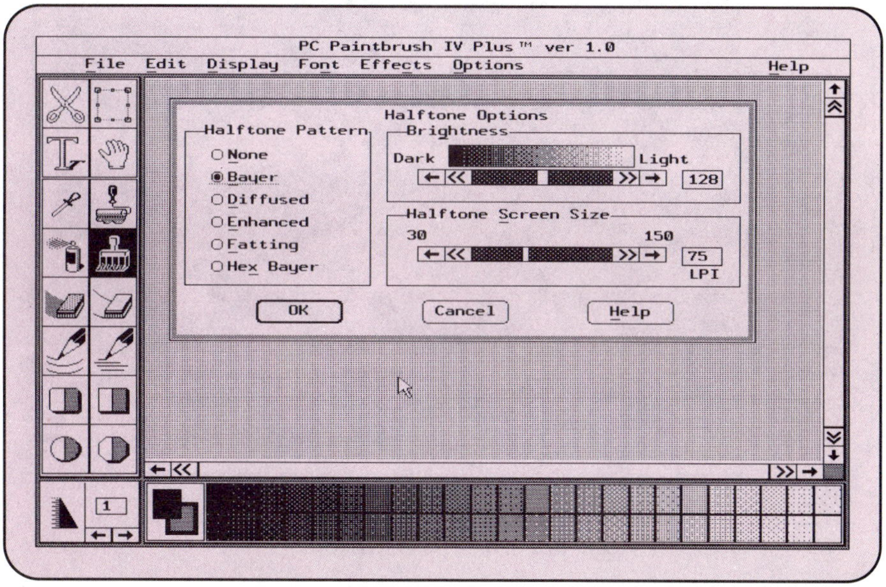

Figure 2.6 The Halftone Options dialog box.

To *halftone* a painting means to express a color or a shade of gray as a series of dots, which makes it possible for you to mimic a large palette with a small number of colors. For example, tiny red dots combined with tiny yellow dots blur together to form orange. This halftone process is used to print photographs in newspapers and magazines. Paintbrush Plus offers six Halftone Pattern options:

- *None*
- *Bayer*
- *Diffused*
- *Enhanced*
- *Fatting*
- *Hex Bayer*

Click the None option or press Alt-N to turn the halftoning off. All colors will appear solid rather than blended, as shown in Figure 2.7.

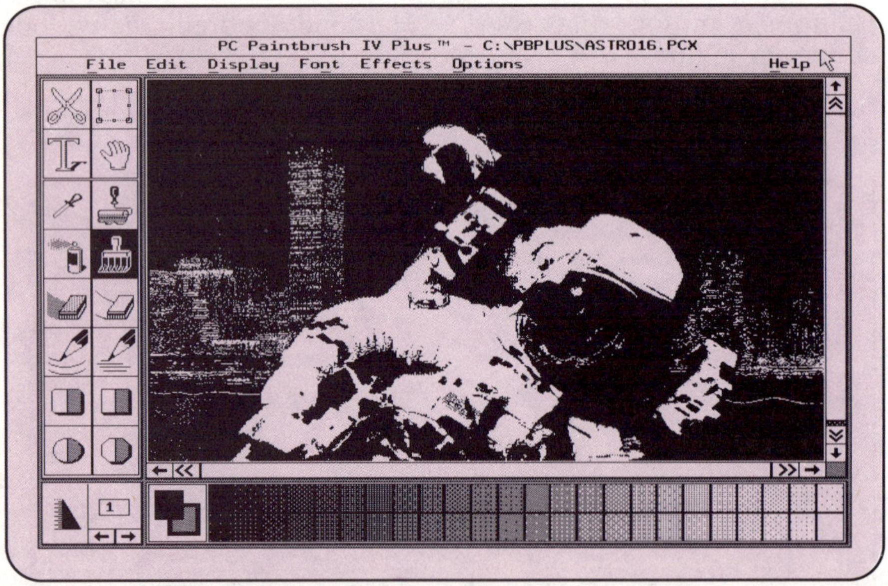

Figure 2.7 A painting opened with the None Halftone Pattern option selected.

Click the Bayer option or press Alt-B to apply a consistent *bit-mapped* pattern to a picture; that is, a pattern composed of a series of dots spaced at regular intervals. This pattern copies well to dot-matrix printers but tends to appear overly geometric when output to a laser printer, as shown in Figure 2.8.

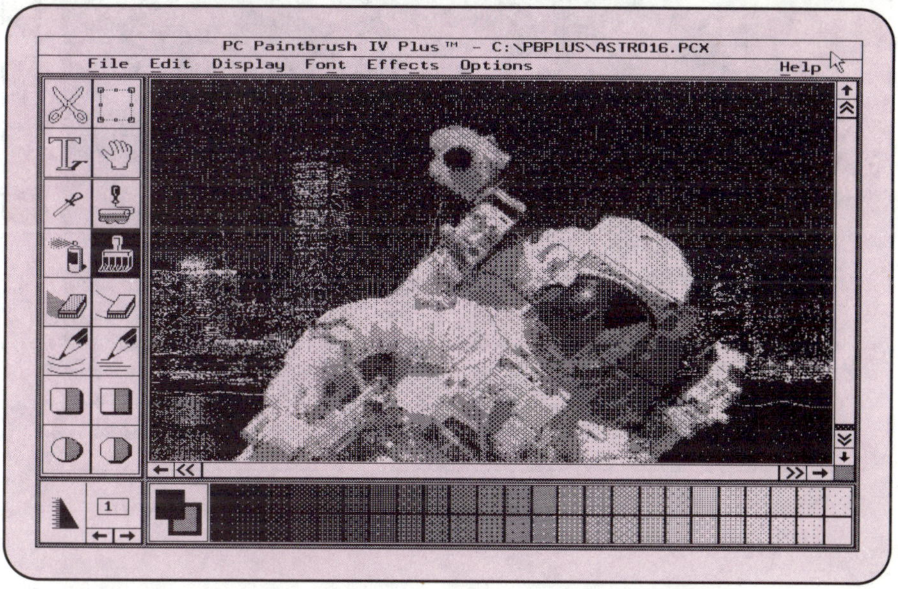

Figure 2.8 A painting opened with the Bayer Halftone Pattern option selected.

Click the Diffused option or press Alt-D to apply a highly textured halftoning pattern to a picture. The pattern is entirely random, as shown in Figure 2.9. This option produces especially fine results when applied to images with lots of contrast.

Click the Enhanced option or press Alt-E to apply a highly textured halftoning pattern to a picture. Like the dots created by the Diffuse option, the dots in this pattern are clustered randomly. In addition, slight outlines are created around bordering colors to make images stand out more, as shown in Figure 2.10.

Click the Fatting option or press Alt-F to apply a *classical screen* dot pattern to a picture. Round halftone dots form the image, as shown in Figure 2.11. This is the halftoning pattern used in newspaper photographs, although the dots here are much larger.

Click the Hex Bayer option or press Alt-X to apply a consistent *bit-mapped* pattern to a picture. This pattern is similar to

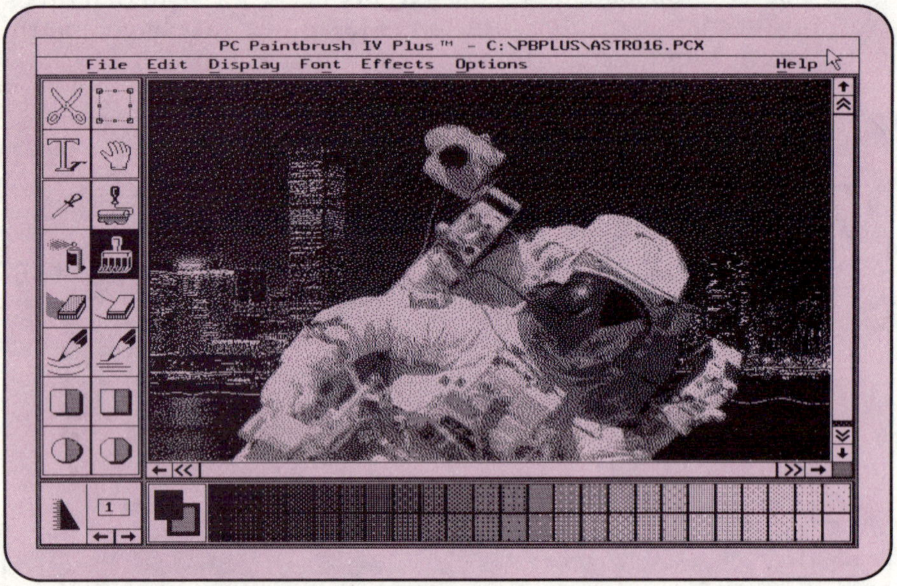

Figure 2.9 A painting opened with the Diffused Halftone Pattern option selected.

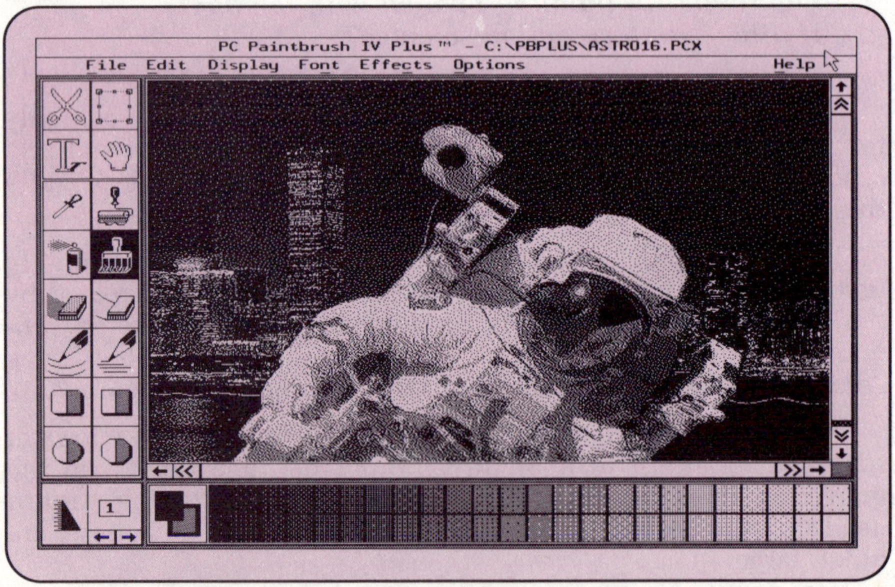

Figure 2.10 A painting opened with the Enhanced Halftone Pattern option selected.

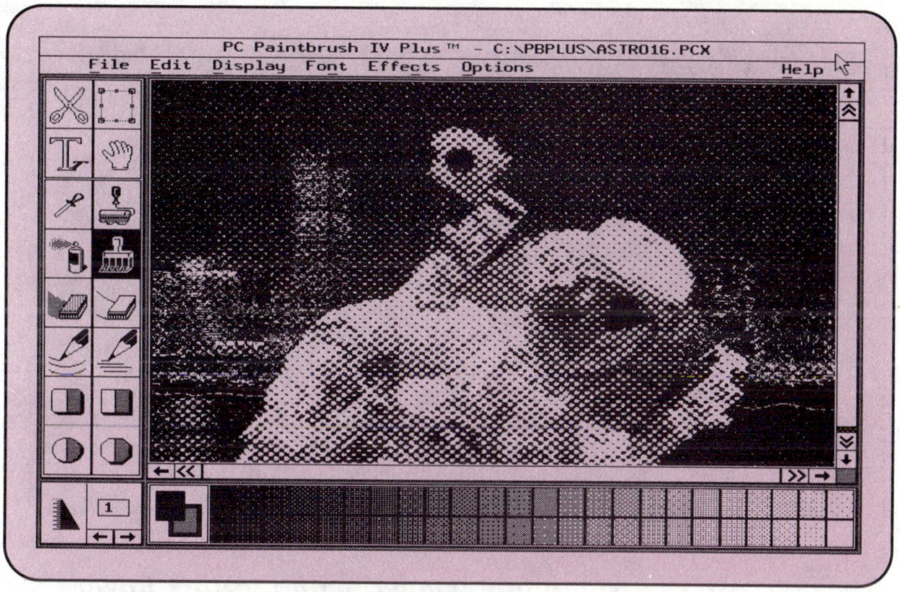

Figure 2.11 A painting opened with the Fatting Halftone Pattern option selected.

that of the Bayer option, but it is applied in hexagonal blocks rather than in rectangular blocks. It copies well to dot-matrix printers but tends to appear overly geometric when output to a laser printer, as shown in Figure 2.12.

The Halftone Options dialog box offers two other options for determining how a color picture is loaded: the Brightness and Halftone Screen Size controls. To adjust either option, you can click the scroll bar arrows, drag the slider in the scroll bar, or enter a value in the option box.

The Brightness controls allow you to determine the lightness or darkness of a picture. The value of this option can range from 1 through 255, 1 being the darkest and 255 being the lightest. In Figures 2.7 through 2.12, the Brightness value was set to 128, medium. Figures 2.13 and 2.14 display darker and lighter values than medium. Both figures use the Enhanced halftone pattern.

The Halftone Screen Size controls allow you to determine the size of individual halftone patterns by specifying the number of *lines* (patterns) per inch. The value for this option can range

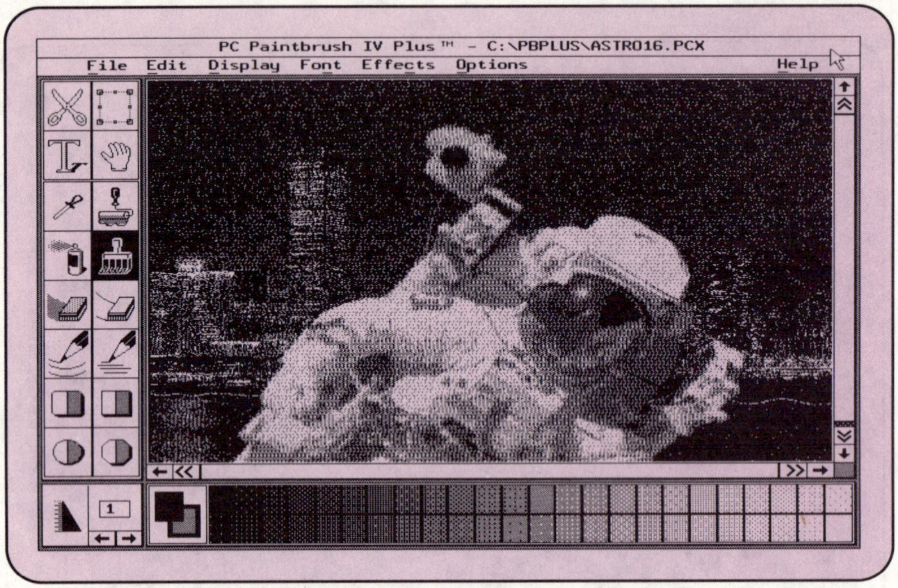

Figure 2.12 A painting opened with the Hex Bayer Halftone Pattern option selected.

between 30 and 150, 30 creating the coarsest patterns and 150 creating the finest patterns. Coarse patterns don't display detail very well, but they allow more levels of gray. Fine patterns show more detail, but they allow fewer levels of gray. In Figures 2.7 through 2.14, the Brightness value was set to 75, medium. Figures 2.15 and 2.16 display coarser and finer values than medium. Both figures use the Fatting halftone pattern.

The Halftone Screen Size option can only be applied to Bayer, Fatting, and Hex Bayer halftone patterns.

The PC Paintbrush Desktop

After you open an existing painting, it appears in the drawing window of the Paintbrush desktop, as in Figures 2.7 through 2.16. In the previous chapter, we discussed the caption bar and the menu bar. In this section, we will cover the other parts of the desktop, including the *toolbox*, the *drawing window*, the *line width box*, and the *color palette*.

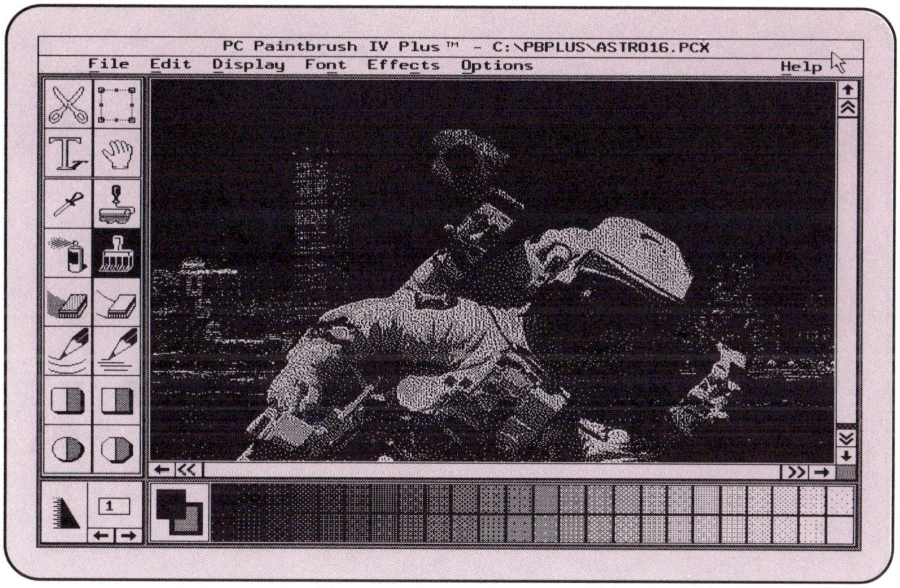

Figure 2.13 A painting opened with a Brightness value of 30.

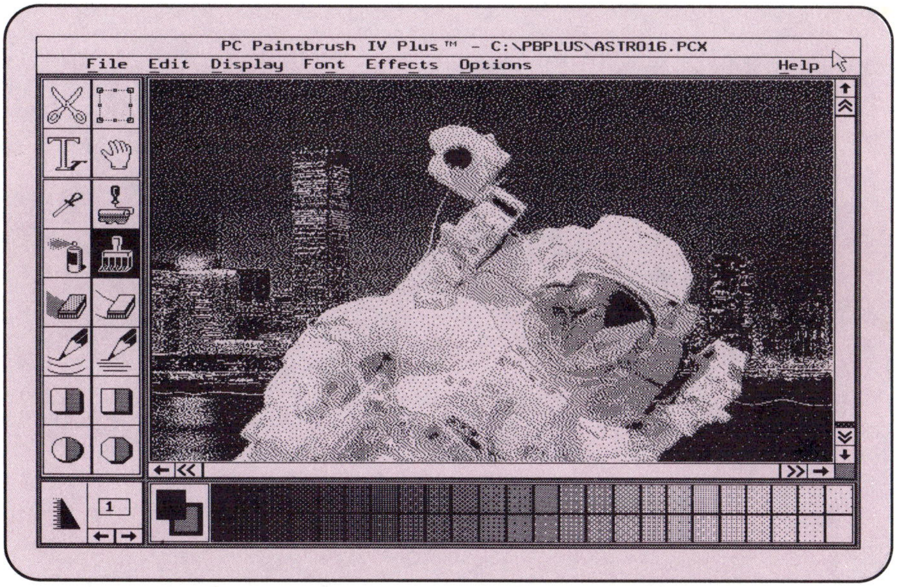

Figure 2.14 A painting opened with a Brightness value of 200.

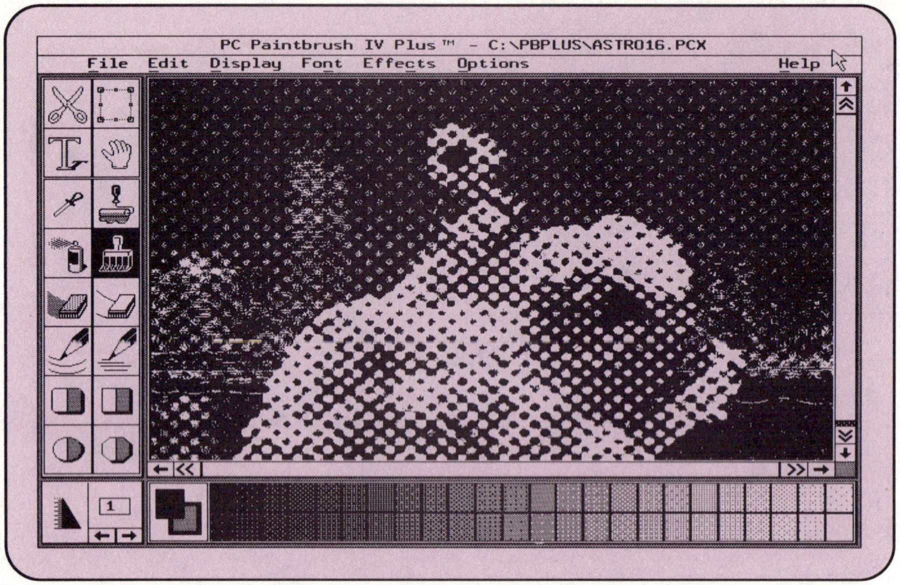

Figure 2.15 A painting opened with a Halftone Screen Size value of 30.

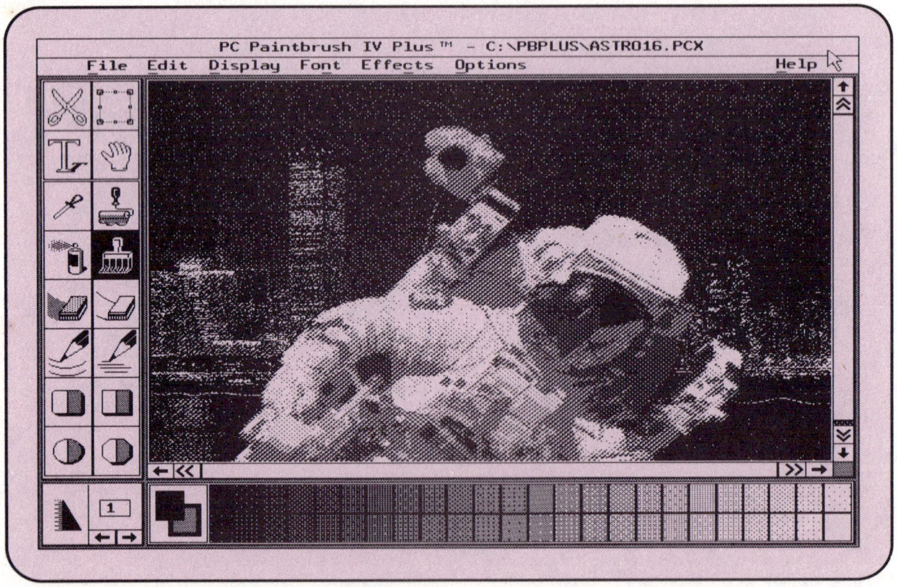

Figure 2.16 A painting opened with a Halftone Screen Size value of 150.

The Toolbox

The *toolbox* is located on the far left side of the desktop. Each of the 16 icons inside the toolbox is called a *tool*. The tools are the primary means for drawing and manipulating images in Paintbrush. Many of them are modeled after real-life drawing tools, like a paintbrush, or an eraser, or a can of spraypaint.

To select a tool for use in the drawing area, position the cursor on it and click. It will become highlighted. For example, when you first start Paintbrush, the Paintbrush tool is highlighted. Drag with the Paintbrush tool inside the drawing window and you will create a free-form line just as if you were drawing with a pencil on a piece of paper. Now select the Eraser tool, directly below the Paintbrush tool in the toolbox. Move the cursor into the drawing area and notice that it has changed to a small white box. Drag the white box over the line you just created with the Paintbrush tool and it disappears, just as if you had erased it with a real-life eraser.

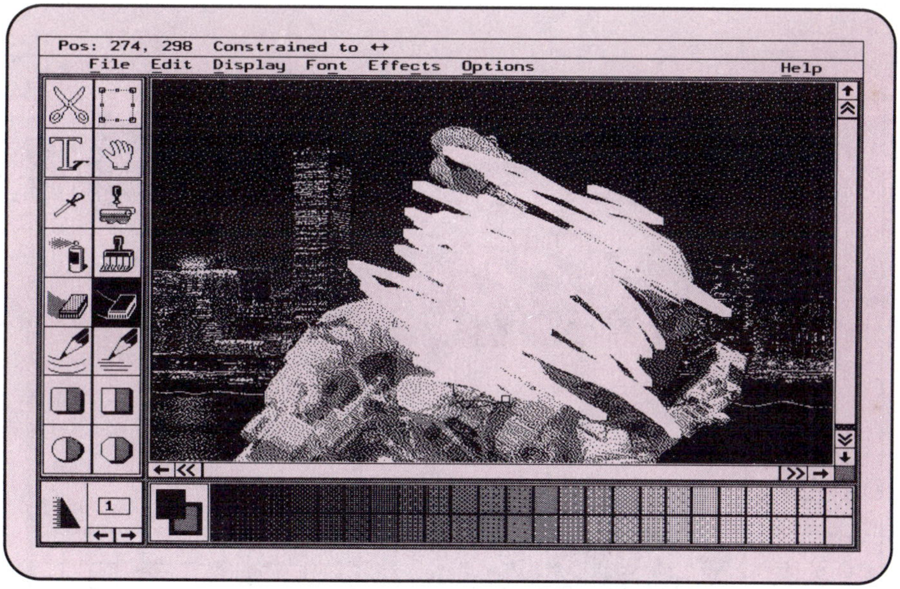

Figure 2.17 Erasing a portion of a picture with the Eraser tool.

You might want to take a moment to select various tools and experiment with them in the drawing window. If you encounter any problems, refer to the following chapter which is devoted entirely to the use of tools.

The Drawing Window

The central portion of the Paintbrush desktop is termed the *drawing window*. All drawing takes place in this area, whether you are creating new images or altering existing images.

4 As you move the cursor inside the drawing window, the caption bar displays the coordinate location of the cursor as well as additional context-sensitive help information. If you get tired of seeing this information, you can turn it off by choosing the Information Line command from the Help menu, or by pressing Alt-H followed by the I key.

Your painting may be larger or smaller than your drawing window. If smaller, a margin of gray space surrounds the painting, as shown in Figure 2.18. You may not draw in this portion of the window.

Figure 2.18 When editing this small painting, you cannot draw in the gray area surrounding the car.

If the painting is larger than the drawing window, as shown in Figure 2.19, only a portion of the painting can be viewed at a time.

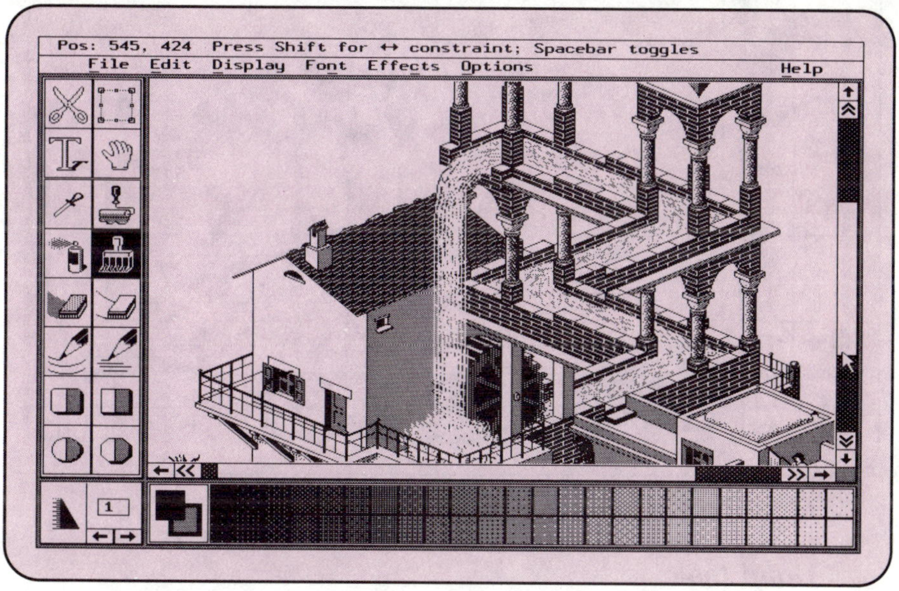

Figure 2.19 Only a portion of this large painting can be viewed in the drawing window at a time.

To view a portion of a painting not currently displayed in the drawing window, use the scroll bars located directly to the right and below the window. As with scroll bars in dialog boxes, you can click a single-arrow icon to scroll the painting in small increments or a double-arrow icon to scroll in large increments. Each scroll bar also includes a slider, which can be dragged up and down or left and right to display hidden portions of a painting.

4 The easiest way to scroll a painting is to use the Hand tool, the second tool down on the right side of the toolbox. When you select this tool and drag in the drawing window, you move the painting with respect to the drawing window. The scroll bars adjust accordingly. Figure 2.20 shows the Hand tool in action.

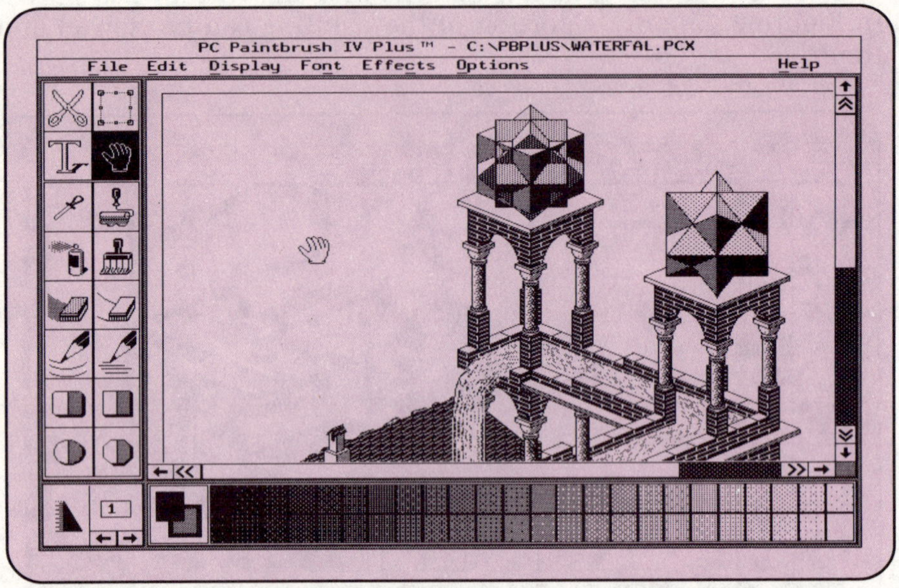

Figure 2.20 To view different portions of a large painting, drag in the drawing window with the Hand tool.

The Line Width Box

4 When using specific drawing tools in Paintbrush IV, you can draw lines between 0 and 40 pixels thick, depending on the size of the cursor. The *line width box*, located in the bottom left corner of the desktop, controls the cursor size.

The line width box is divided into two parts: the *line width triangle* on the left and the *line width display* on the right. Unlike in older versions of Paintbrush, in Paintbrush IV you don't adjust an arrow next to the triangle to set the line width. Now the triangle is simply an icon that you click to display the new Set Line Width dialog box.

To use the line width display, enter a value between 0 and 40 in the option box or click the arrow icons to increase or decrease the line width in 1-pixel increments.

For complete information about line width and the special tools which can alter it, see the *Paintbrush Tool* section in Chapter 3.

The Color Palette

The *color palette* is the area along the bottom of the desktop where colors are selected. The number of colors displayed (up to 256) depends on the monitor configuration you specified during the installation procedure. You can change the number of colors in the palette by quitting Paintbrush and rerunning the Pbsetup program. For complete information about the color palette, refer to Chapter 4, *Using Colors.*

Three colors are selected at all times: the *primary color*, the *secondary color*, and the *background color*. Generally, the primary color is used by lines and outlines, the secondary color is used to fill objects, and the background color is used by the Eraser tool. In the color palette shown in Figure 2.21, the primary, secondary, and background colors are black, white, and gray, respectively. To select a different primary color, click a color box in the palette. The new primary color will be displayed in the forward box on the left side of the palette. To select a different secondary color, right-click a color box in the palette. The new secondary color will be displayed in the rear box on the left side of the palette. To select a different background color, shift-click a color box in the palette. The new background color will be displayed behind the primary and secondary colors on the left side of the palette.

Changing the Screen Layout

The caption bar, menu bar, toolbox, drawing window, line width box, and color palette are all displayed when you first start Paintbrush. But you are free to customize your *screen layout* to include only those parts of the desktop that you need.

To change the screen layout, choose the Set Screen Layout... command from the Display menu. The Set Screen Layout dialog box, shown in Figure 2.22, will display. This dialog box contains five screen display options:

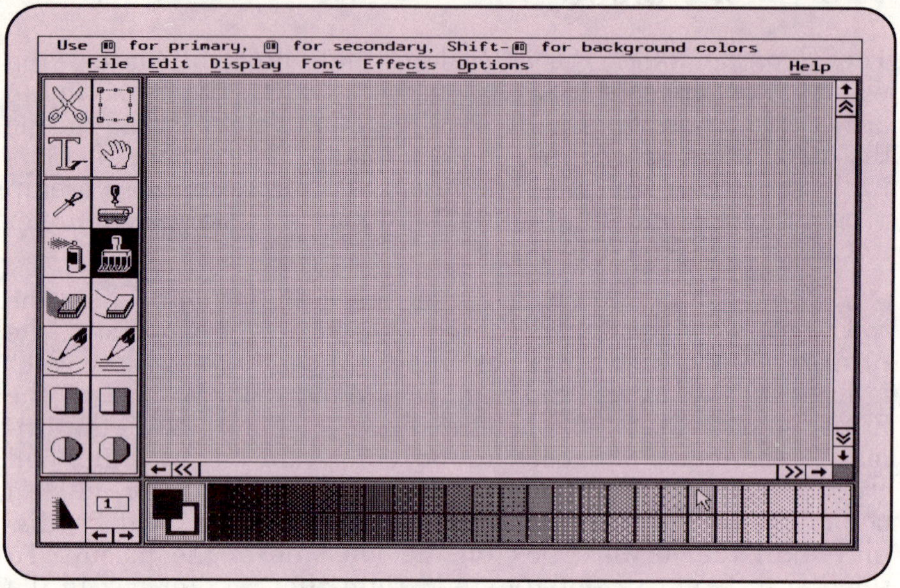

Figure 2.21 In this color palette, black is the primary color, white is the secondary color, and gray is the background color.

- *Caption bar*
- *Menu*
- *Palette*
- *Scroll Bars*
- *Tools*

Click the Caption bar option or press the C key to hide the caption bar or display it at the top of the screen. When the caption bar is hidden, the menu bar moves up into the position previously occupied by the caption bar and the drawing window expands to fill the available space, as shown in Figure 2.23.

Click the Menu option or press the M key to hide the menu bar or display it under the caption bar. When the menu bar is hidden, the drawing window expands to fill the available space. To restore the menu, press Alt-D.

Click the Palette option or press the P key to hide the color palette or display it at the bottom of the desktop. When the color palette is hidden, the drawing window expands vertically downward, as shown in Figure 2.24.

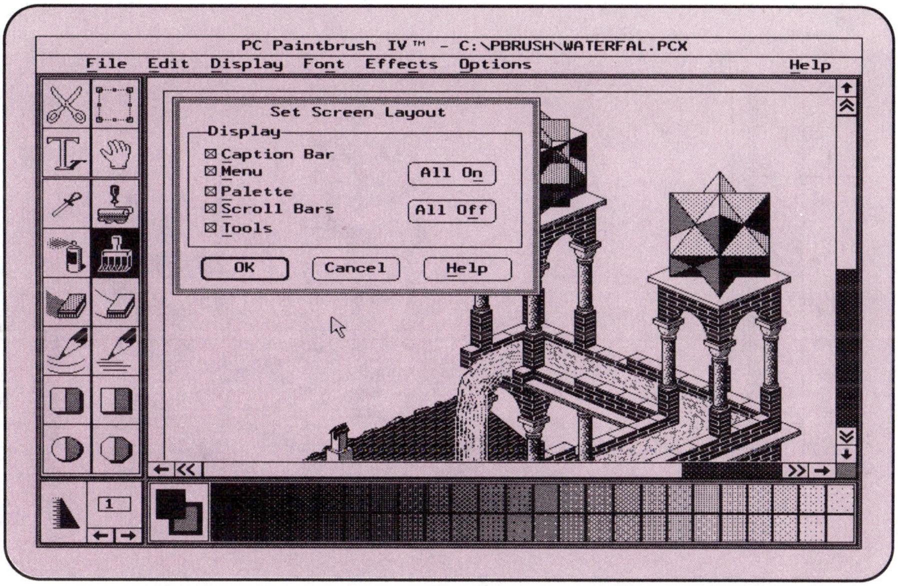

Figure 2.22 The Set Screen Layout dialog box.

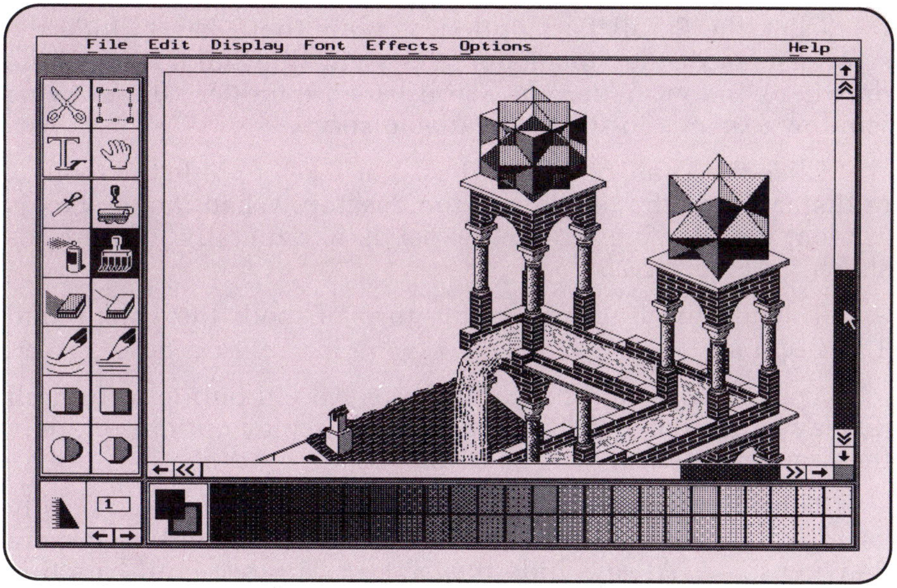

Figure 2.23 The desktop with the caption bar hidden.

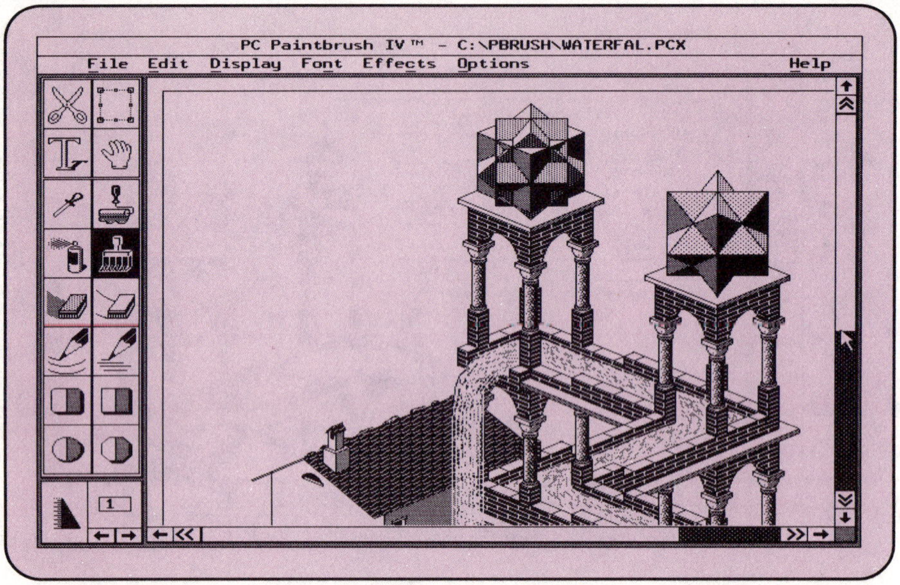

Figure 2.24 The desktop with the color palette hidden.

Click the Scroll Bars option or press the S key to hide the scroll bars or display them along the right side and bottom of the drawing window. When the scroll bars are hidden, the drawing window expands to fill the available space.

Click the Tools option or press the T key to hide the toolbox or display it on the left side of the desktop. When the toolbox is hidden, the drawing window expands horizontally leftward, as shown in Figure 2.25.

To hide the line width box, turn off both the Palette and Tools options.

You can also select the All On or All Off button to turn all display options on or off. If you turn all display options off, only the drawing window will be displayed.

This capability to hide portions of the desktop is especially useful when you are working on a large painting and need more drawing space. Always hide the caption bar and scroll bars first since these portions of the desktop are not needed for drawing. You can do without the context-sensitive help and coordinate information in the caption bar, and you can use the Hand tool

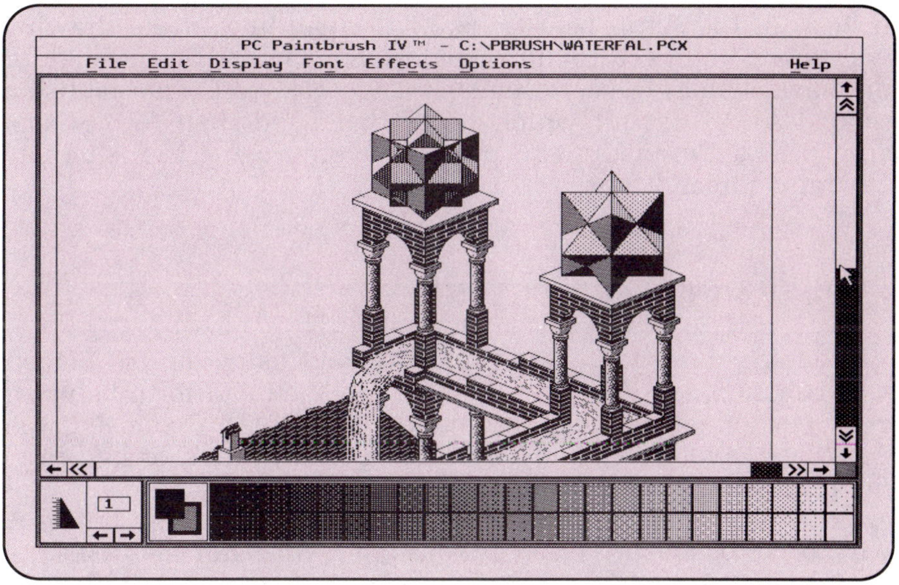

Figure 2.25 The desktop with the toolbox hidden.

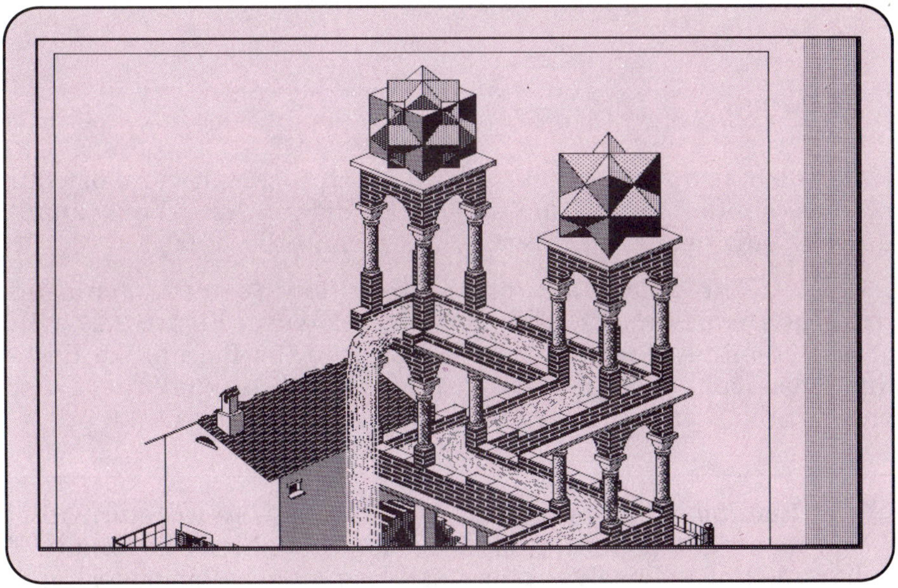

Figure 2.26 When the All Off screen layout button is selected, only the drawing window appears in the desktop.

instead of the scroll bars to scroll the painting in the drawing window. If you need to hide desktop items which are needed for drawing, such as the color palette or toolbox, you can establish a second screen layout which hides them and then toggle back and forth between the two custom layouts using the Alternate Layout command.

Toggling between Layouts

4 After you customize the screen layout using the Set Screen Layout... command, you can toggle back and forth between your custom layout and the standard layout by choosing the Alternate Layout command from the Display menu or by pressing Control-A. If you choose the Set Screen Layout... command again and customize a second screen layout, pressing Control-A will toggle between the second custom layout and the first.

If you choose the Alternate Layout command without first specifying a custom layout, the command will toggle back and forth between the standard layout and the drawing-window-only layout, as shown in Figure 2.26.

Full-Screen View

Paintbrush also allows you to display a full-screen view of your picture, similar to the one shown in Figure 2.26. You cannot draw or edit images in this view; you can only look.

For a full-screen view, choose the Show Screen... command from the Display menu. The alert box shown in Figure 2.27 will appear, reminding you how to get back to the Paintbrush desktop when you're done viewing. Press Enter to continue. After viewing the painting, press Escape to return to the desktop.

> **Caution:** Pressing Escape is the *only* way to return to the desktop from the full-screen view. Many beginners have found themselves completely stranded after choosing the Show Screen... command.

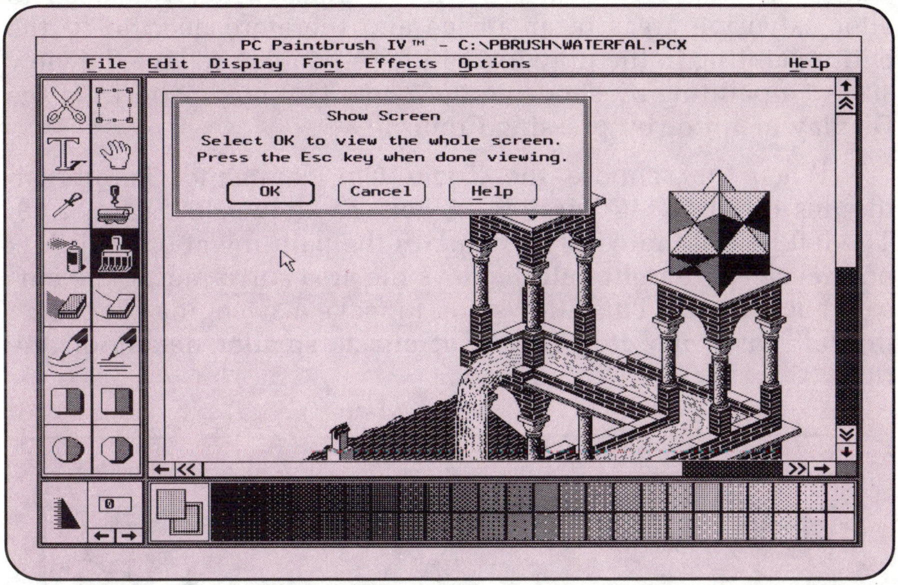

Figure 2.27 The Show Screen alert box reminds you to press Escape to return to the desktop from a full-screen view.

Generally, this command isn't very useful. The drawing-window-only view provides the same view and, in addition, allows you to draw using the mouse and to access menu commands using keyboard equivalents.

Changing the View Size

Hiding portions of the desktop is not the only way to change the screen display. You can also reduce or enlarge the view size of the painting in the drawing window by altering the magnification level.

Zooming Out

If your painting is very large, some portions will remain hidden even in the drawing-window-only screen layout, as demonstrated in Figure 2.27. There will be times when you need to alter extensive areas of an image and therefore need to fit the entire painting in the drawing window. You can reduce the view size of a painting by choosing the Zoom Out command from the Display menu or by pressing Control-O.

When you choose the Zoom Out command, Paintbrush divides the drawing window in half, as shown in Figure 2.28. The left half of the window displays the painting at one third its normal size, the right half displays the area surrounding the cursor at actual size. This allows you to make a sweeping change on the left while monitoring how it effects smaller details on the right.

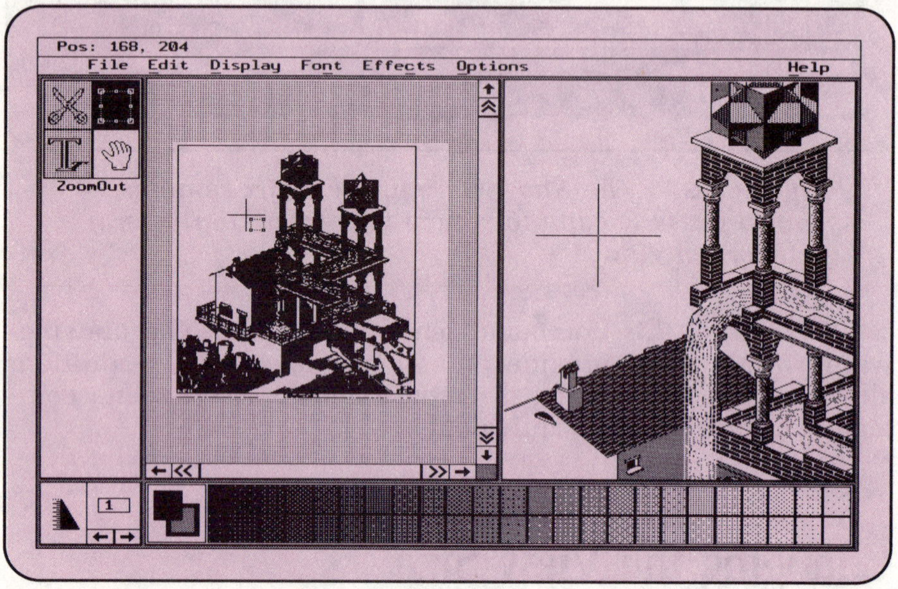

Figure 2.28 Reduce the view size of a painting by choosing the Zoom Out command.

As you can see in Figure 2.28, many of the tools disappear from the toolbox at this view size. In fact, the Gadget Box and Hand tools are the only tools you can use in a reduced view size. Using the Gadget Box tool, you can move, clone, copy, or paste a selected image, but you cannot transform it or apply any of the special effects described in Chapter 7. For complete information about the Gadget Box tool, see Chapter 5, *Manipulating Images*.

Zooming In

To return to the normal view size, choose the Zoom In command from the Display menu or press Control-Z. If you choose the Zoom In command a second time, you will magnify the painting inside the drawing window, as shown in Figure 2.29.

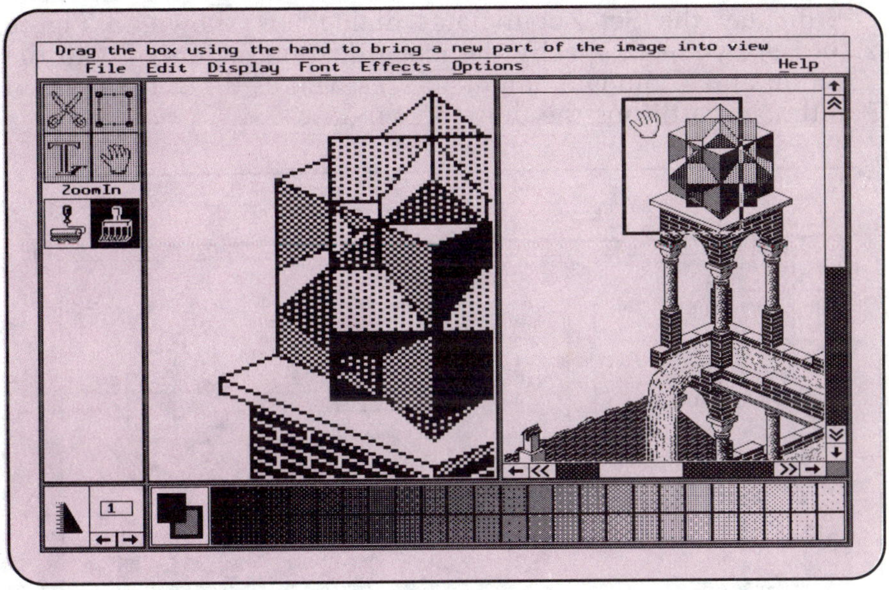

Figure 2.29 Magnify the view size of a painting by choosing the Zoom In command.

If you choose the Zoom Out command, Paintbrush again divides the drawing window in half. You can use the Paintbrush tool or the Paint Roller tool to make precise alterations to the magnified image in the left half of the window. You can then view the results of your changes on the actual-size display in the right half of the window. When you move the cursor from the left half to the right half of the drawing window, it changes to a Hand tool icon, which can be used to reposition the rectangular border and thereby magnify a different portion of the painting. To return to the normal view size, press Control-O or choose the Zoom Out command.

+ In Paintbrush Plus, the Eyedropper tool is also available in a magnified view size.

Zoom Particulars

By default, the Zoom Out command reduces the view size of your painting to one third its normal size, while the Zoom In command enlarges the view size of your painting to three times its actual size. However, other magnification factors can be used.

4 Choose the Set Zoom command from the Display menu to display the Set Zoom Rates dialog box shown in Figure 2.30. Here you can specify the magnification factors of both the Zoom In and Zoom Out commands, as well as the way in which Paintbrush partitions the drawing window.

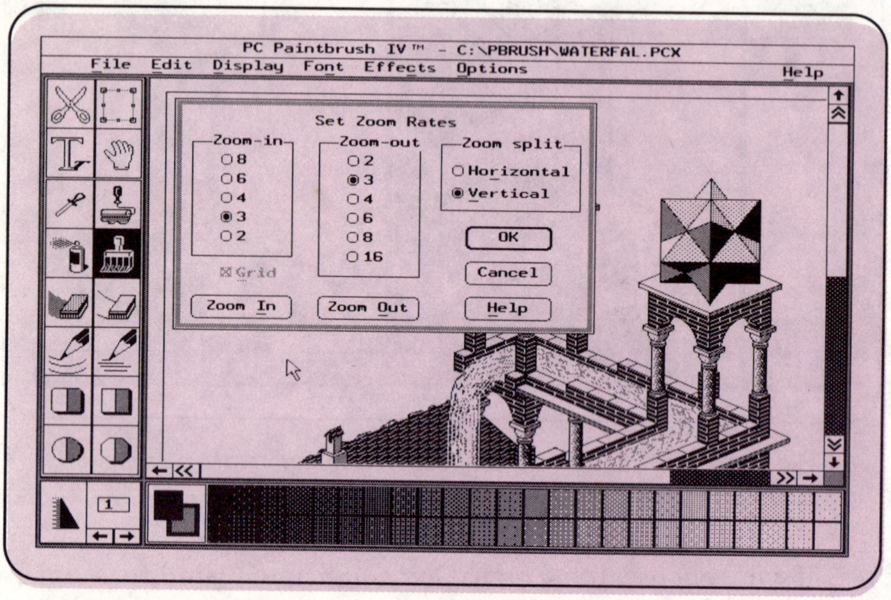

Figure 2.30 The Set Zoom Rates dialog box.

To specify how close you can zoom in to a painting, select one of the Zoom-in options. You can magnify a picture from twice its normal size (Zoom-in option 2) to eight times its normal size (Zoom-in option 8). If you select a magnification factor of 4 or greater, you also have the option to display a *grid*. When the Grid option is selected, a checkerboard of horizontal and vertical lines appears in the left half of the drawing window, as shown in Figure 2.31.

If you want to zoom in immediately after selecting a Zoom-in option, click the Zoom In button or press the I key.

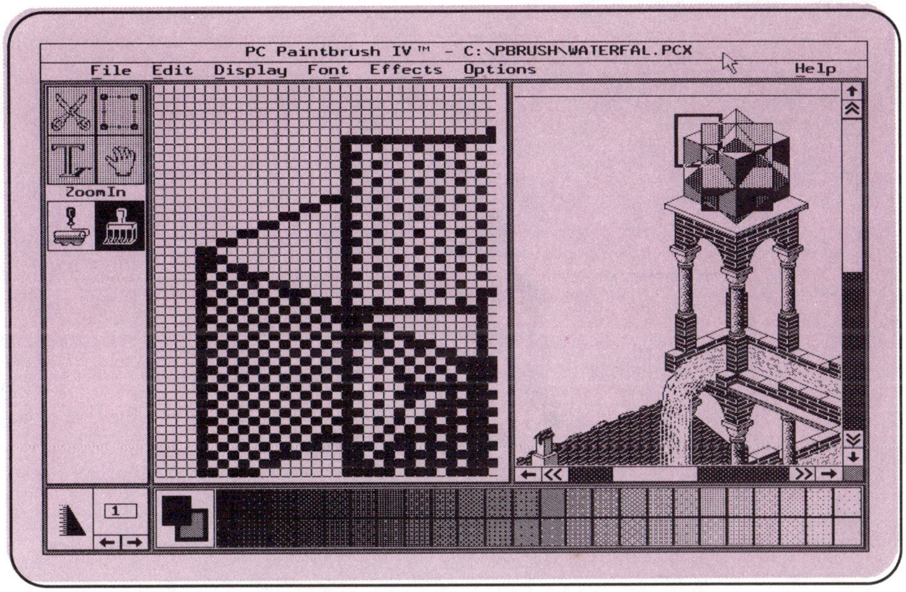

Figure 2.31 A grid can be displayed to help distinguish individual pixels.

To specify how far you can zoom away from a painting, select one of the Zoom-out options. You can reduce a picture from 1/2 its normal size (Zoom-out option 2) to as small as 1/16 its normal size (Zoom-out option 16). If you want To zoom out immediately after selecting a Zoom-out option, click the Zoom Out button or press the O key.

The two Zoom split options determine how the drawing window is apportioned when you choose the Zoom In or Zoom Out command. Vertical is the default option and divides the window vertically, as shown in Figures 2.28, 2.29, and 2.31. If you select the Horizontal option, the window will be divided horizontally, as shown in Figure 2.32.

Undoing Mistakes

Paintbrush provides many ways to create and alter images in the drawing window. By magnifying a painting, you can make

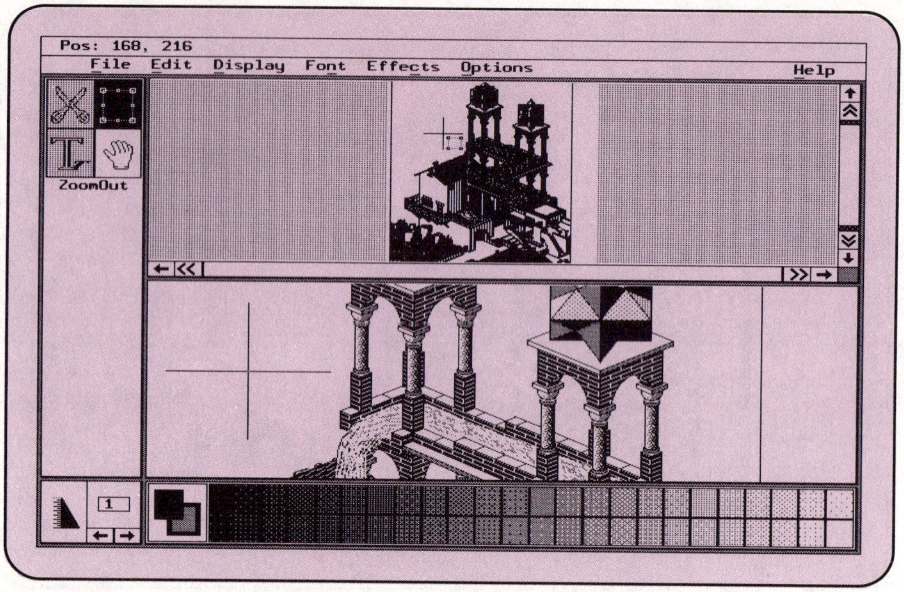

Figure 2.32 Splitting the drawing window horizontally during a zoom.

detailed adjustments to a line or shape. But because we all occasionally make big mistakes, the program also provides two commands for "undrawing" images: the Undo and Local Undo commands.

Both the Undo and Local Undo commands are extremely useful. But you should keep in mind that both commands only remove the effects of your most recent manipulation. For example, suppose you draw a line. Then you select a different tool. Whoops, now it's too late to use either command. As soon as you click anywhere in the toolbox, choose a command from the Display menu, or so much as use the scroll bars, you lose the ability to undo the effects of the last tool.

> **Caution:** You cannot undo the results of choosing the Undo or Local Undo command by again choosing Undo or Local Undo. Once a detail or image is erased, it's erased for good.

The Undo Command

Suppose you want to add a happy face to the astronaut image included with Paintbrush. You're going along fine until, all of a sudden, your mouse careens out of control. "Oh no!" you scream, yanking out your few remaining hairs, "I've *ruined* it!"

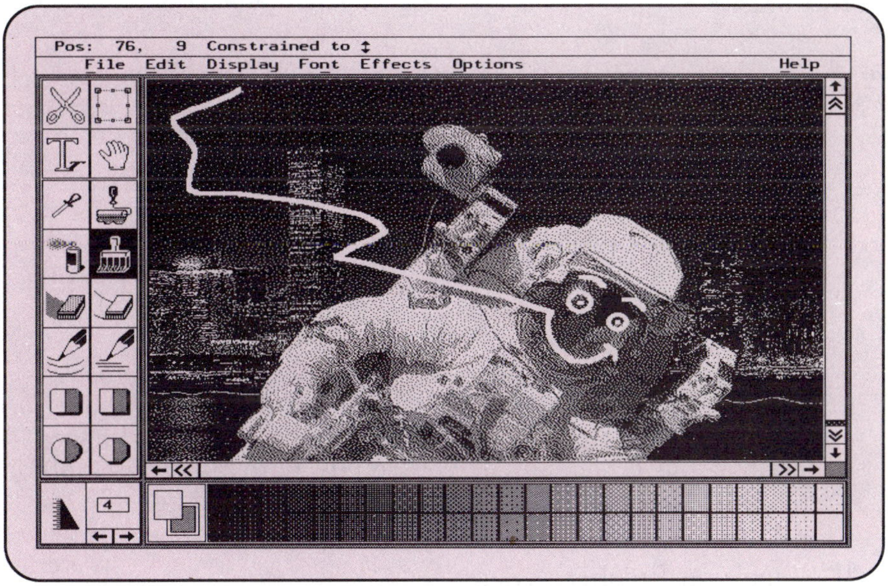

Figure 2.33 An electronic mishap.

Fortunately, a line drawn is just as easily erased. Rather than aggravate your ulcer, you can simply choose the Undo command from the Edit menu or press Control-U. The line will be erased and you can start over.

Unlike undo commands in other programs, the Undo command in Paintbrush erases all changes made since the last time you selected a tool. If you drew the entire face with the same tool without once clicking in the toolbox, choosing the Undo command will erase the entire face. The exceptions to this rule are the Text, Scissors, and Gadget Box tools, in which case choosing the Undo command only erases the image currently selected.

To undo more selectively, choose the Local Undo command.

The Local Undo Command

The Local Undo command allows you to undo specific portions of a drawing rather than undoing everything created with the current tool. You can use this command to undo a mistake only if, after making the mistake, you do not select a different tool or reselect the same tool or change the screen layout or use the scroll bars.

Q Using Local Undo

1. Make a mistake while drawing with any tool. — Momentary panic.
2. Choose the Local Undo command or press Control-L. — Most of the toolbox disappears and the cursor changes to a box with an "X" in it, as shown in Figure 2.34.
3. Use the cursor to erase a specific portion of your mistake. If the cursor is too small or too large, adjust its size using the options in the line width box. — As you drag, you erase images made with the current tool while images made with previous tools remain unchanged.
4. When you finish, press Control-L to return to the desktop.

□

As long as you don't select another tool, you can continue to undo details you created before choosing the Local Undo command. You can go back and forth between drawing and using the Local Undo command, fine-tuning one image without affecting others.

Creating a New Painting

When you first start Paintbrush, you are presented with the option to load (and therefore edit) an existing painting. If you pass on this by selecting the Cancel button or by pressing Escape, a second dialog box will appear, as shown in Figure 2.35, allowing you to cre-

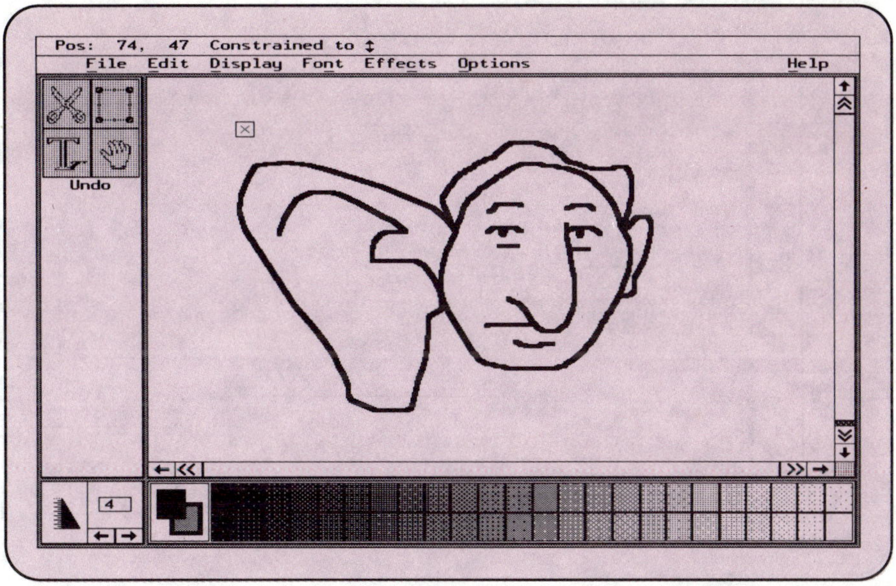

Figure 2.34 The local undo cursor is a box with an "X" in it.

ate a new painting. This dialog box also appears when you choose the New... command from the File menu.

Q Creating a New Painting File

1. Choose the New... command from the File menu or press Alt-F followed by the N key.
   The Create a New Picture dialog box displays.
2. Specify Width and Height values.
   Determines the size of your prospective painting.
3. Select a Number of Colors option.
   16 selects the full array of colors allowed under the current monitor configuration. 2 uses a black and white palette for your painting.
4. Make sure the Memory Available value is greater than the Memory Required value or go back to step 2 and reenter smaller Width and Height values.

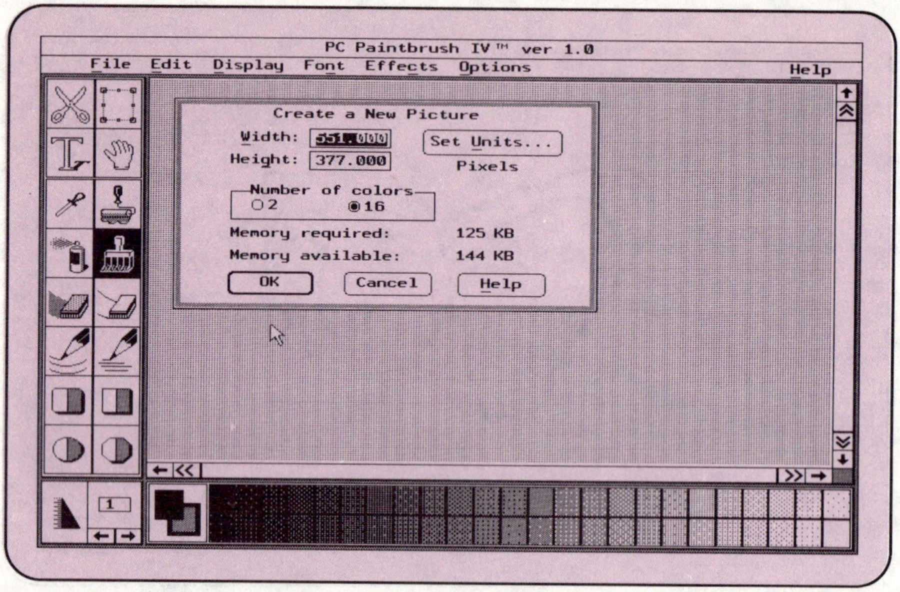

Figure 2.35 The Create a New Picture dialog box.

5. Press Enter or click OK to create the new file.

If, despite the warning in step 4, you try to create an image too large for your system, an alert box appears, warning `Not enough memory to create image`. If this alert does not appear, skip ahead to the result side of step 6.

6. Press Enter or click OK to close the alert box. Then enter smaller Width and Height values and press Enter or click OK again.

If a painting is already open and if you have made changes to it, an alert box displays, asking if you want to create a new painting without saving the current one. If this alert does not appear, an empty drawing window appears in the desktop.

7. Press the Y key or click Yes or press the N key or click No.

The Y key discards the changes and displays an empty drawing window in the desktop. The N key cancels the New... command and allows you to continue editing the current painting. □

Because Paintbrush IV can only access your computer's 640K of standard memory, the default values for the Width and Height options generally represent the largest image you can create using the current color configuration. In Paintbrush Plus, which can access expanded and virtual memory, you can use values higher than the defaults.

The values for the Width and Height options are normally displayed in *pixels*, which are the individual dots on your computer screen. However, you can change the unit of measure to something more familiar than pixels by selecting the Set Units... option in the Create a New Picture dialog box. This displays the Set Unit of Measure dialog box, shown in Figure 2.36, which allows you to choose from Inches, Centimeters, Points (1/72 of an inch), Picas (12 points or 1/6 of an inch), or Pixels for your Width and Height measurements. Press Enter after you make your choice.

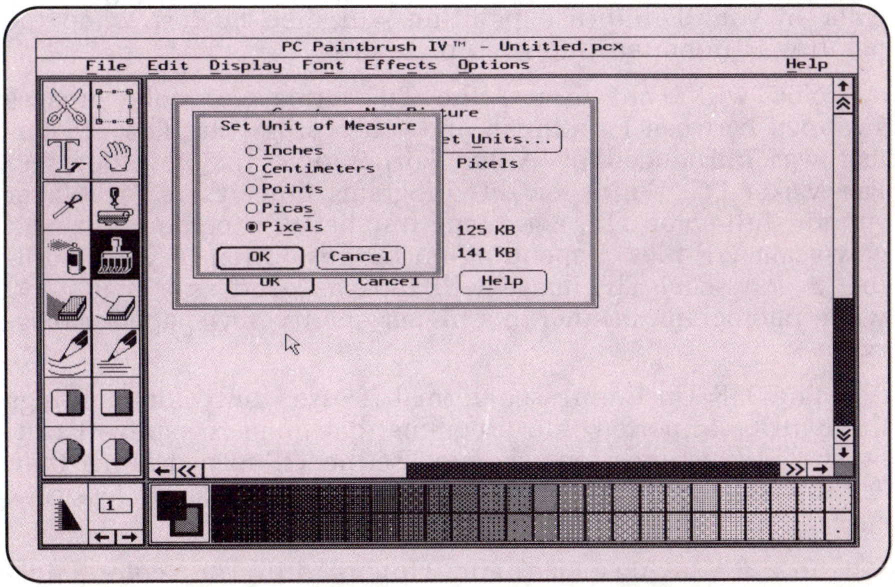

Figure 2.36 The Set Unit of Measure dialog box.

Saving a Painting

After you finish drawing a new painting or enhancing an existing painting, you will probably want to save it to disk for future use. This can be accomplished using either the Save or Save As... command, available from the File menu.

Saving a Painting in PCX or TIF Format

4 Paintbrush IV is capable of storing images in two widely used file formats: PCX, Paintbrush's native file format, and TIF, the tag image file format.

The PCX format is recognized by almost every desktop publishing, presentation, and graphics program designed for the PC. Therefore, if you create a painting in Paintbrush and save it as a PCX file, you will also be able to use it in an animated video or as an illustration in a newsletter. The PCX format has become the universal painting format for the PC.

However, the overwhelming majority of programs that read PCX files can only read them as black and white images. The color in your Paintbrush painting will then be lost when the painting is imported into such programs.

You will want to use the TIF format for color images swapped between Paintbrush and other programs. The TIF format was introduced by Aldus Corporation, the developers of PageMaker PC. While few PC programs other than PageMaker support full-color TIF, a growing number of programs can read gray-scale TIF files. Depending on the resolution of your painting, a gray-scale TIF image will look as good as a black and white photograph printed in a higher-quality newspaper or magazine.

The TIF Uncompressed format is used only for paintings that will be imported into programs that don't recognize Paintbrush's TIF compression scheme. Use the TIF format rather than TIF uncompressed if you can because TIF files occupy less disk space.

So when saving a black and white painting, or a color painting that you will use only in Paintbrush, use the PCX format. It will take less time to save a painting in PCX format because Paintbrush defaults to the PCX format in Save and Load dialog boxes. PCX is also a better choice for Paintbrush files because you'll know at once where a file called ANT.PCX comes from when you look at it years from now, whereas ANT.TIF might have come from any of several programs. When creating gray-scale images to import into other programs, save your painting as a TIF file.

Q Saving a Painting to Disk

1. Choose the Save command from the File menu or press Control-S.
   If you have saved the current painting previously, an alert box appears, asking if you want to save over the existing copy of the painting; proceed to step 2. If the current painting is new, the Save a Picture to Disk dialog box appears, as shown in Figure 2.37; skip to step 3.
2. Press the Y key or click Yes or press the N key or click No. (After answering No, you could choose the Save As... command to save the file under a new name.)
   The Y key saves the painting to disk over the old painting, using the Image Format of the old file; skip the remaining steps. The N key cancels the Save command.
3. Press Alt-P, Alt-T, or Alt-U or click on PCX, TIF, or TIF Uncompressed to select the correct Image Format option.
   Alt-P selects the PCX format, Alt-T the TIF format, and Alt-U the TIF Uncompressed format.
4. Enter a file name in the Filename option box. The file name cannot contain more than eight characters and must have a .PCX or .TIF extension.
5. Press Enter or click Save.
   Saves the painting to disk under the name specified and in the selected format. □

Saving a Painting under a New Name

1. Choose the Save As... command from the File menu or press Alt-F followed by the A key.	The Save a Picture to Disk dialog box appears, as shown in Figure 2.37.
2. Press Alt-P, Alt-T, or Alt-U or click on PCX, TIF, or TIF Uncompressed to select the correct Image Format option.	Alt-P selects the PCX format, Alt-T the TIF format, Alt-U the TIF Uncompressed format.
3. Enter a file name in the Filename option box. The file name cannot contain more than eight characters and must have a .PCX or .TIF extension.	
4. Press Enter or click Save.	Saves the painting to disk under the new name and in the selected format. □

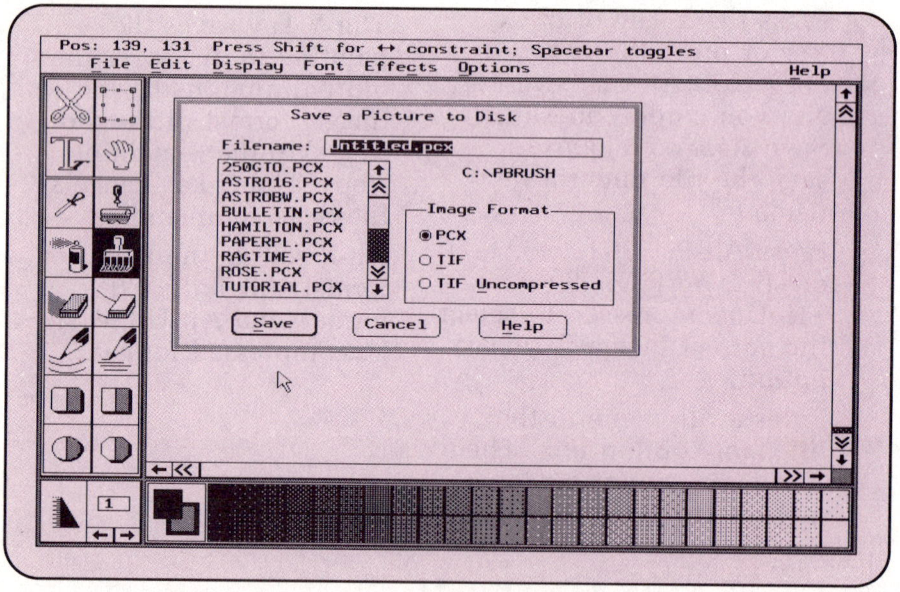

Figure 2.37 The Save a Picture to Disk dialog box.

Opening and Saving Workspaces

4 Just as you can open and save a painting, you can also open and save the various settings that make up the Paintbrush environment, which is known as the *workspace*. We've already discussed some of these settings, such as whether or not the caption bar, menu bar or color palette appears on the desktop. Following is a list of all the workspace settings you can adjust, in the order they are discussed in this book:

- Screen layout—Chapter 2
- Zoom magnification factors—Chapter 2
- Painting unit of measure—Chapter 2
- Selected Image Format—Chapter 2
- Current brush shape—Chapter 3
- Line width—Chapter 3
- Current color palette—Chapter 4
- Color model—Chapter 4
- Copy To directory—Chapter 5
- Active fonts in Font menu—Chapter 6
- Selected Font Format option—Chapter 6
- Current font, specifications, and style—Chapter 6
- Font directory—Chapter 6
- Effects mode—Chapter 7
- Set Tile Pattern directory—Chapter 7
- Halftone printing options (Paintbrush Plus only)—Chapter 8
- Printing aspect ratio—Chapter 8

Once you have customized the workspace settings to your satisfaction, choose the Save Workspace... command from the File menu to store them to disk. Workspaces are saved in an .INI file extension.

To load an existing workspace, choose the Open Workspace... command from the File menu. The previous settings will be replaced by new ones without harming the current painting. You *cannot* open workspaces saved under a monitor configuration different from the current one.

Summary

In this chapter, you've learned:

- Paintbrush Plus users can convert color paintings to black and white using halftone controls.
- You can hide the context-sensitive help in the caption bar by pressing Alt-H followed by the I key.
- You can select a new primary color by clicking a color box in the palette, a new secondary color by right-clicking a color box, a new background color by Shift-clicking a color box.
- You can make more room for the drawing window on the desktop by changing the screen layout using the Set Screen Layout... command from the Display menu.
- Pressing Control-A toggles the screen layout between the standard layout and a custom layout or between two custom layouts.
- You can magnify the view size of a painting in the drawing window so that you can adjust individual pixels by pressing Control-Z. Pressing Control-O reduces the view size of the painting.
- The Undo command undoes actions taken since you last selected the current tool, used the scroll bars, or changed the view size.
- Black and white paintings, or a color painting to be used only in Paintbrush, should be saved in the PCX file format. Gray-scale images to be imported into other programs should be saved in the TIF format.

Chapter 3

The Drawing Tools

What You Will Learn

- *Painting with the Paintbrush*
- *Drawing lines and shapes*
- *Filling in an area with the Paint Roller*
- *Creating special effects with the Spraycan*
- *Using the Standard and Color Erasers*

This chapter explains how to use 11 of the 12 drawing tools provided in Paintbrush IV as well as how each tool is affected by various factors such as line width and brush shape. (The Eyedropper tool is described in Chapter 4.) All 12 drawing tools are located in the lower portion of the Paintbrush toolbox.

The Paintbrush Tool

The Paintbrush tool, the fourth tool down on the right side of the toolbox, is the primary means for creating and editing images in Paintbrush. As the following Quick Steps demonstrate, this tool is precise, versatile, and easy to use.

Q Painting with the Paintbrush

1. Click a color in the color palette to select the primary color, right-click a color to select the secondary color.	The primary color appears in the forward box on the left side of the palette, the secondary color appears in the rear box on the left side of the palette.
2. Double-click the Paintbrush tool.	The Select a Brush Shape dialog box appears.
3. Select a brush shape. Select the square, round, or diamond brush shape to draw thick, consistent lines. Select a flat brush shape to create calligraphic lines.	
4. Specify a line width in the line width box, located in the lower-left corner of the desktop.	Determines the size of the cursor.
5. Draw lines by dragging or right-dragging.	Dragging creates lines in the primary color, right-dragging creates lines in the secondary color.
6. Press the Shift key while dragging to draw straight horizontal or vertical lines. Press the Spacebar to toggle between horizontal and vertical.	
7. Click on any tool in the Toolbox if you're satisfied with the lines you just drew.	Protects the lines you just drew from being deleted by the Undo command. □

Tip: To emulate real-life drawing and erasing, select black for the primary color and white for the secondary color.

Changing the Brush Shape

You paint with the Paintbrush tool much as you would with a real-life paintbrush: Dip the brush in paint, press the tip of the brush against the surface of the page, and make a brush stroke. In another respect, however, the Paintbrush tool doesn't so much imitate its real-life counterpart as surpass it. For example, a traditional artist utilizes many paintbrushes of different shapes and sizes. With a thick, soft brush, an artist can draw heavy outlines and create bold flourishes, or with a delicate, stiff-tip brush, add fine detail and touch up mistakes. In Paintbrush, the Paintbrush tool is a hundred brushes in one. With a few clicks of a mouse button, you can change the shape and size of the brush to satisfy any artistic impulse.

To change the brush shape, double-click the Paintbrush tool to display the Select a Brush Shape dialog box, shown in Figure 3.1. Or if you prefer, you can display this dialog box by choosing the Set Brush Shape command from the Options menu.

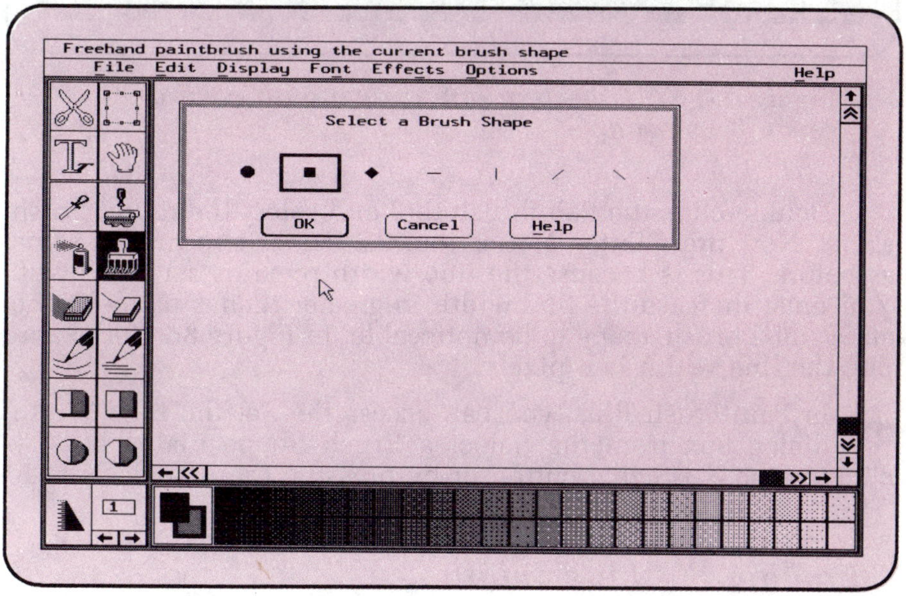

Figure 3.1 The Select a Brush Shape dialog box.

You can select one of seven cursor, or brush, shapes. Each shape produces a different effect, as demonstrated in Figure 3.2. To select a brush shape, click on it and press Enter. To select a brush shape and return to the desktop simultaneously, double-click a brush shape.

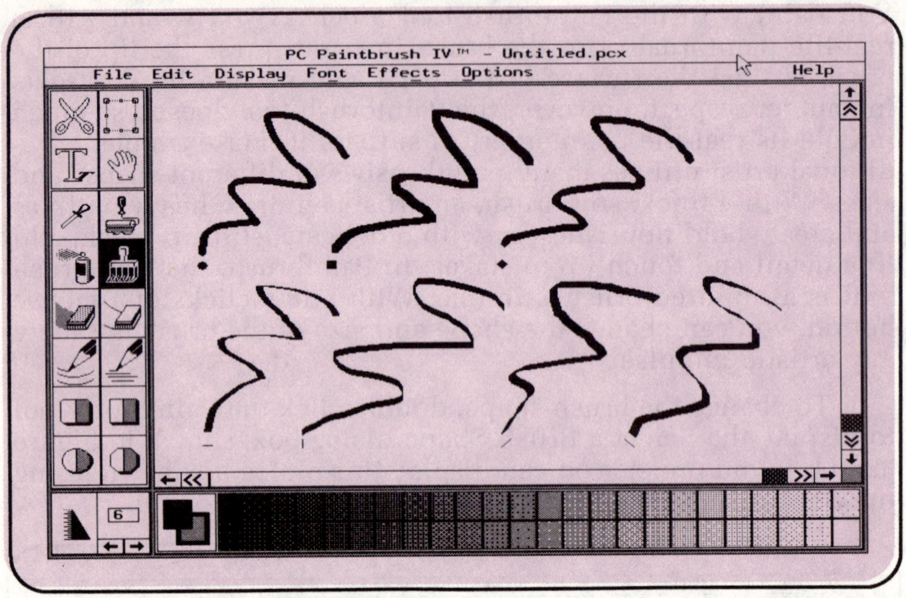

Figure 3.2 A free-form line drawn with each of the seven brush shapes.

Double-click the Paintbrush tool and select the round brush shape. Now press Enter. Notice that the cursor appears the same as before. This is because the line width remains set at 1 pixel. You must increase the line width to greater than 1 pixel for the effects of a brush shape to be noticeable. In Figure 3.2, for example, the line width is 6 pixels.

+ In Paintbrush Plus, you can access the Set the Line Width dialog box from the Select a Brush Shape dialog box by clicking the Set Size... button or by pressing the S key.

Changing the Line Width

4 You can change the line width by using the line width box located in the lower-left corner of the desktop. As we mentioned in Chapter 2, the line width box is divided into two parts: the line width triangle on the left and the line width display on the right. The following Quick Steps demonstrate three methods

to alter the line width using either or both parts of the line width box.

Entering a New Line Width Value

1. Drag the cursor over the line width value in the line width display. — Highlights the line width value.
2. Type a whole number between 0 and 40 and press Enter. — Changes the line width to the new value measured in pixels. □

Using the Line Width Arrow Icons

1. Click the left arrow in the line width display to decrease the line width in 1-pixel increments, click the right arrow to increase the line width in 1-pixel increments. — The value in the line width display changes.
2. Click on either arrow icon while holding the mouse button down to decrease or increase the line width more rapidly. Release the mouse button when the line width is the required thickness. — The value in the line width display becomes lower or higher. □

Using the Set Line Width Dialog Box

1. Click the line width triangle or choose the Set Line Width command from the Options menu. — The Set the Line Width dialog box, shown in Figure 3.3, appears.
2. Click the Set Units... button to change the unit of measure. — The Set Units of Measure dialog box, shown in Figure 2.36 of Chapter 2, appears.

3. Choose Inches, Centimeters, Points, Picas, or Pixels as the unit of measure and press Enter.	The selected unit of measure displays to the right of the Set Units... button.
4. Use the scroll bar to increase or decrease the line width value or enter a new value in the Line width option box.	The line width value changes. The dialog box below the Line width option box displays the line width in pixels, regardless of the current unit of measure. The large cross hairs to the right illustrate the current line width value.
5. Press Enter or click OK.	Accepts your changes and returns you to the desktop. □

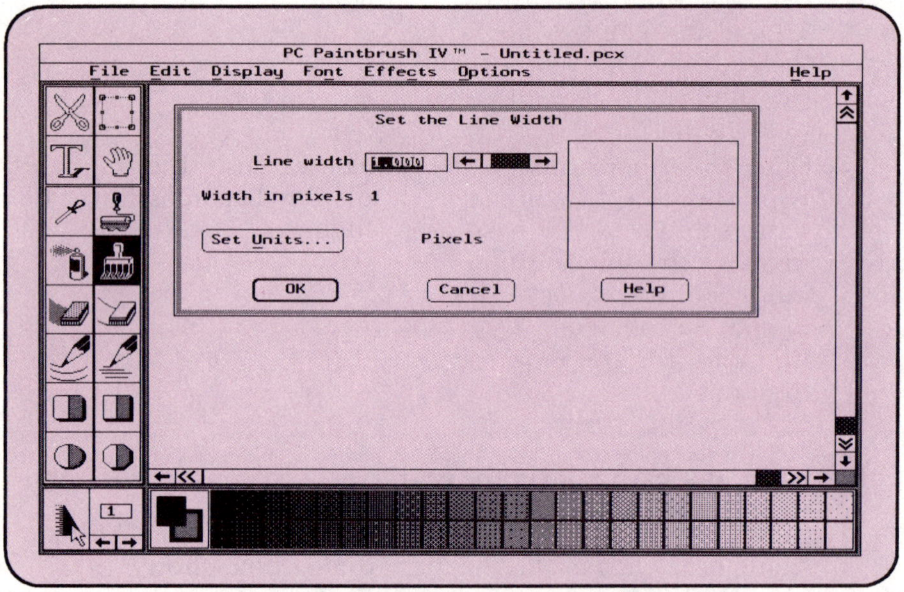

Figure 3.3 The Set the Line Width dialog box.

Although you can enter a fractional value in the Set Line Width dialog box, it will always round off to the nearest whole-pixel value. Figure 3.4 shows several sample line widths, ranging between 1 and 13 pixels. Line widths above 13 pixels are rarely useful.

> ▶ **Note:** When using the Paintbrush tool, a line width of 0 produces the same effect as a line width of 1: a single-pixel line.

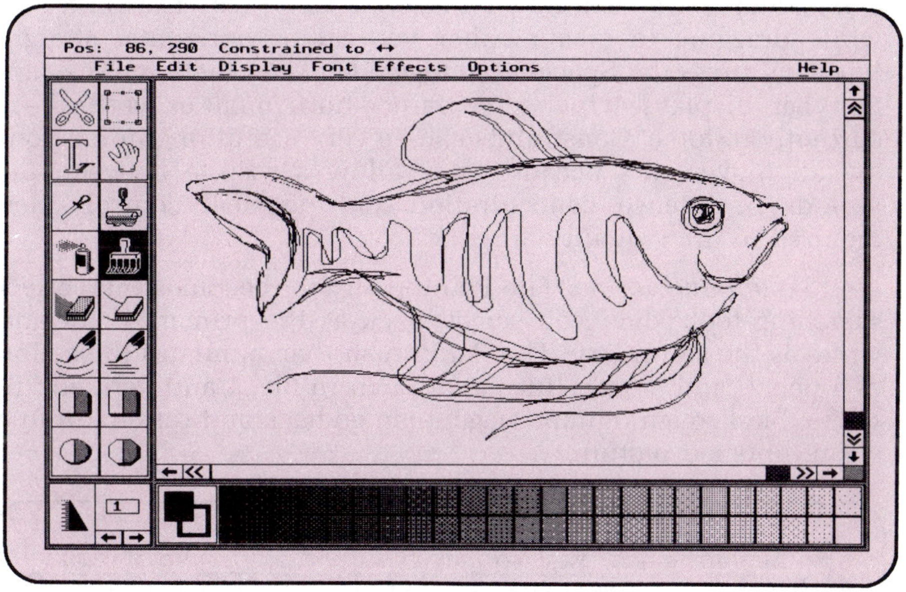

Figure 3.4 Line widths from 1 to 13 pixels.

The current brush shape is also used by the Straight Line tool, as discussed in *The Line Tools* section later in this chapter. The current line width is also used by both the Straight and Curved Line tools, the four shape tools, the Eraser tool, the Spraycan tool, and the Local Undo cursor (described in Chapter 2).

Painting Technique

Depending on your experience, you may at first find it difficult to create clean, consistent lines with the Paintbrush tool. But with practice, you will be able to master this tool. You can improve your painting technique more quickly by following these suggestions:

Draw slowly. Drawing with a mouse when you're used to drawing with a pencil is like driving a Greyhound when you're used to a Honda. You will draw more accurately if you take it slow and easy.

Use the Shift key to constrain your movements. In earlier Quick Steps, we mentioned that you can press the Shift key while dragging to create either vertical or horizontal straight lines and press the Spacebar to toggle between the two. The caption bar displays which constraint—horizontal or vertical—is currently in force. Constraints can be very useful in guiding your overall movements because they allow a respite between the periods of intense concentration and physical control often required to draw quality artwork.

Sketch and refine. The Paintbrush tool becomes the perfect sketching tool when you select black as the primary color and white as the secondary. The Paintbrush then emulates the action of a pencil and eraser; lines are drawn in black and "erased" in white. First rough out an image, then go back and refine it into a clean, finished picture.

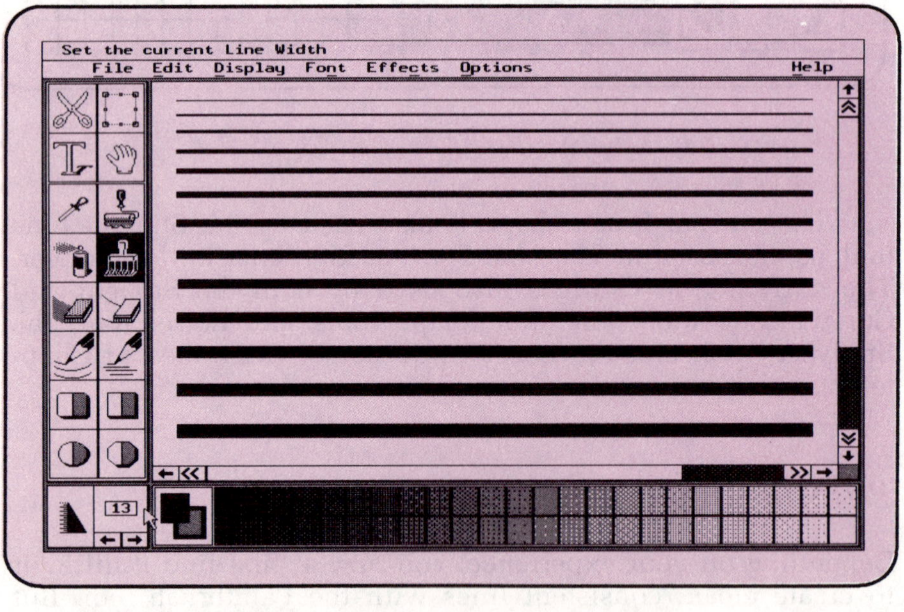

Figure 3.5 A sketch created quickly and approximately with the Paintbrush tool.

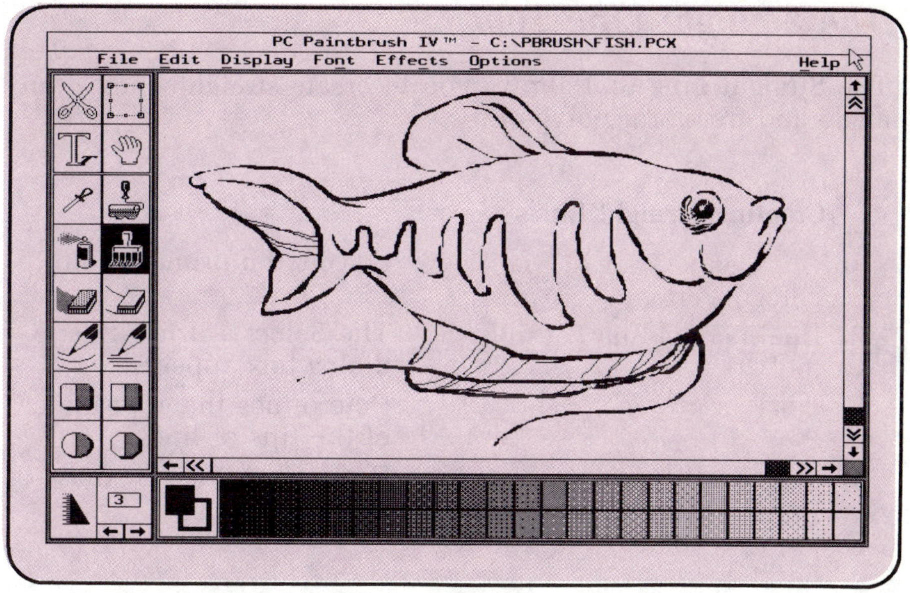

Figure 3.6 The finished image, refined by alternately drawing and erasing with the Paintbrush tool.

The Line Tools

The two line tools are the Straight Line tool and the Curved Line tool, which appear in the toolbox as a pencil drawing straight lines and a pencil drawing curved lines, respectively. Both tools create smooth, crisp lines of consistent thicknesses. Use these tools when you want to create geometric and curvilinear outlines. The traditional counterpart of the Straight Line tool is a ruler; the Curved Line tool performs like a French curve.

4 Both line tools have been enhanced in Paintbrush IV. Both tools are now capable of drawing multi-line images, the left and right mouse buttons perform different functions than in previous versions, and the Curved Line tool provides more control.

The Straight Line Tool

The Straight Line tool allows you to create straight lines at any angle and free-form polygons.

Q Creating Straight Lines

1. Click on a color in the color palette.	Selects the primary color.
2. Double-click the Paintbrush tool.	The Select a Brush Shape dialog box appears.
3. Select a brush shape.	Determines the appearance of the tips of lines.
4. Specify a line width in the line width box, located in the lower-left corner of the desktop.	Determines the thickness of lines.
5. Select the Straight Line tool.	Highlights the Straight Line tool.
6. Press the left mouse button to mark the beginning of a line and drag. Press the Shift key as you drag to draw lines at 45° angles. Release at the point where you want a line to end.	The caption bar shows the coordinate of the cursor, the coordinate at which the line begins, the length of the line, and its angle, as shown in Figure 3.7.
7. Continue right-clicking, right-dragging, and releasing to create a free-form polygon.	Figure 3.8 shows a polygon created with the Straight Line tool.
8. Press the Control key and right-click several times to create a ray.	Rays emanate from the first point in the polygon, as shown in Figure 3.9.
9. If you have finished drawing lines, select any tool.	Protects the lines you just drew from being deleted by the Undo command. □

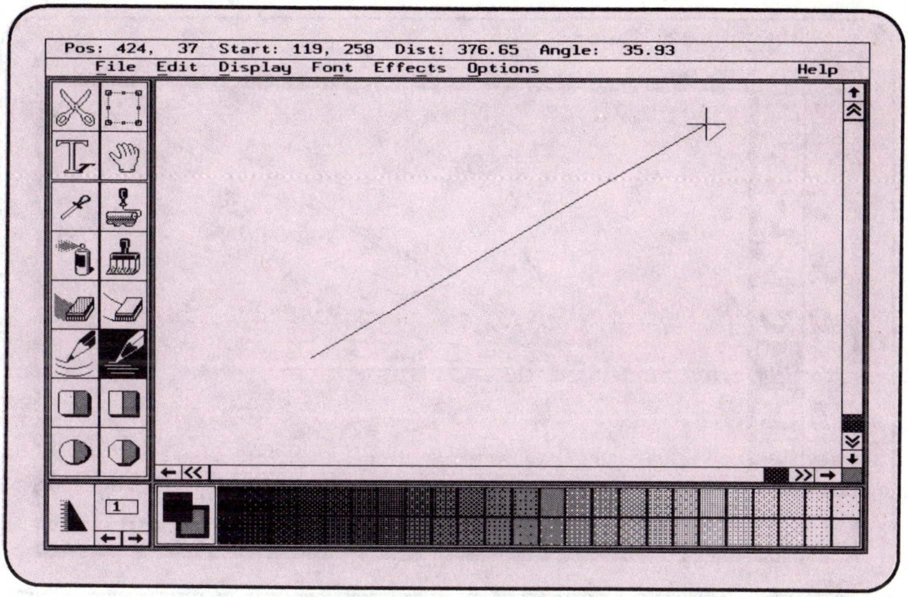

Figure 3.7 Dragging with the Straight Line tool.

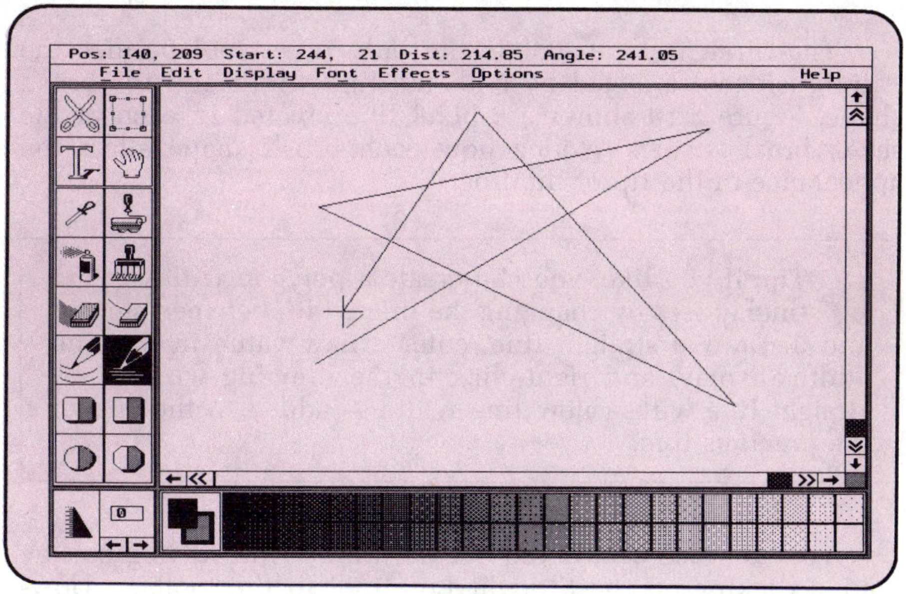

Figure 3.8 Right-dragging with the Straight Line tool.

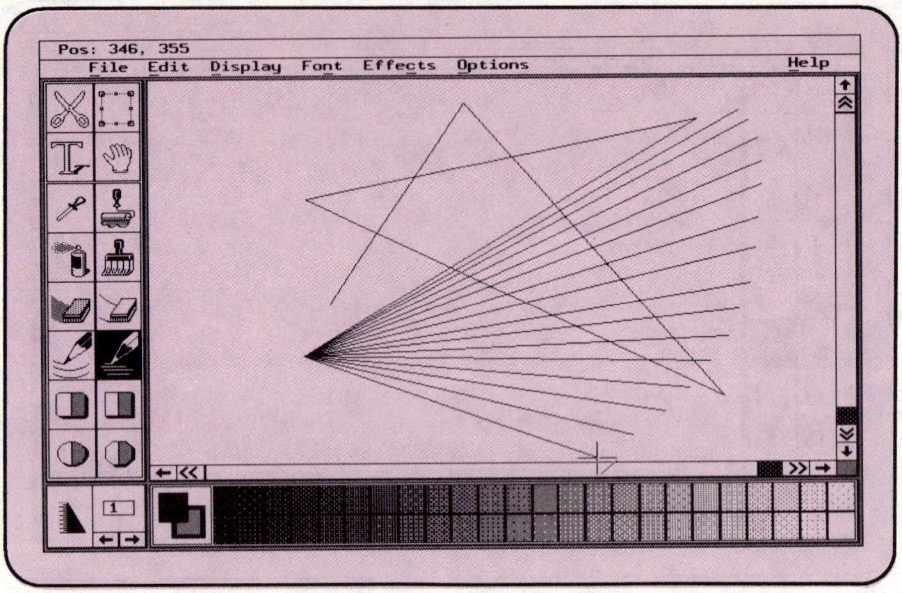

Figure 3.9 Control-right-clicking with the Straight Line tool.

The Straight Line tool is the only other tool besides the Paintbrush tool affected by both the line width and the brush shape. Figure 3.10 shows a 6-pixel line created in each of the seven brush shapes. Notice how each brush shape alters the appearance of the tip of the line.

Tip: If you like, you can create a polygon with varying thicknesses by changing the line width between steps 4 and 5. Draw a straight line, enter a new value in the line width display, and right-click in the drawing window. A straight line with a new line width is added to the end of the previous line.

You can also access the Set the Line Width dialog box by double-clicking on the Straight Line tool in the toolbox. However, if you change the line width in this way, you will no longer be able to append lines to the current polygon by right-clicking.

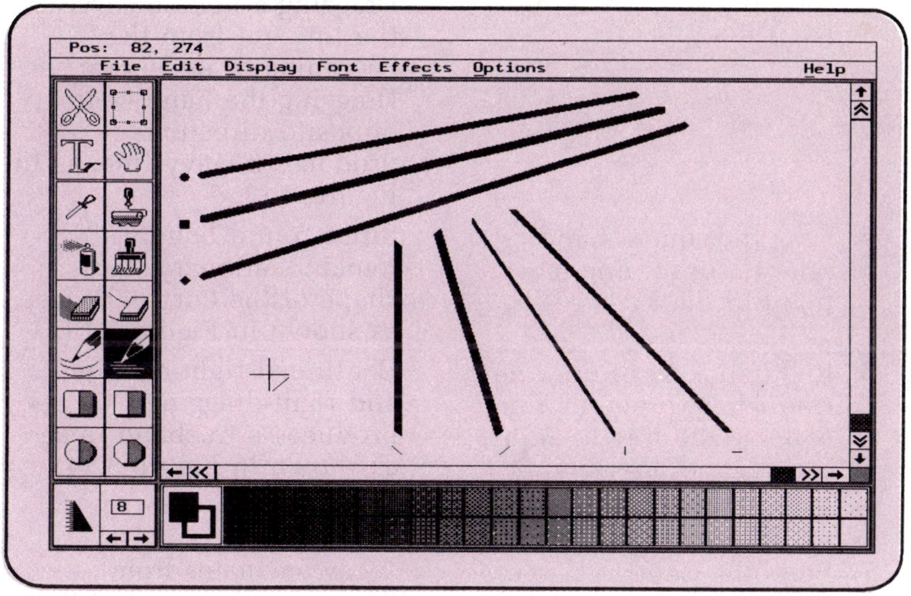

Figure 3.10 Each of the seven brush shapes applied to straight lines.

The Curved Line Tool

The Curved Line Tool is the third tool from the bottom on the left side of the toolbox. You can use the Curved Line tool to create meticulous curving lines as well as freehand images composed of several curving lines.

Creating Curved Lines

1. Select a primary color.	
2. Specify a line width in the line width box.	Determines the thickness of lines.
3. Select the Curved Line tool and drag to create a straight line, as if using the Straight Line tool.	Caption bar displays line information. When you release, four hollow handles appear on the line, as in Figure 3.11.

4. Drag the round handles to bend the line.	Dragging a handle curves the line out from the beginning or end point. Dragging the handles in opposite directions produces a wavy line, as in Figure 3.12.
5. Drag the square handles to relocate beginning or end point of the line.	Since round handles remain stationary, the shape of the curve changes, as shown in Figure 3.13.
6. Right-click to begin a new line where previous line ends. Right-drag to adjust the angle of the line. Drag the handles to adjust the curvature and end points.	Continued right-clicking and right-dragging produces a freehand image as shown in Figure 3.14.
7. Press the Control key and right-click to create a curved ray. Drag the handles to adjust the ray.	A ray emanates from the beginning point of the first line drawn, as in Figure 3.15.
8. Click outside the curve to fix the completed image in place.	All handles disappear.
9. Select any tool.	Protects lines you just drew from the Undo command. □

As with the Straight Line tool, you can change the line width between steps 5 and 6 to create a freehand image of varying thicknesses. Draw a line, enter a new value in the line width display, and right-click in the drawing window. A curved line with a new line width will be added to the end of the previous line.

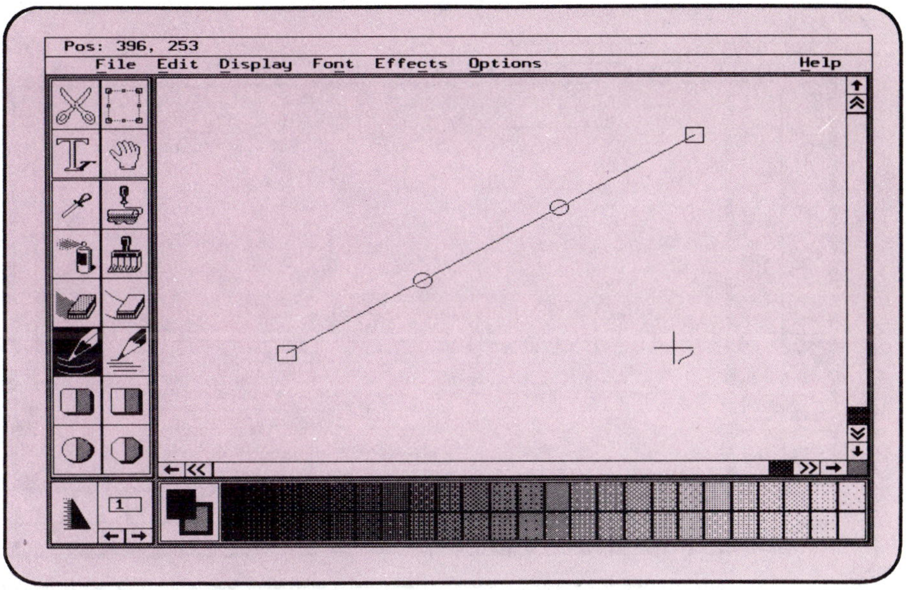

Figure 3.11 Dragging with the Curved Line tool creates a straight line with handles.

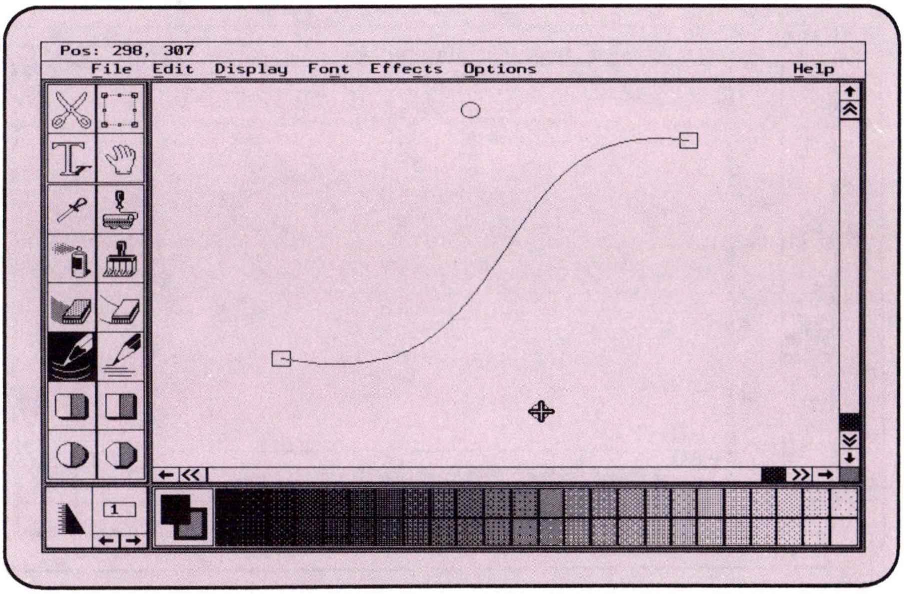

Figure 3.12 Drag the round handles to make the line curve in the direction of the handle.

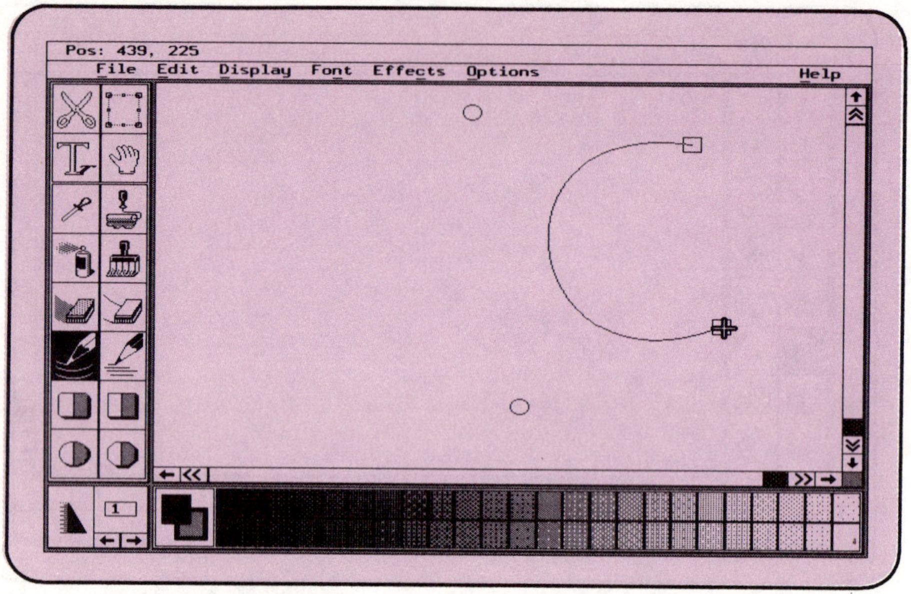

Figure 3.13 Drag the square handles to move the ends of the curved line.

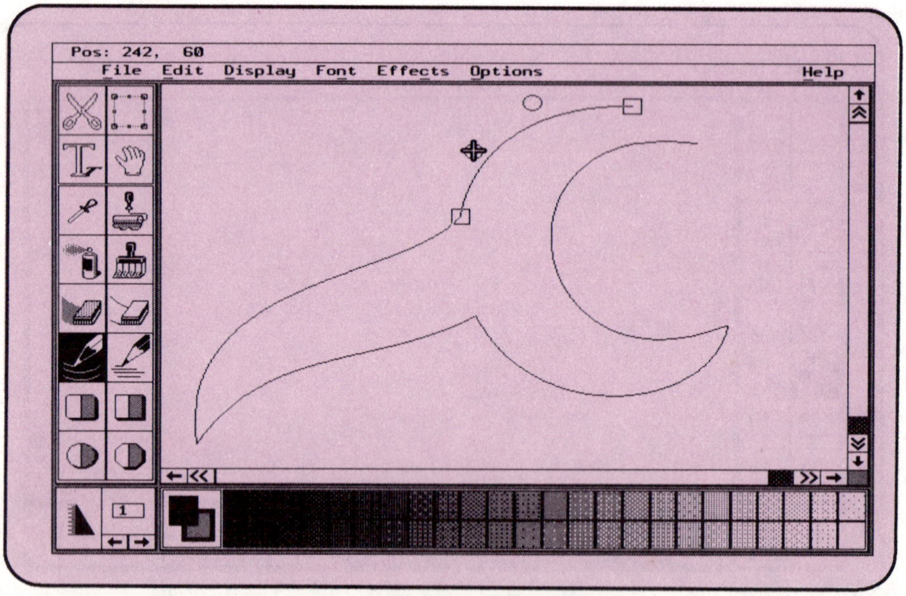

Figure 3.14 Right-dragging with the Curved Line tool appends a curved line to the end of the previous line.

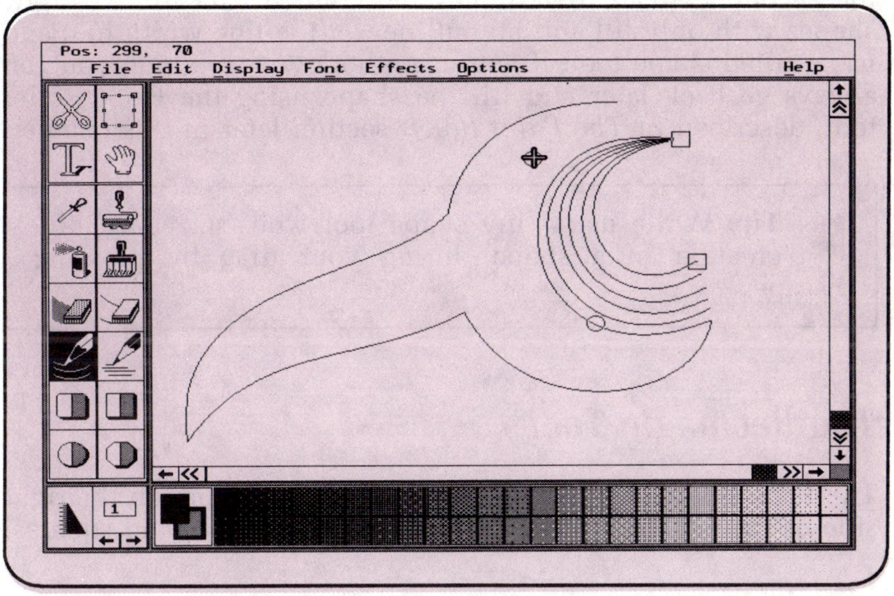

Figure 3.15 Control-right-clicking with the Curved Line tool produces a curved ray.

Caution: When creating a series of curved lines, do not drag the first point in a line unless you want to create a gap in your image between the end of the previous line and the beginning of the new line. Dragging a square handle does not move the end of the previous line.

The Shape Tools

The shape tools include the Rectangle tool, the Rounded Rectangle tool, the Ellipse tool, and the Polygon tool, located in the bottom four slots of the toolbox. All four tools are available in a hollow and a filled form. To create a hollow shape, click in the left half of the tool icon. To create a filled shape, click in the right half of the tool icon. The half you select will become highlighted.

The shape tools are easy to use. The primary color determines the color of the outline. If you select a filled shape tool, the secondary color determines the color of the fill. To draw shapes with only fill and no outline, set the line width to 0 and use a filled shape tool. If you use a hollow shape tool, you can always go back later and fill the shape using the Paint Roller tool, described in *The Paint Roller* section later in this chapter.

> **Tip:** While using any shape tool, you can cancel the creation of a shape during your drag by pressing Escape.

The Rectangle Tool

The Rectangle tool, the second tool from the bottom on the right side of the toolbox, allows you to create rectangles and squares.

Drawing a Rectangle

1. Click a color in the color palette to select the primary color, right-click a color to select the secondary color.	The primary color appears in the forward box on the left side of the palette, the secondary color appears in the rear box.
2. Specify a line width in the line width box, located in the lower-left corner of the desktop.	The line width determines the thickness of the rectangle's outline.
3. Click the hollow or filled Rectangle tool.	Highlights the left or right half of the Rectangle tool.
4. Press the left mouse button to set the first corner of the rectangle, then drag.	The caption bar indicates the coordinate of the cursor, the coordinate of the first point, and the width and height of the rectangle (labeled "Delta"), as shown in Figure 3.16.

5. Press the Shift key as you drag to constrain the shape to a perfect square. Release when the rectangle is the correct size and shape.

6. Select any tool if you are satisfied with the rectangle you drew.

Protects the rectangle from being deleted by the Undo command. □

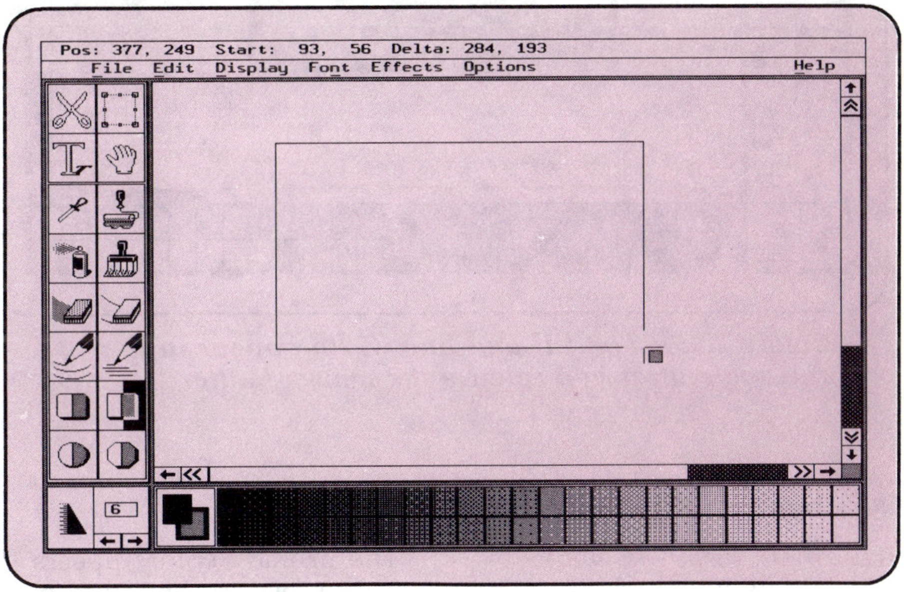

Figure 3.16 Dragging with the Rectangle tool.

> **Note:** If your squares do not appear as perfect squares on screen, it is because you have tampered with the aspect ratio, which is discussed in Chapter 8, *Printing a Painting*.

The Rounded Rectangle Tool

The Rounded Rectangle tool, the second tool from the bottom on the left side of the toolbox, allows you to create rectangles and squares with rounded corners.

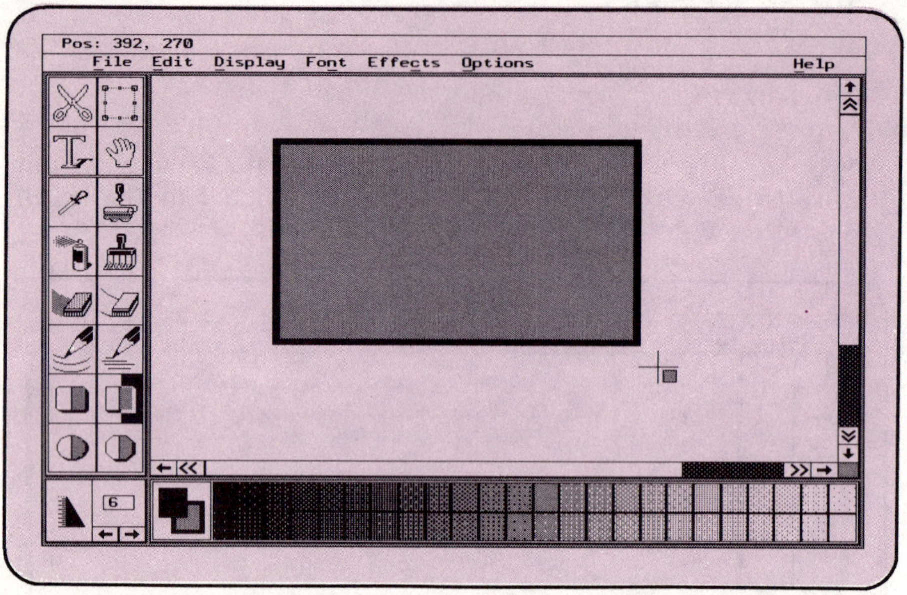

Figure 3.17 The fill and line width appear in the rectangle after you release the mouse button.

Q Drawing a Rectangle with Rounded Corners

1. Click a color in the color palette to select the primary color, right-click a color to select the secondary color.

   The primary color appears in the forward box on the left side of the palette, the secondary color appears in the rear box.

2. Specify a line width in the line width box, located in the lower-left corner of the desktop.

   The line width determines the thickness of the rectangle's outline.

3. Click the hollow or filled Rounded Rectangle tool.

   Highlights the left or right half of the Rounded Rectangle tool.

4. Press the left mouse button to set the first corner of the rectangle and drag.

The caption bar indicates the coordinate of the cursor, the coordinate of the first point, and the width and height of the rectangle (labeled "Delta"), as shown in Figure 3.18.

5. Press the Shift key as you drag to constrain the shape to a rounded square. Release when the rectangle is the correct size and shape.

6. Select any tool if you are satisfied with the rounded rectangle you just drew.

Protects the rounded rectangle from being deleted by the Undo command. □

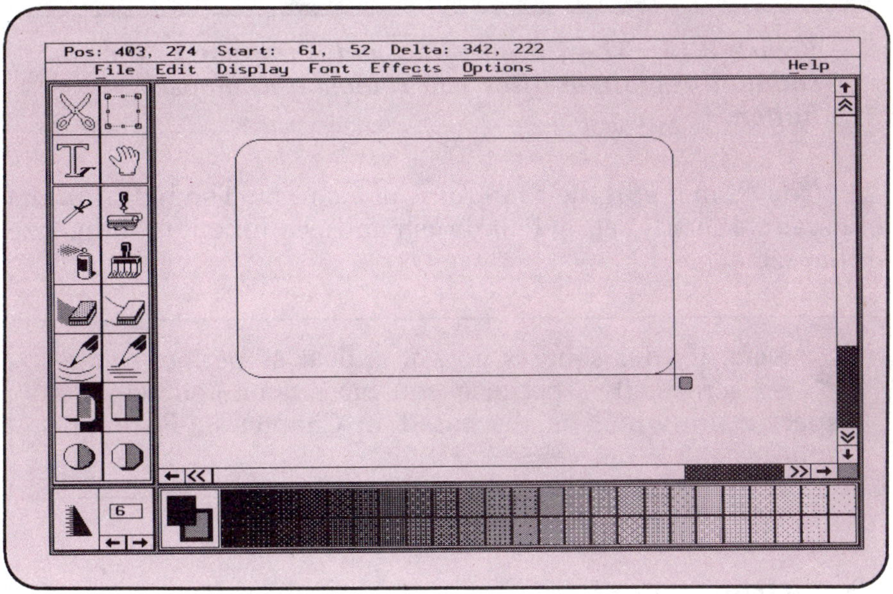

Figure 3.18 Dragging with the Rounded Rectangle tool.

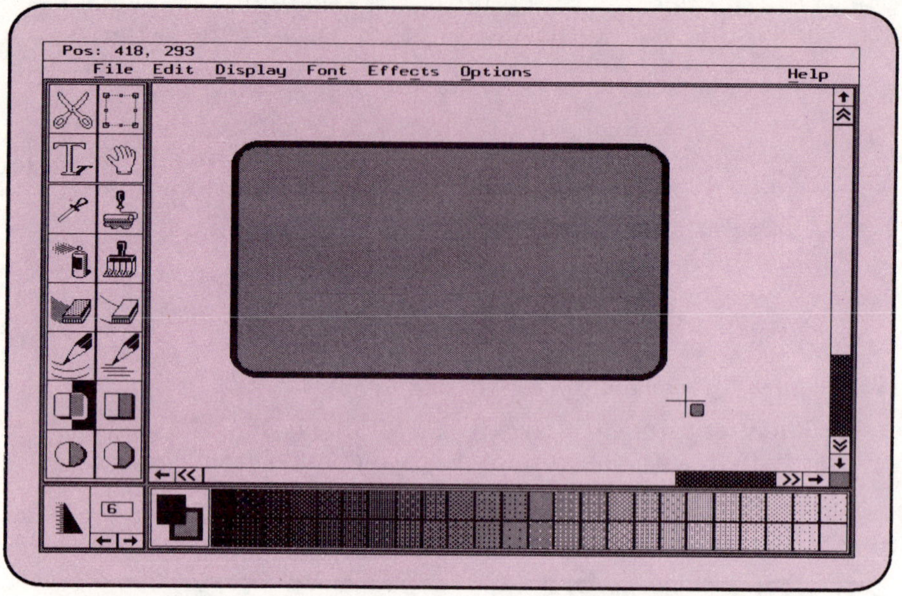

Figure 3.19 The fill and line width appear in the rounded rectangle after you release the mouse button.

You cannot edit the roundness of a corner. The radius of the circular corners is set by Paintbrush and is a function of the size of the rectangle.

> **Note:** If your squares do not appear as perfect squares on screen, it is because you have tampered with the aspect ratio, which is discussed in Chapter 8, *Printing a Painting*.

The Ellipse Tool

4 The Ellipse tool, the lowest tool on the left side of the toolbox, allows you to create ellipses (ovals) and circles. Paintbrush IV includes a new feature which allows you to create concentric ellipses and circles. The following Quick Steps explain how to draw with the Ellipse tool.

Q Drawing an Ellipse

1. Click on the color palette to select the primary color, right-click a color to select the secondary color.

   The primary color appears in the forward box on the left side of the palette, the secondary color appears in the rear box.

2. Specify a line width in the line width box.

   The line width determines the thickness of the ellipse outline.

3. Click the hollow or filled Ellipse tool.

   Highlights the left or right half of the Ellipse tool.

4. Press the left mouse button to specify the center of the ellipse and drag.

   The caption bar indicates the coordinate of the cursor, the coordinate of the center point, and the horizontal and vertical radius of the ellipse (half the width and height), as shown in Figure 3.20.

5. Press the Shift key as you drag to constrain the shape to a perfect circle. Release when the ellipse is the correct size and shape.
6. Right-click to create an ellipse that shares the same center point as the previous shape.
7. Right-drag to adjust the size and shape of the ellipse as you create it, then release.

   Continued right-clicking, right-dragging, and releasing created the concentric ovals shown in Figure 3.22.

8. Select any tool if you are satisfied with the ellipse you just drew.

   Protects the ellipse from being deleted by the Undo command. □

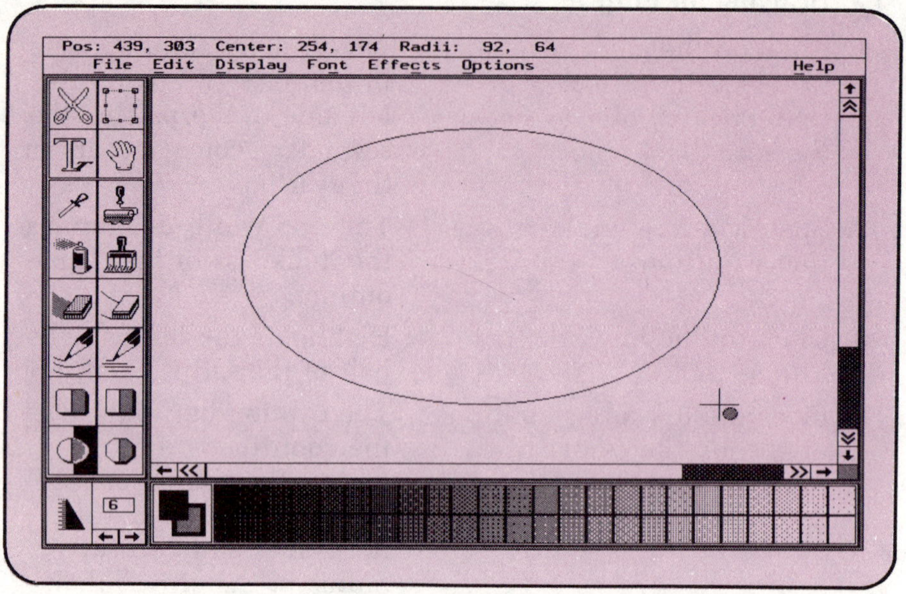

Figure 3.20 Dragging with the Ellipse tool.

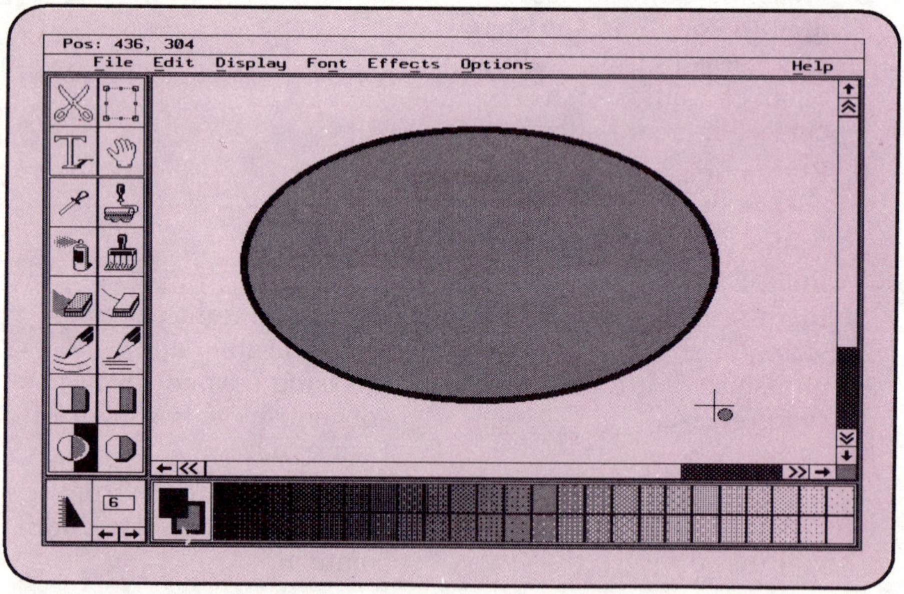

Figure 3.21 The fill and line width appear after you release your mouse button.

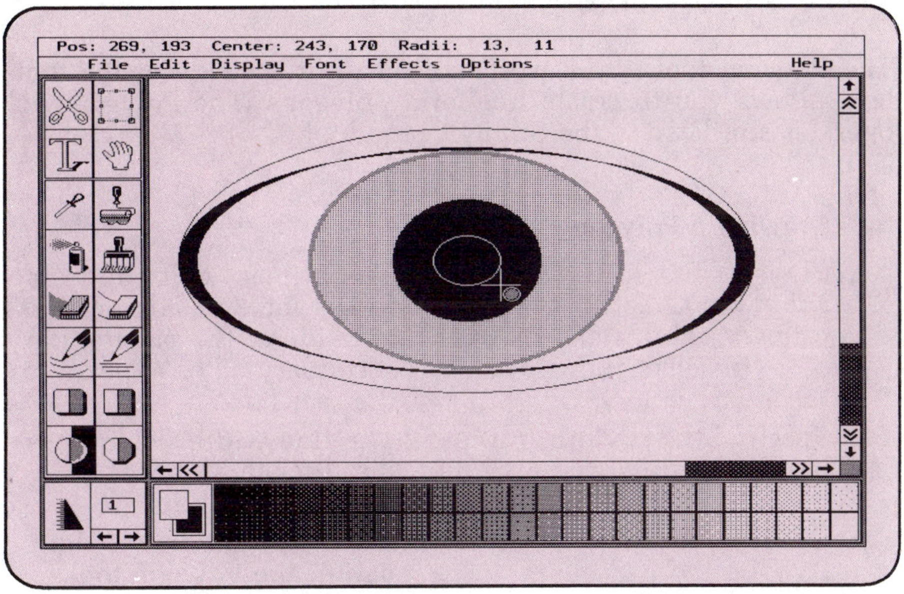

Figure 3.22 Right-dragging with the Ellipse tool creates concentric circles.

> **Note:** If your circles do not appear as perfect circles on screen, it is because you have tampered with the aspect ratio, which is discussed in Chapter 8, *Printing a Painting*.

You can change the line width between steps 4 and 5 to assign different thicknesses to your concentric ovals. Draw an ellipse, enter a new value in the line width display, and right-click in the drawing window. An ellipse with a new line width will share the same center point as the previous shape.

If you want to create concentric ovals with the filled Ellipse tool, be sure to create the outermost ovals first and work inward. This way, you will not cover up your previous shapes with new ones. If you change from the filled Ellipse tool to the hollow Ellipse tool, you will no longer be able to create concentric ellipses by right-clicking.

The Polygon Tool

The Polygon tool, the lowest tool on the right side of the toolbox, allows you to create free-form polygons. The Polygon tool operates similarly to the Straight Line tool.

Q Drawing a Polygon

1. Click a color in the color palette to select the primary color, right-click a color to select the secondary color.	The primary color appears in the forward box on the left side of the palette, the secondary color appears in the rear box.
2. Specify a line width in the line width display.	The line width determines the thickness of the polygon's outline.
3. Click the hollow or filled Polygon tool.	Highlights the left or right half of the Polygon tool.
4. Draw the first side of the polygon: Press the left mouse button to mark the beginning of the line and drag, release where you want the line to end. Press the Shift key as you drag to draw lines at 45° angles.	The caption bar indicates the coordinate of the cursor, the coordinate at which the line begins, the length of the line and its angle, as shown in Figure 3.23.
5. Click (do not right-click) to create another line that begins where the previous line ends, drag to adjust the angle of the line as you create it.	Continued clicking, dragging, and releasing created the free-form polygon shown in Figure 3.24.
6. Double-click to close the polygon.	A straight line connects the point at which you double-click to the first point in the polygon. If you used the filled polygon tool, overlapping portions of the polygon are not filled, as shown in Figure 3.25.
7. Select any tool if you are satisfied with the polygon you just drew.	Protects the polygon from being deleted by the Undo command. □

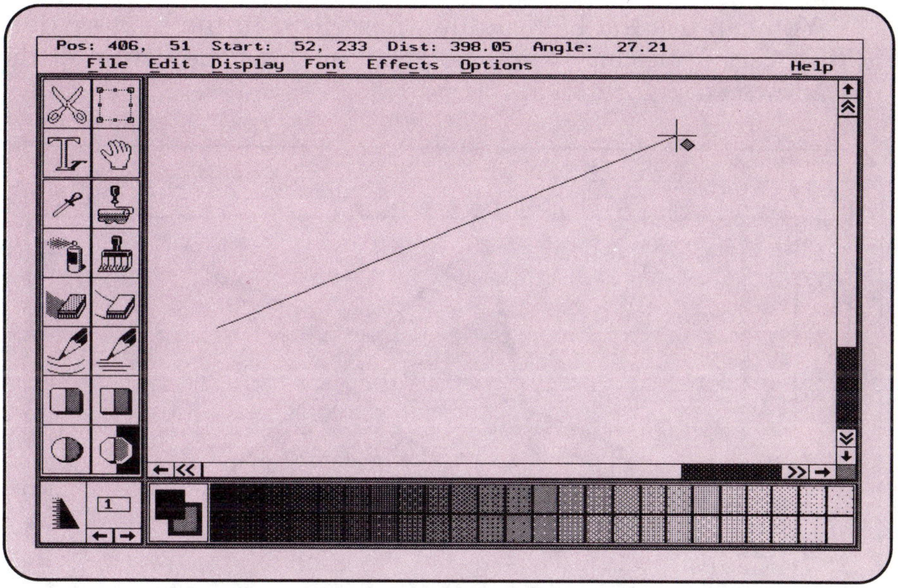

Figure 3.23 The caption bar provides information about the cursor and line as you drag with the Polygon tool.

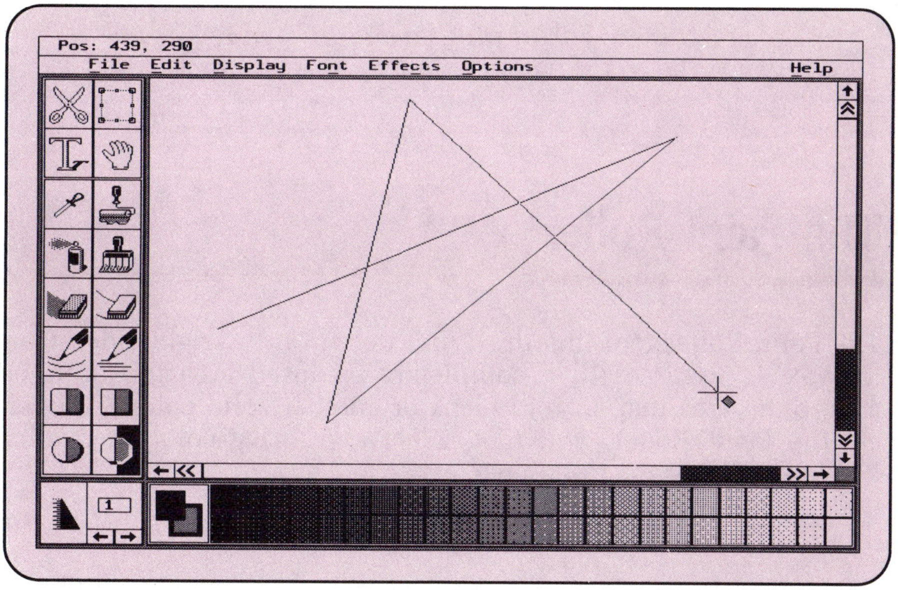

Figure 3.24 A free-form polygon created with the Polygon tool.

You can use the Paint Roller, described in the next section, to fill overlapping areas in a polygon, such as the center of the star shown in Figure 3.25.

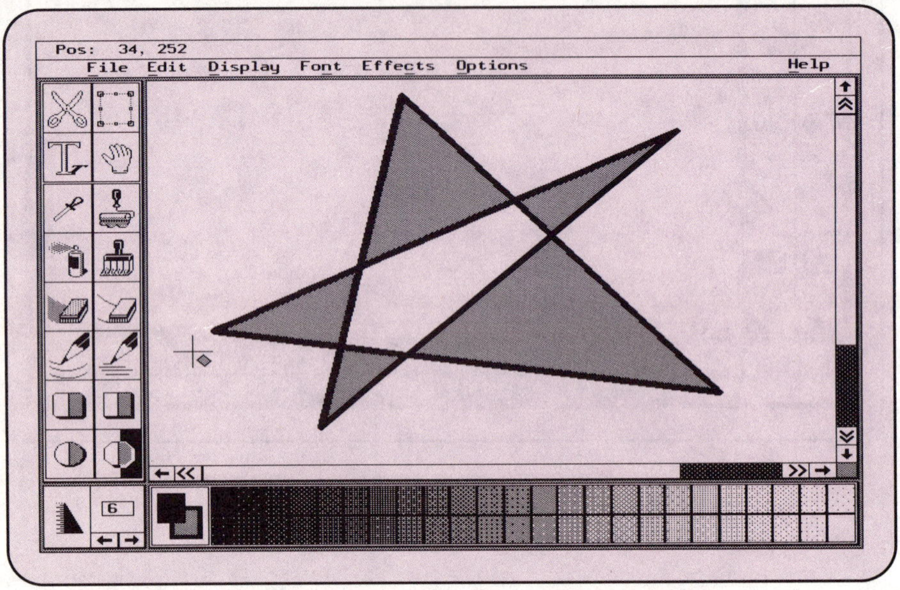

Figure 3.25 Overlapping areas in a polygon are never filled, as demonstrated by the center of this star.

The Paint Roller

The Paint Roller tool, the third tool down on the right side of the toolbox, is used to fill a completely enclosed area (an outlined area) or an area that is solid black or another solid color. To operate the Paint Roller, you first select a primary color then click inside a solid or enclosed area.

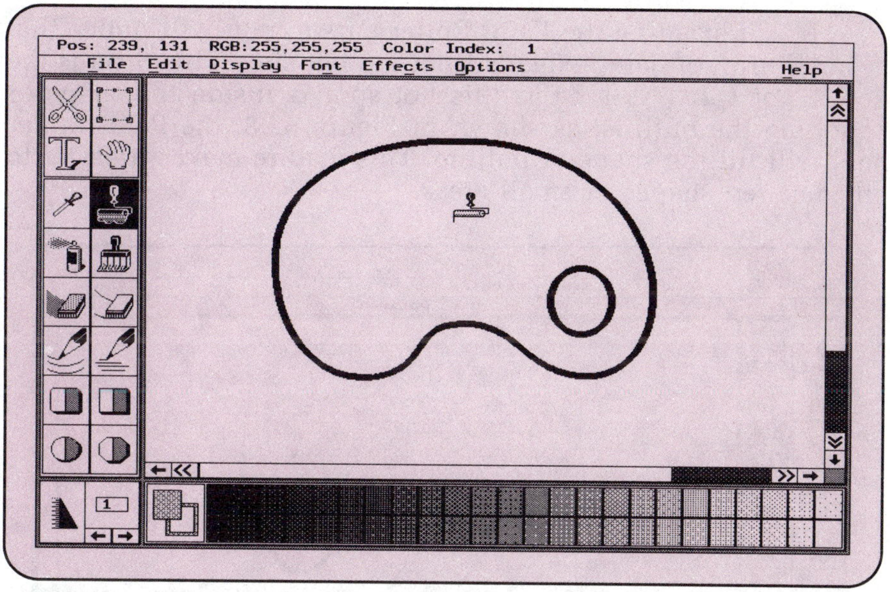

Figure 3.26 Position the Paint Roller cursor inside the shape to be filled and click.

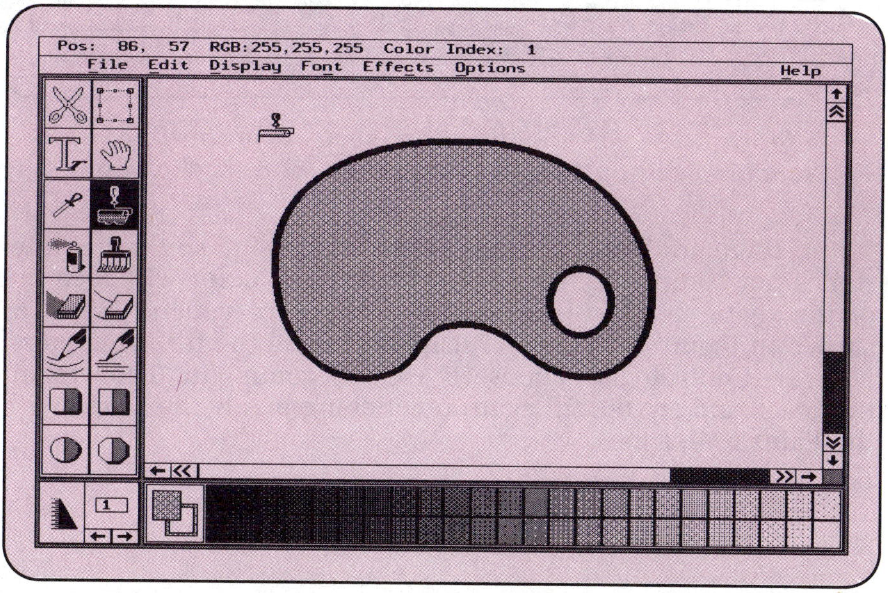

Figure 3.27 The Paint Roller fills the shape with the primary color.

If you examine the Paint Roller cursor, you will notice that a small drop of paint extends from the left side. This drop is the tool's *hot spot*. As long as this hot spot is inside the shape or touching the outline, as shown in Figure 3.28, the Paint Roller tool will fill the shape or outline. This feature makes it easier to fill detailed shapes or small areas.

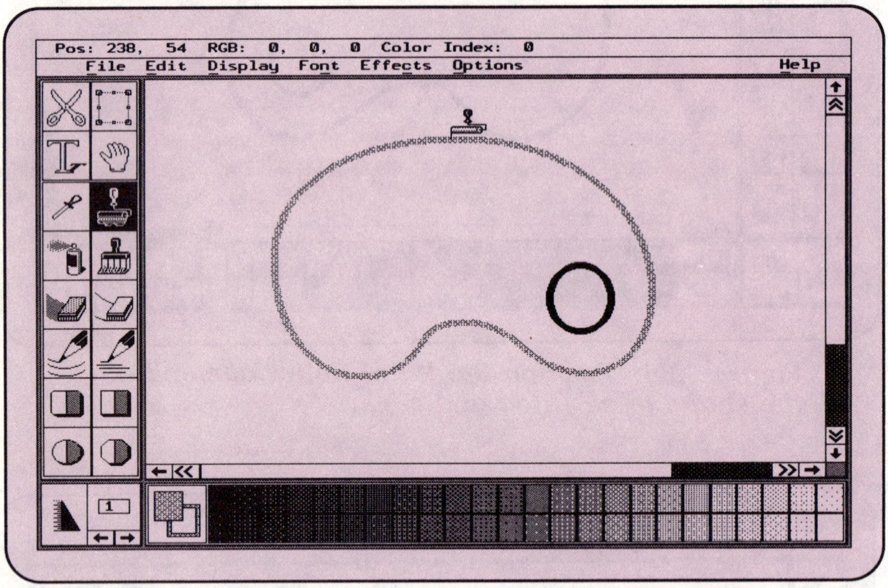

Figure 3.28 Fill a solid area, such as an outline, by touching the outline with the hot spot and clicking.

If there are breaks in the outline of a shape so that its interior is not completely enclosed, the primary color will seep out of the shape and spill into other portions of your drawing, as shown in Figure 3.29. Press Escape to cancel the fill in progress, or press Control-U to choose the Undo command. Then repair the break and try the fill again by clicking inside the shape with the Paint Roller tool.

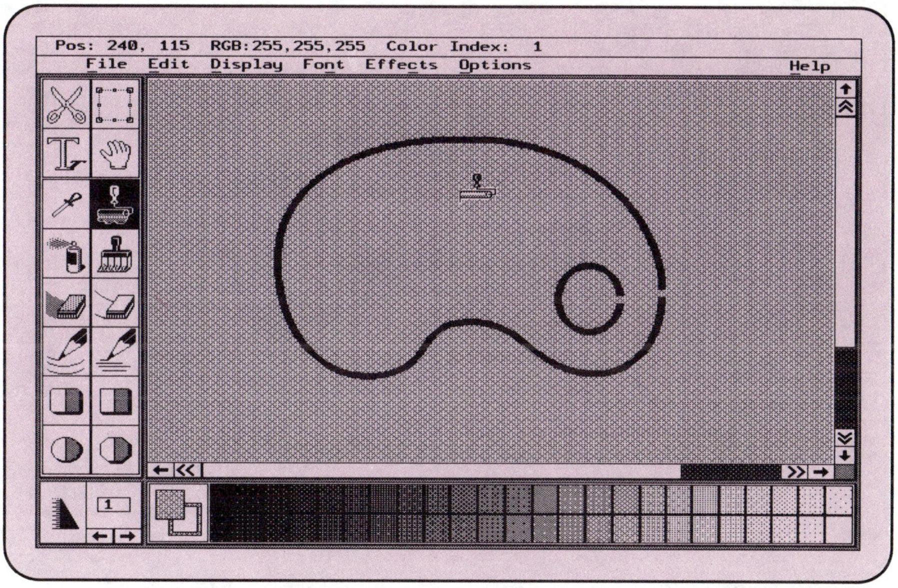

Figure 3.29 Breaks allow the primary color to spill out of the shape.

If a shape is filled with a *pattern* (an area which is not solid but contains pixels of different colors), you can refill this area with a darker pattern or a solid color by right-clicking with the Paint Roller. For example, the shape shown in Figure 3.27 is filled with a pattern. If you select a darker pattern as the primary color and right-click inside this shape with the Paint Roller tool, you will produce the result shown in Figure 3.30. If you right-click on the filled outline shown in Figure 3.28, you will produce Figure 3.31. Right-clicking with the Paint Roller tool instructs Paintbrush to fill in any area that is not a solid color.

Q Filling Shapes and Outlines

1. Click a color in the color palette to select a primary color. — The primary color appears in the forward box on the left side of the palette.
2. Click the Paint Roller tool. — Highlights the Paint Roller tool.

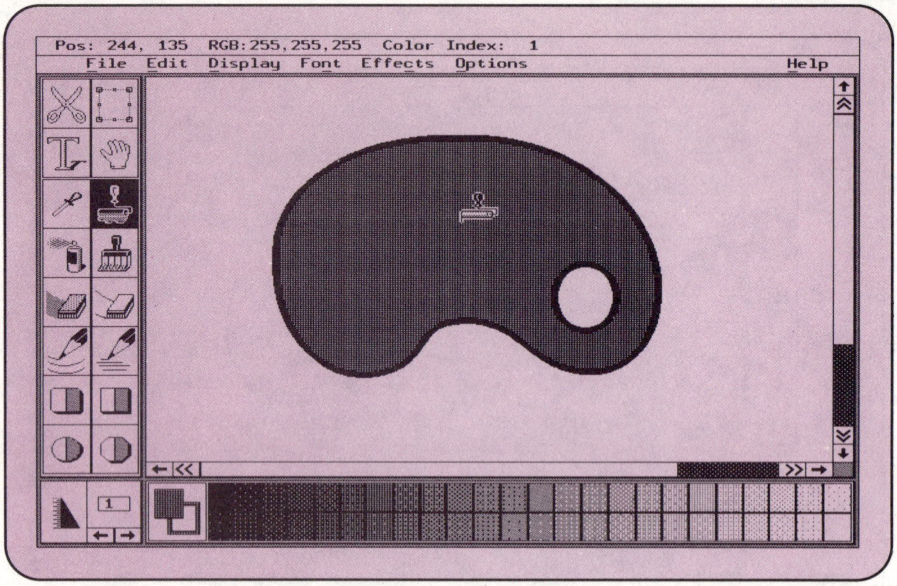

Figure 3.30 Right-click with the Paint Roller tool to fill in a pattern.

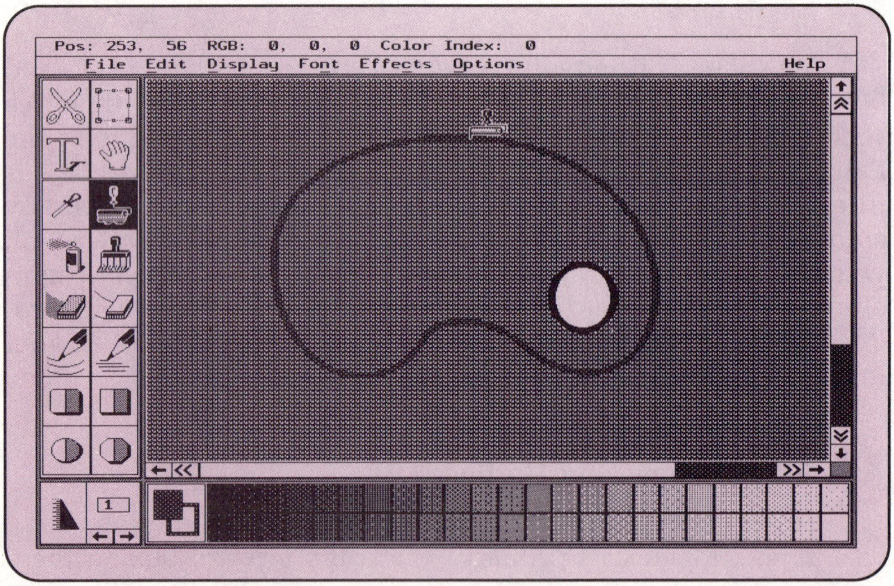

Figure 3.31 When you right-click outside a shape, the Paint Roller tool fills all areas not protected by a solid outline.

3. Position the hot spot (the drop of paint extending from the cursor) inside the enclosed or solid area.

   The caption bar displays the coordinate of the cursor, the RGB values, and the color index number for the color under the cursor. (See the *Using Colors* chapter for information on the last two items.)

4. Click to fill the area under the hot spot. Right-click to fill an area containing a pattern.

   Fills the area with primary color.

5. Select any tool if you are satisfied with the results of your fill.

   Protects the fill from being deleted by the Undo command. □

The Spraycan Tool

The Spraycan tool, the fourth tool down on the left side of the toolbox, is a special-effects version of the Paintbrush tool. As with the Paintbrush, you create free-form images with the Spraycan simply by dragging in the drawing window and you change the width of the cursor using the controls in the line width box. But unlike the Paintbrush, which produces a constant line, the Spraycan produces a random pattern of dots, as shown in Figure 3.32. You can paint light areas by dragging quickly or paint dark areas by dragging slowly. If you drag at the same location for a prolonged period, the area will fill with more and more color, much as it would if you were using a real airbrush.

Q Painting with the Spraycan

1. Click a color in the color palette to select the primary color, right-click a color to select the secondary color.

   The primary and secondary colors appear in the front and rear boxes in the left side of the palette.

2. Specify a line width in the line width box.

   The line width determines the size of the cursor.

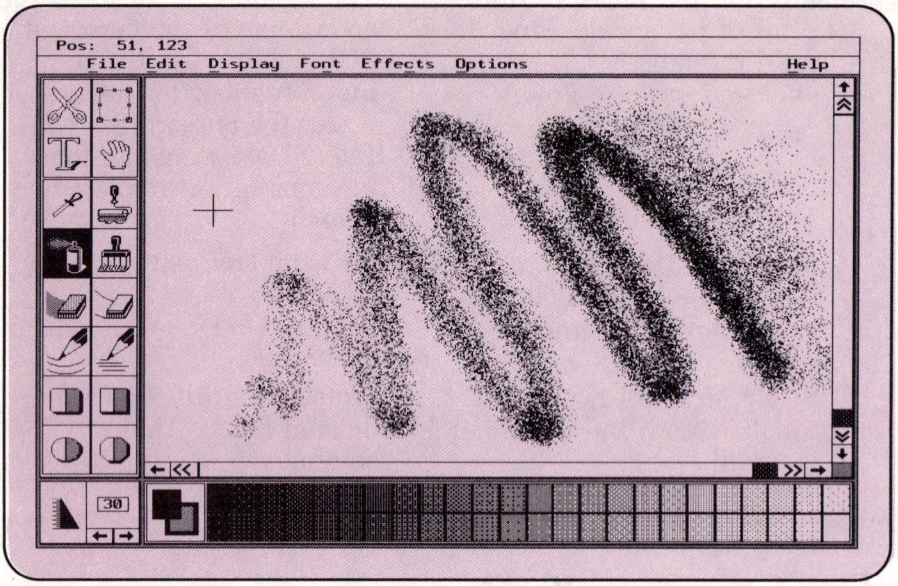

Figure 3.32 An image drawn with the Spraycan tool.

3. Click the Spraycan tool. — Highlights the Spraycan tool.
4. Drag in the drawing window to create lines of spray in the primary color, right-drag to create lines in the secondary color.
5. Select any tool if you're satisfied with the images created. — Protects your images from being deleted by the Undo command.

> **Tip:** For best results, use line widths of 15 or greater with the Spraycan tool.

The Spraycan tool is a powerful shading tool. In Figure 3.33, we used the Spraycan to color in portions of the fish created with the Paintbrush tool (shown in Figure 3.6).

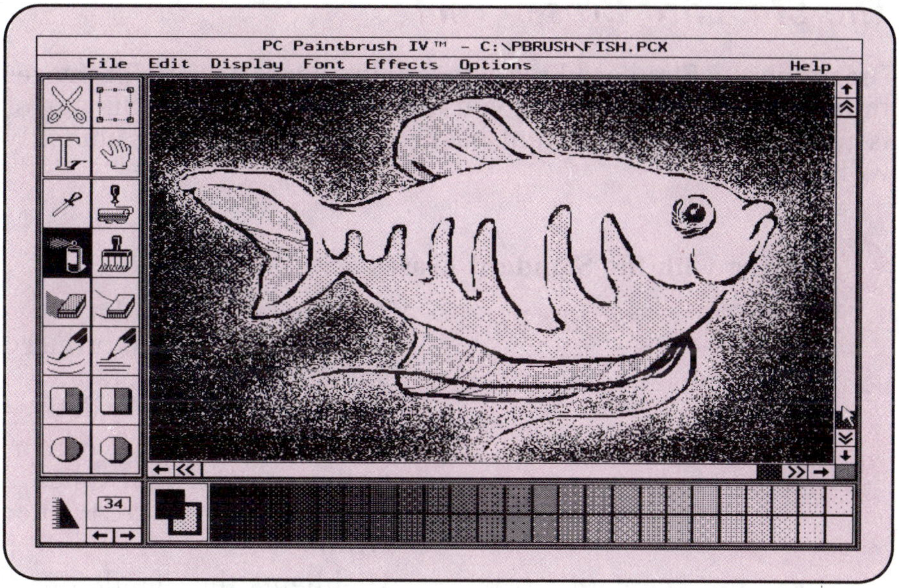

Figure 3.33 A fish shaded with the Spraycan tool.

Since images drawn with the Spraycan tool appear to fade from dark to light, they are perfectly suited to representing the differences between light and dark areas of a three-dimensional object. The Spraycan is also useful for drawing shadows, clouds, and other fuzzy images.

The Erasers

Paintbrush provides two erasers: the Standard Eraser tool and the Color Eraser tool. The icon for both tools is a chalkboard eraser. The Standard Eraser tool is located below the Paintbrush tool in the toolbox and the Color Eraser tool below the Spraycan tool. Both tools erase images in the drawing window by replacing them with either the background color (the Standard Eraser) or with another color from the palette (the Color Eraser). You can constrain the area erased to a vertical or horizontal line by pressing the Shift key while you drag; pressing the Spacebar toggles between the two constraints.

The Standard Eraser Tool

Drag with the Standard Eraser to delete images or parts of images in the drawing window. As you drag, any color under the cursor is replaced with the current background color, most commonly white.

Q Erasing with the Standard Eraser

1.	Shift-click a color in the palette to select the background color.	The background color appears behind the primary and secondary colors on the left side of the palette.
2.	Specify a line width in the line width box.	The Standard Eraser cursor becomes about four times as thick as the current line width.
3.	Click the Standard Eraser tool.	Highlights the Standard Eraser tool.
4.	Drag over the images in the drawing window that you want to erase.	The images are replaced by the background color.
5.	Select a different tool or reselect the Standard Eraser when you have finished erasing.	The images erased cannot be restored by the Undo command. □

> **Tip:** To erase an entire painting and start over, double-click the Standard Eraser tool to display the Create a New Picture dialog box and press Enter or click OK. Then answer Yes to the dialog box query.

The Color Eraser Tool

Drag with the Color Eraser to replace occurrences of the primary color with the secondary color. Colors other than the primary color are not affected by the Color Eraser. For example, suppose that the fish in Figure 3.33 is vivid orange and the sea around the fish is deep blue. If you select deep blue as the primary color and light purple as the secondary color and then drag across the fish painting with the Color Eraser tool, you'll change portions of the sea to light purple but leave the fish unaltered, as demonstrated by Figure 3.34.

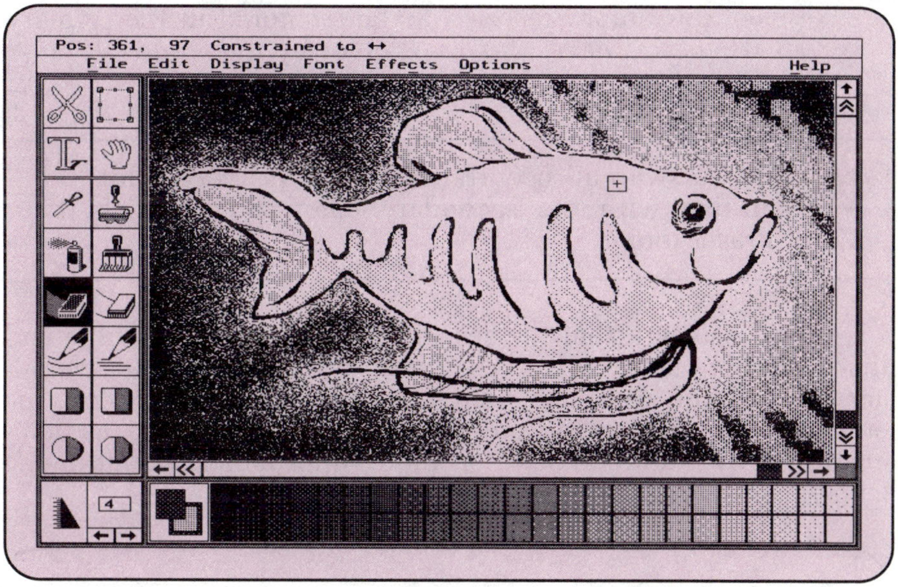

Figure 3.34 Using the Color Eraser to "erase" portions of the sea using the secondary color.

Q Erasing with the Color Eraser

1. Click a color in the color palette to select the primary color and right-click a color to select the secondary color.	The primary color determines the color you will erase, the secondary color determines the color which will replace the primary color.
2. Specify a line width in the line width box.	The Color Eraser cursor becomes about four times as thick as the current line width.
3. Click the Color Eraser tool.	Highlights the Color Eraser tool.

4. Drag over the images in the drawing window that you want to erase.

Pixels colored in the primary color are now colored in the secondary color.

5. Select a different tool or reselect the Color Eraser tool when you have finished erasing.

The images erased cannot be recolored in the primary color by the Undo command. □

> **Tip:** To swap all occurrences of the primary color in a painting with the secondary color, double-click the Color Eraser tool.

Suppose again that the sea in Figure 3.33 is deep blue and that deep blue is the primary color and light purple the secondary color. If you were to double-click the Color Eraser icon, the entire sea would change from deep blue to light purple, as demonstrated by Figure 3.35. For more information about using color, refer to Chapter 4, *Using Colors*.

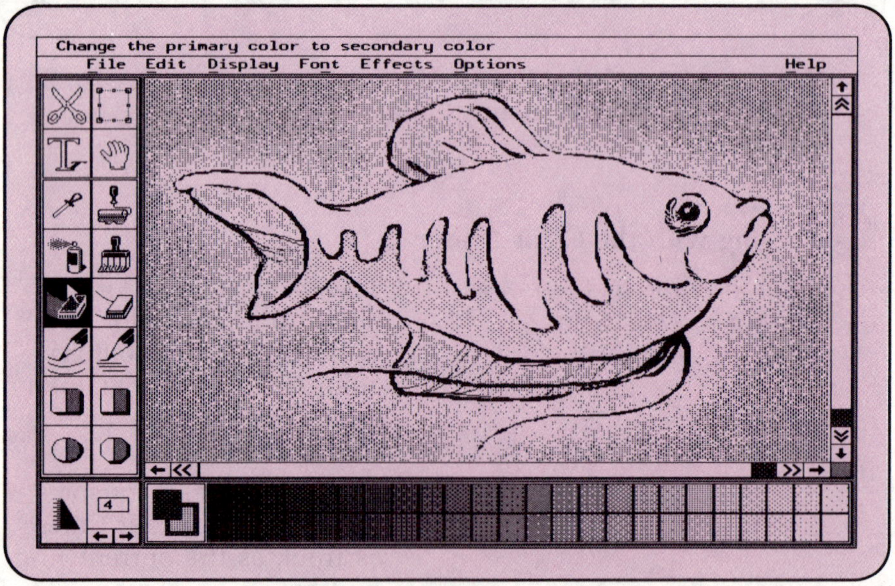

Figure 3.35 Double-clicking the Color Eraser changes the color of the sea from the primary to the secondary color.

Summary

In this chapter, you've learned:

- Dragging with the Paintbrush or Spraycan tool creates lines in the primary color and right-dragging creates lines in the secondary color.
- You can draw a straight horizontal or vertical line with the Paintbrush, Eraser, or Color Eraser by pressing the Shift key as you drag. By pressing the Spacebar, you can toggle between these two constraints.
- The brush shape affects both the Paintbrush and Straight Line tool cursors. To change the brush shape, double-click the Paintbrush tool, select a brush shape, and press Enter.
- The line width must be greater than 1 pixel for a brush shape to produce its effect. You change the line width using controls in the line width box. The current line width affects almost all drawing tools.
- You can create additional lines with the line tools by right-clicking. Control-right-clicking creates rays.
- After drawing a straight line with the Curved Line tool, you curve the line by dragging the round handles.
- Right-dragging with the ellipse tool creates concentric ovals and circles.
- Double-clicking the Standard Eraser tool effectively erases the entire drawing window because it allows you to create a new file. Double-clicking the Color Eraser tool replaces the primary color in the drawing window with the secondary color.

Chapter 4

Using Colors

What You Will Learn

- ▶ *Customizing the color palette*
- ▶ *Color theory*
- ▶ *Using the Eyedropper Tool*
- ▶ *Changing, saving, and loading palettes*

In previous chapters, you performed a few tasks related to the use of color in Paintbrush. You configured your monitor to display 2, 4, 8, 16, or 256 colors in Chapter 1 and you selected primary, secondary, and background colors in connection with tool use in Chapter 3. In this chapter, you will delve more deeply into the Paintbrush color network and learn, for example, how to alter individual colors and how to load and save entire palettes.

The Color Palette

The color palette, located along the bottom of the desktop, is your color control center. It contains every color you can use in the current painting. If a color is missing, you can't use it without first editing one or more colors in the palette, a process discussed later in this chapter.

If you have configured Paintbrush to display only 2 colors —black and white—or if you specified a 2-color display when you created a new file, the color palette will contain 48 *color patterns*, as shown in Figure 4.1. Each of these patterns imitates a shade of gray using a cluster of dots. The fewer the dots, the lighter the shade of gray.

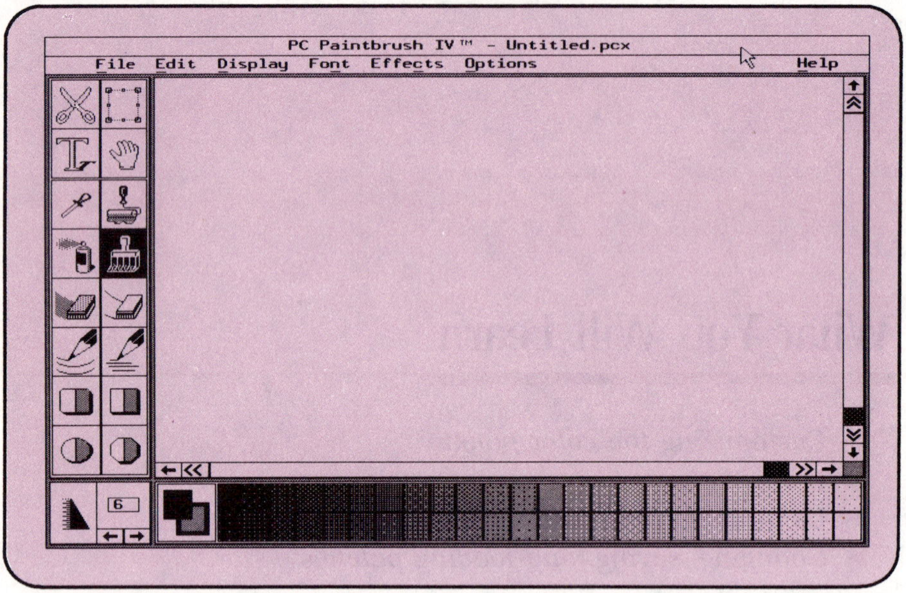

Figure 4.1 When PC Paintbrush is configured to display 2 colors, the color palette contains 48 patterns.

4 If you have configured Paintbrush to display 4 or more colors, the color palette will contain 256 color patterns, as shown in Figure 4.2. Unless your monitor is configured for 256 colors, most of the color patterns will not be *true colors*—solid red or solid blue, for example—but will be *blended* colors containing red dots mixed with blue dots, and so on.

Depending on the resolution of your monitor, the differently colored dots in a color pattern will blend together to form a single, unique color. If you prefer to view only the true colors in the palette, choose the Solid Colors Only command from the Display menu. If your monitor is configured to display 16 colors, the palette will appear as shown in Figure 4.3.

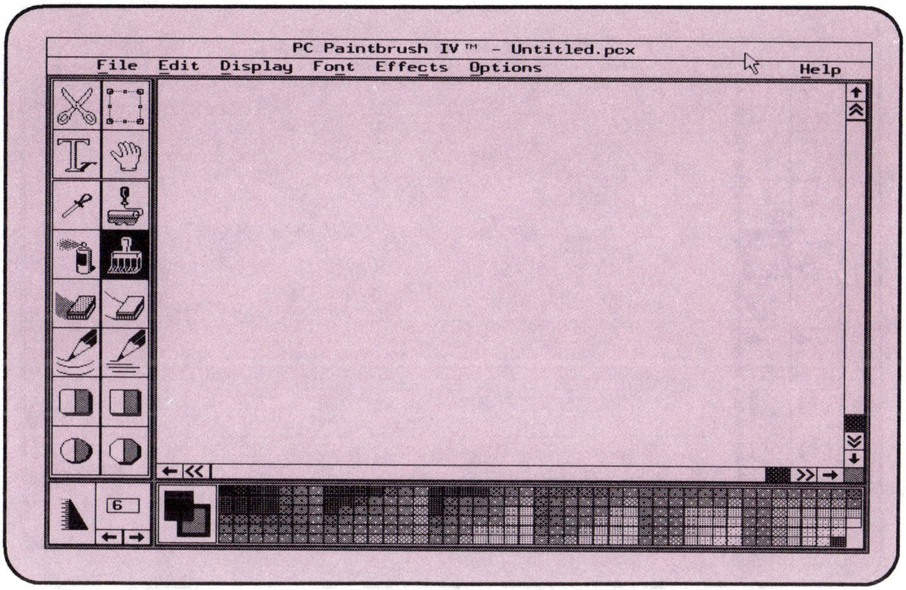

Figure 4.2 When PC Paintbrush is configured to display more than 4 colors, the color palette contains 256 patterns.

If your monitor is configured for 256 colors, choosing the Solid Colors Only command will produce no effect because the color palette already contains only true colors. The Solid Colors Only command will be *dimmed*, indicating that it is not available for use, if you have set up Paintbrush to display only 2 colors or if you specify a 2-color display when creating a new painting.

Accessing Colors

4 When you first start Paintbrush, three colors are selected from the palette: black is selected as the primary color, red or gray as the secondary color, and white as the background color. The next section summarizes the conditions under which Paintbrush applies each of these colors in the drawing window. Some of the information will be familiar to you from previous chapters and some of the information is new—all conditions are covered.

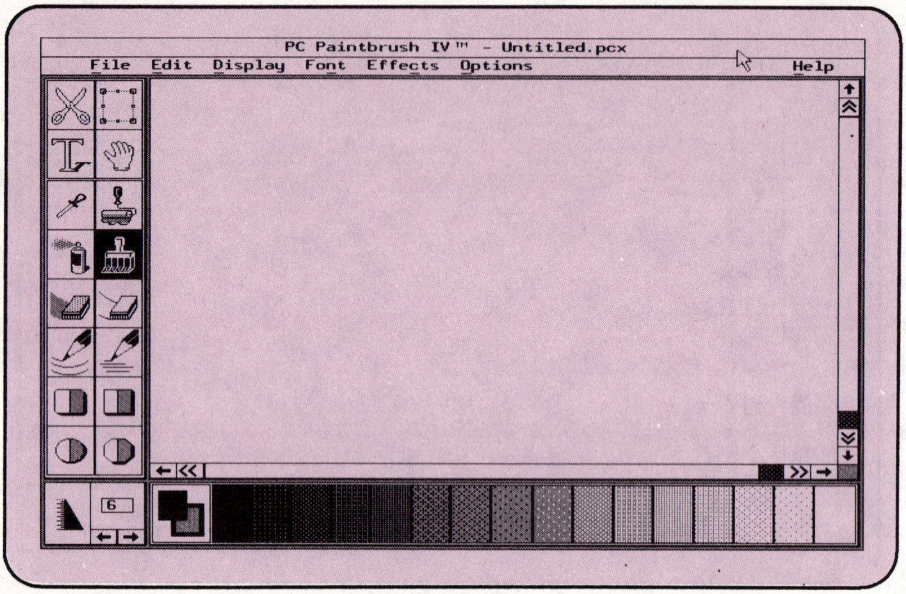

Figure 4.3 Choosing the Solid Colors Only command reduces the color palette to the number of true colors.

Applying Colors

The primary, secondary, and background colors affect the performance of all drawing tools as well as the operation of several commands. By understanding each color's sphere of influence, you can better predict the results of your actions.

The primary color is applied in the drawing window as follows:

- Dragging with the Paintbrush, Straight Line, or Curved Line tool creates a line in the primary color.
- Dragging with a shape tool creates an outline in the primary color.
- Dragging with the Spraycan creates a random spray of pixels in the primary color.
- Clicking with the Paint Roller fills a solid or enclosed area with the primary color.
- Outlines around type are created in the primary color.

The secondary color is applied in the drawing window in these ways:

- Right-dragging with the Paintbrush creates a line in the secondary color.
- Dragging with a filled shape tool creates a shape filled with the secondary color.
- Right-dragging with the Spraycan creates a random spray of pixels in the secondary color.
- Dragging with the Color Eraser tool changes occurrences of the primary color to the secondary color.
- Type is created in the secondary color.
- Gradient effects fade from the secondary color to the background color.

The influence of the background color is broader:

- Dragging with the Eraser tool creates lines in the background color.
- When you create a new painting, the entire drawing area is filled with the background color.
- Shadows behind type are created in the background color.
- Gradient effects fade from the secondary color to the background color.
- When you select an image with the Scissors or Gadget Box tool, right-dragging the selected image treats pixels in the background color as transparent.

The tools and techniques relating to the primary, secondary, and background colors are discussed in detail elsewhere in this book. Consult the index for specific page numbers.

Selecting Colors

As you may recall, you select colors from the color palette in one of three ways: click a color to select it as the primary color, right-click to select the secondary color, and shift-click to select the background color.

Selecting colors becomes more complicated, however, if you use a large palette of colors. Suppose you want to edit an image you created a few days ago. Exactly what shade of green were you using?

4 One of Paintbrush IV's new tools is the Eyedropper tool, the third tool down on the left side of the toolbox. This useful tool allows you to select colors directly from the drawing window. Select the Eyedropper, then click on a color in the drawing window. The solid color directly under the cursor will become the primary color. Right-click on a color to select the secondary color and shift-click on a color to select the background color.

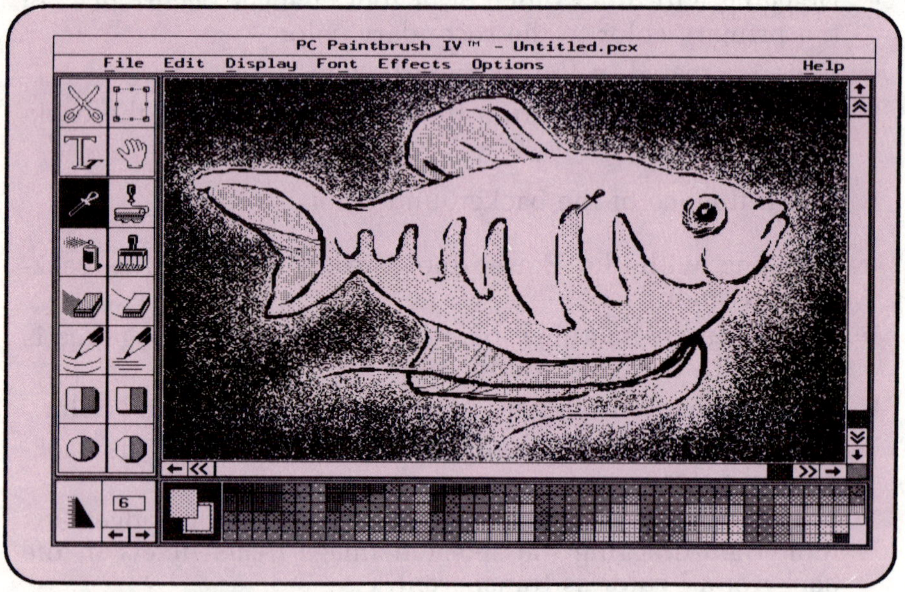

Figure 4.4 Clicking with the Eyedropper tool selects colors from the current painting.

> **Note:** The Eyedropper can be used to select solid colors only. To select a blended color pattern, you must select from the palette.

Color Index Numbers

As you move the Eyedropper tool across your painting, you will notice that the caption bar displays the *RGB* (red-green-blue) breakdown for the color under the cursor as well as the color's *color index number*. This information can be helpful in locating matching colors in a painting. For example, suppose you want to use the Color Eraser tool to replace a color in one portion of your painting but you don't want to alter this same color elsewhere. You can locate other occurrences of this exact color by moving the Eyedropper cursor over similar colors and examining their RGB and color index values.

When Paintbrush is configured for 256 colors, the color index number corresponds to a color's exact location in the palette, from top to bottom and then left to right (rows), counting from 0 to 255. For example, the first color in the first row is color 0. The first color in the sixth row (the last row) is color 5. The second color in the first row is color 6, and so on.

When Paintbrush is configured for 16 or fewer colors, the correspondence between color index number and palette doesn't work out so nicely. For example, when Paintbrush is configured for 16 colors, the color index numbers start at 0 and end at 15. However, these numbers do not reflect the order of the colors in the 256-color pattern palette nor their order in the 16-color palette that displays when you choose Solid Colors Only from the Display menu. The color index numbering system corresponds to the order of the colors in the palette only when you choose either the Set Entire Palette or Set Palette command from the Options menu. Both of these commands are discussed later in this chapter.

Like the color index number, the RGB values can be useful for identifying matching colors. However, this is far from their intended purpose—color editing. To use the RGB values successfully in color editing, you must first understand the basics of color theory, including the RGB color scheme.

Color Theory

A basic knowledge of color theory is essential to creating color paintings in Paintbrush. If you already have a thorough knowledge of additive and subtractive primary colors, and of the RGB and HLS color schemes, skip to the *Editing Colors* section of this chapter. Otherwise, read on.

Whether they appear on a television screen or in a magazine advertisement, all colors are created by mixing two or more *primary hues*. The identity of these primary hues is a function of the current *color model*. If you create colors on a sheet of paper, you use the *subtractive primary model*. If you create colors with light, as on a computer screen, you use the *additive primary model*. Both color models are described in the next section.

Coloring with Pigments

In nature, colors are created according to the subtractive color model. Sunlight contains all visible colors. When sunlight is directed at an object, the object absorbs (subtracts) some of the light and reflects the rest. This reflected light is the color that you see. For example, a fire engine is red because it absorbs all other colors from the white light spectrum.

Pigments on a sheet of paper work the same way. A purple crayon absorbs all non-purple colors; green ink absorbs all colors that aren't green. As a child, you learned that you can make any color using red, yellow, and blue. Red and yellow mix to create orange, yellow and blue make green, and so on. This is the subtractive primary model.Unfortunately, what you learned in elementary school is only an approximation of the truth. Did you ever mix a vivid red with a bright yellow only to produce a disappointingly drab orange?

And the very idea that deep blue and vivid red make purple is almost laughable. The true result is more a washed-out gray.

The true subtractive primary model used by commercial artists and printers consists of four hues: cyan (pale greenish blue), magenta (bright purplish pink), yellow, and black, each of which is applied to white paper. In this *CMYK* color scheme, the primary hues are mixed as follows:

- Equal amounts of cyan and magenta make violet. Additional cyan pigment produces blue; additional magenta pigment produces purple.
- Equal amounts of magenta and yellow make red. Additional magenta pigment produces carmine; additional yellow pigment produces orange.

- Equal amounts of yellow and cyan make green. Additional yellow pigment produces chartreuse; additional cyan pigment produces turquoise.
- Equal amounts of cyan, magenta, and yellow make brown.
- Black pigmentation added to any other pigment darkens the color.
- No pigmentation results in white (assuming white is the color of the paper).

Coloring with Light

Colors on a computer screen work very differently than in nature or on paper. Recall that sunlight appears white because it includes all colors in the visible spectrum. In the subtractive color model, hues added to each other produce darker colors; in the additive color model, hues mixed together produce lighter colors. Because computer monitors and other projection devices, such as televisions, use light rather than pigments to display colors, they work according to the additive model.

The additive primary model consists of only three hues: red, green, and blue. In this *RGB* color scheme, the primary hues are mixed as follows:

- Equal intensities of red and green make yellow. Subtract some red light to produce chartreuse; subtract some green light to produce orange.
- Equal intensities of green and blue make cyan. Subtract some green light to produce turquoise; subtract some blue light to produce jade.
- Equal intensities of blue and red make purple. Subtract some blue light to produce magenta; subtract some red light to produce violet.
- Equal intensities of red, green, and blue make gray or white.
- No light results in black (or darkness).

The Color Wheel

Paintbrush allows you to specify the amounts of red, green, and blue light in a color. It also provides a second model for adjusting the amount of light in a color. This *HLS* color scheme, as it is called, makes use of the properties of *hue*, *lightness*, and *saturation*. The hue of a color is measured on an imaginary wheel representing the entire color spectrum. Paintbrush divides this *color wheel* into 360 equal slices, each representing a unique hue. Some of the most popular hues are found at the following numeric locations:

- Red is 0.
- Orange is 30.
- Yellow is 60.
- Chartreuse is 90.
- Green is 120.
- Jade is 150.
- Cyan is 180.
- Blue is 240.
- Violet is 270.
- Purple is 300.
- Magenta is 330.

Lightness is merely the lightness or darkness of a color. A lightness of 0 results in black; a lightness of 1 results in white. A lightness of 0.5 is used to achieve each of the colors listed previously. If the hue is red, a lightness of 0.25 produces dark red, 0.5 produces bright red, and 0.75 produces vivid pink.

Saturation represents the purity of a color. A saturation of 0 produces gray; a saturation of 1 is required to produce each of the colors listed previously. You can think of the saturation value as the difference between a black and white and a color television. When the saturation value is low, all the information about a color is expressed except the hue. Most natural colors require moderate saturation values. Highly saturated colors appear very bright or fluorescent.

Editing Colors

4 Editing colors is a concept new to Paintbrush IV. This upgrade in the program allows you to edit any of the color

patterns or true colors in the palette using the Set Color Pattern... or Set Palette... command, respectively.

Choosing the Set Color Pattern command displays the Edit Color Pattern dialog box shown in Figure 4.5. Choosing the Set Palette command displays the Adjust Individual Hardware Palette Color dialog box shown in Figure 4.6. Because the RGB option is selected, both dialog boxes contain Red, Green, and Blue scroll bars. These bars can be adjusted to any value between 0 (no intensity) and 255 (full intensity).

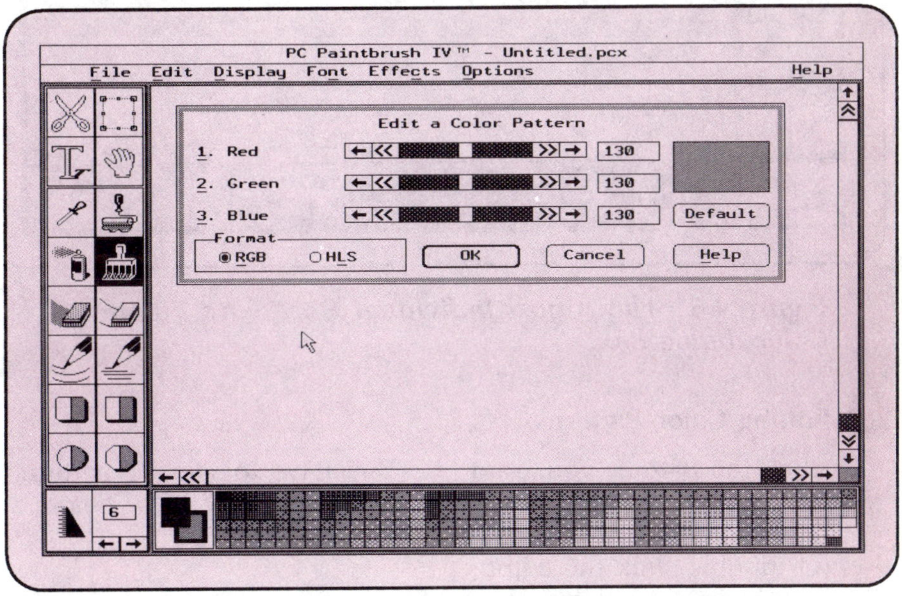

Figure 4.5 The Edit Color Pattern dialog box.

If you select the HLS option, the names of the scroll bars change to Hue, Lightness, and Saturation. The value for Hue can range from -1 to 360, while the Lightness and Saturation values can be set between 0 and 1 in 0.001 increments.

Note: If you have configured Paintbrush to display 256 colors, all of the colors in the palette will be true colors, so you will not be allowed to choose the Edit Color Pattern command.

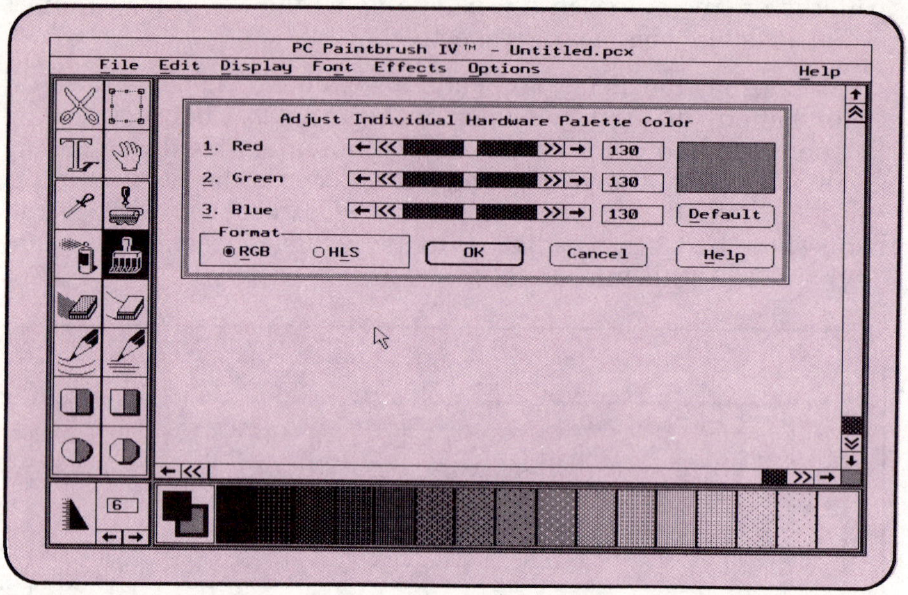

Figure 4.6 The Adjust Individual Hardware Palette Color dialog box.

Q Editing Color Patterns

1. Click the pattern you want to edit. Be sure to select a pattern and not a true color. (Or double-click the color pattern in the palette and skip step 2.)

   You have to select a pattern as the primary color before you can edit it.

2. Choose the Set Color Pattern command from the Options menu.

   Displays the Edit Color Pattern dialog box.

3. Enter values in the Red, Green, and Blue option boxes (or Hue, Lightness, and Saturation option boxes in the HLS color scheme) or drag the sliders in the scroll bars. Press Alt-1, Alt-2, or Alt-3 to move between option boxes.

   Sets the intensity of the red, green, and blue dots in the pattern being edited. (In HLS, Sets the hue, lightness, and saturation of the dots in the pattern.)

4. If you make a mistake and want to start over, select the Default button.

   The scroll bars return to their original values.

5. Press Enter or click OK.

   The color pattern in the palette changes according to your specifications. □

Editing True Colors

1. Click the true color you want to edit.

   You have to select a color as the primary color so that you can edit it. If you select a color pattern, Paintbrush edits the closest true color.

2. Choose the Set Palette command from the Options menu.

   Displays the Adjust Individual Hardware Palette color dialog box.

3. Enter values in the Red, Green, and Blue option boxes (or Hue, Lightness, and Saturation option boxes in the HLS color scheme) or drag the sliders in the scroll bars. Press Alt-1, Alt-2, or Alt-3 to move between option boxes.

   Sets the intensity of the red, green, or blue dots in the color being edited. (In HLS, Sets the hue, lightness, and saturation of the dots.)

4. If you make a mistake and want to start over, select the Default button.

   The scroll bars return to their original values.

5. Click another color in the palette to edit a new color. Repeat steps 3 and 4 for the new color.

6. Press Enter or click OK.

   True colors edited during this session change according to your specifications. Depending on your alterations, Paintbrush adjusts several color patterns to maintain a consistent palette. □

> ⊘ **Caution:** In changing true colors, you change all occurrences of those colors in your painting. You also run the risk of altering the colors Paintbrush uses to display portions of the desktop.

Paintbrush uses various true colors to display elements of the desktop. Each element is tagged to a specific color index number. If you change the true color associated with that index number, you will also change the color of the desktop element. The colors that Paintbrush uses to define the desktop vary, depending on how you have configured Paintbrush. Table 4.1 identifies the color index numbers of each desktop element when Paintbrush is configured to display 16 colors.

Table 4.1 True Colors Used to Display Desktop Elements

Color Index	Default Color	Desktop Elements Using This Color
0	Black	Borders and command and option names
1	Dark blue	Scroll bars
2	Dark green	None
3	Dark cyan	None
4	Dark red	Highlighted tools and commands
5	Dark purple	None
6	Dark orange	Tool details
7	Gray	Tool details
8	Dark gray	None
9	Blue	Tool details and caption bar
10	Green	None
11	Cyan	Tool backgrounds, menu bar, scroll bars, and buttons
12	Red	None
13	Purple	None
14	Yellow	Tool detail
15	White	Tool details, dialog boxes, caption bar titles

If you change two colors used in the desktop such that they appear similar, you may diminish the legibility of the desktop. For example, when 16 colors are displayed, the menus are displayed in cyan (color index 11) and the command names are displayed in black (color index 0). If you change cyan and black to similar shades of red using the Set Palette command, you will have difficulty distinguishing a command name from its background.

Changing the Entire Palette

4 If editing individual colors is too time-consuming, you can edit the entire palette at once. Choose the Set Entire Palette command from the Options menu to display the Adjust the Entire Hardware Palette dialog box shown in Figure 4.7. In Paintbrush Plus, this dialog box appears slightly different, as shown in Figure 4.8.

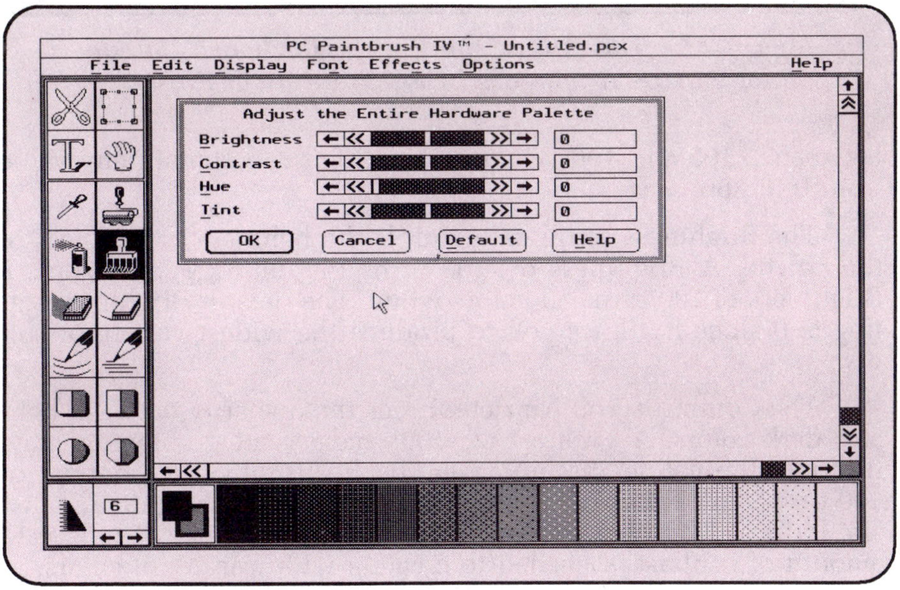

Figure 4.7 The Adjust the Entire Hardware Palette dialog box as it appears in PC Paintbrush.

Both versions of this dialog box contain four scroll bars whose settings affect every true color in the palette. The values for the Brightness, Contrast, and Tint (or Amount) scroll bars can vary

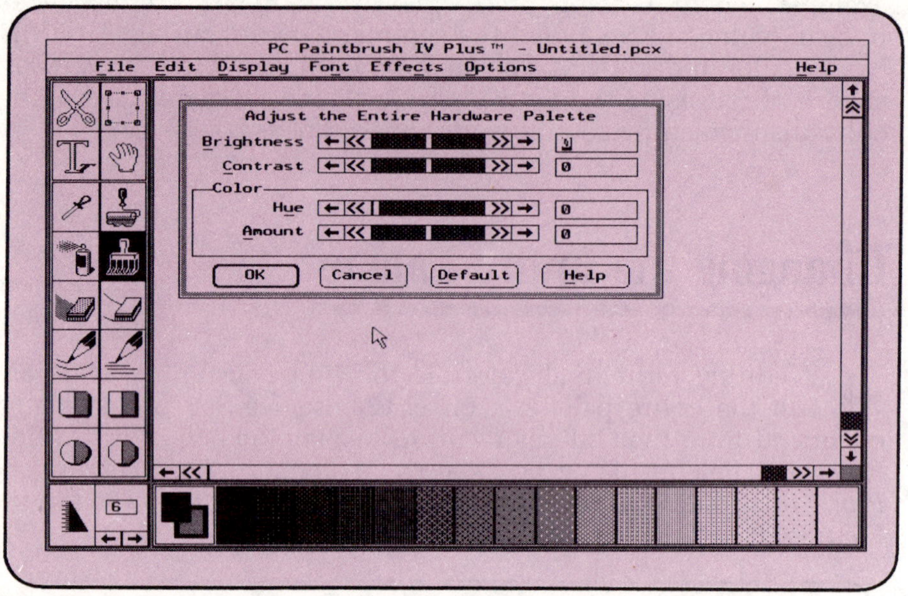

Figure 4.8 The Adjust the Entire Hardware Palette dialog box as it appears in PC Paintbrush Plus.

between −100 and 100. The Hue scroll bar can contain any value from 0 to 360.

The Brightness scroll bar controls the lightness or darkness of the palette. A Brightness of -100 turns the entire palette black; a Brightness of 100 turns all colors white. The default Brightness setting is 0 since it allows you to produce the widest variety of colors.

The Contrast scroll bar determines the disparity between light and dark colors. A Contrast of -100 changes most colors to gray, thereby eliminating dissimilarities between colors; a Contrast of 100 turns dark colors black and light colors white, heightening dissimilarities. The default Contrast setting is 0, since a moderate amount of contrast is needed to create a wide variety of colors.

The Hue scroll bar determines the principal color in the palette. Recall that the hue of a color depends on its numeric location in the color wheel; a value of 0 is red, 60 is yellow, 120 is green, and so on. Refer to *The Color Wheel* section earlier in this chapter for the locations of other popular hues. However, changing the Hue value produces no effect unless you also adjust the Tint (Paintbrush) or Amount (Paintbrush Plus) value.

The Tint (or Amount) scroll bar controls the amount of Hue color applied to the palette. A Tint of 100 overwhelms the entire palette with the Hue color, so that every color has an apparent tint. A Tint of −100 overwhelms the palette with the color opposite to the current hue. A color's opposite is the hue halfway around the color wheel from it. To determine this color, add 180 (half of a circle) to the current Hue value. For example, since red has a Hue value of 0, its opposite has a Hue value of 180, which is cyan. The opposite of chartreuse, which has a Hue value of 90, is, violet, Hue value 270.

Q Editing Whole Palettes

1. Choose the Set Entire Palette command from the Options menu. — Displays Adjust Entire Hardware dialog box.
2. Enter values in the Brightness, Contrast, Hue, and Tint (Amount in Paintbrush Plus) option boxes or adjust the values in these boxes by dragging the sliders in the scroll bars. Press Alt-B, Alt-C, Alt-H, and Alt-T to move between option boxes in Paintbrush. Press Alt-B, Alt-C, Alt-U, and Alt-A to move between option boxes in Paintbrush Plus.
3. If you make a mistake and want to start over, select the Default button. — The scroll bars return to their original values.
4. Press Enter or click OK. — All true colors in the palette change according to your specifications. □

Palette Problems

In using the Set Entire Palette command to edit the color palette, you may notice that some of the high-intensity colors like cyan and yellow don't seem to change regardless of your alterations.

This is one of the serious drawbacks of this command. You may prefer not to use the Set Entire Palette command unless you are certain of your results. To get a feel for how each option in the Adjust the Entire Hardware Palette dialog box affects the other options, load the GRAYS.PAL palette file (following the load palette instructions in the next section) before experimenting with each scroll bar. Since the GRAYS.PAL palette only contains shades of gray, it provides a neutral starting point from which you can observe the effects of your palette alterations.

You may encounter a second problem with the Set Entire Palette command if Paintbrush is configured for 16 or fewer colors. Your palette may turn completely black (or some other color) when the program attempts to recalculate the color patterns in an altered palette. Simply choose the Sold Color Only command from the Display menu to get your colors back. However, you will not be able to use any of the color patterns in your altered palette.

Caution: Because the Set Entire Palette command will affect all colors in the current painting, use this command only before creating a new painting. Even then, you may not want to use this command because of possible palette problems.

Loading and Saving Palettes

Most users will find the Set Entire Palette command unpredictable and even destructive. If you want to adjust your palette, you will find it quicker, easier and safer, in general, to use one of the alternative palettes included with Paintbrush.

Loading a Palette

Just as you can load a painting or a workspace, you can also open and save custom palette files. You can then access different combinations of colors without having to go through the rigmarole of adjusting true colors, patterns, or whole palettes. Loading new palettes is not only a quick and easy approach to editing colors but generally a more successful one as well.

Q Loading an Alternative Palette

1. Choose the Get Palette... command from the Options menu.	The Load Color Patterns from Disk dialog box displays, as shown in Figure 4.9.
2. Press Alt-C, Alt-P, or Alt-B or select the Color, Palette, or Both Items option.	Alt-C loads only the color patterns of the alternate palette. Alt-P loads only the true colors of the alternate palette. Alt-B loads both new color patterns and new true colors.
3. Select a palette from the scrolling Filename field. (Change to a different drive or directory to change the display in the Filename field.)	Highlights the selected palette file.
4. Press Enter to open the highlighted file.	If the number of colors in the palette is compatible with your monitor configuration, the patterns and/or true colors of the selected palette will appear in the current palette. If not, you will be unable to open the palette. □

The Items options in the Load Color Patterns from Disk dialog box allow you to load only a portion of a palette or an entire palette. The Color Patterns option will load only the color patterns of the selected palette and retain the true colors of the current palette. Select the Hardware Palette option if you want to load the true colors of the alternative palette but retain the color patterns of the current palette. Select the Both option if you want to load new color patterns and new true colors.

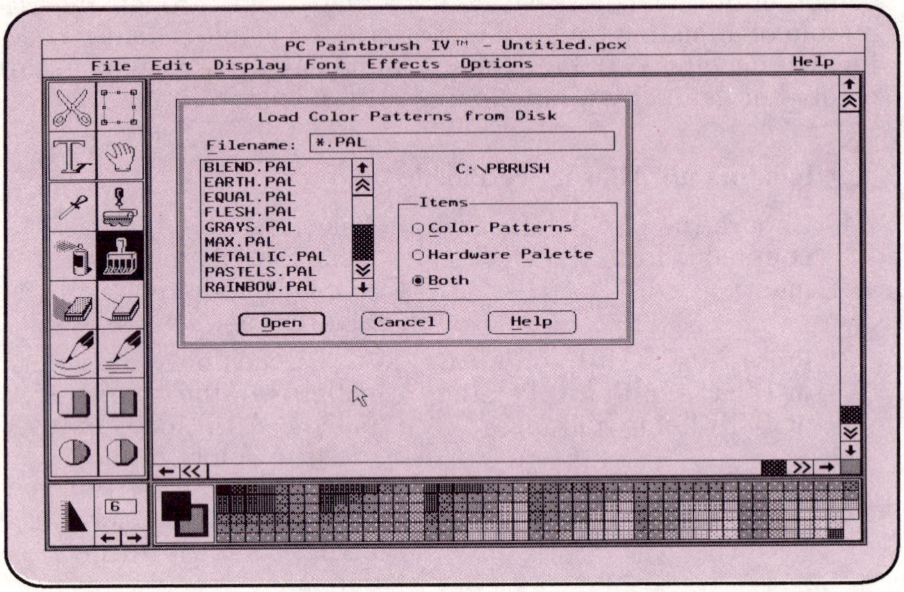

Figure 4.9 The Load Color Patterns from Disk dialog box.

Since the variety and ultimate utility of a palette are equally dependent on the palette's true colors and color patterns, you will generally want to select the Both option. If you plan to use the Color or Palette option, we recommend that you first experiment with various combinations of patterns and true colors to determine which palettes are compatible.

Saving a Palette

If you have created a special palette for a particular painting, you can save it to disk for use in future paintings by choosing the Save Palette... command from the Options menu. You can also adjust one of the alternative palettes included with Paintbrush and save your customized version of the palette. A saved palette always includes both true colors and color patterns.

Q Saving the Current Palette

1. Choose the Save Palette... command from the Options menu. — The Save Color Patterns to Disk dialog box displays, as shown in Figure 4.10.

2. Enter a file name in the Filename (Filename in Paintbrush Plus) option box. The file name is limited to eight characters and must have a .PAL extension.
3. Press Enter or click Save.

   If the palette you are saving is new, save the palette to disk under the name specified. If you are saving an existing palette which you have altered, an alert box appears asking if you want to save over the existing copy of the file.

4. Press the Y key or click Yes or press the N key or click No.

   The Y key saves the altered palette over the old file. The N key cancels the Save Palette... command. □

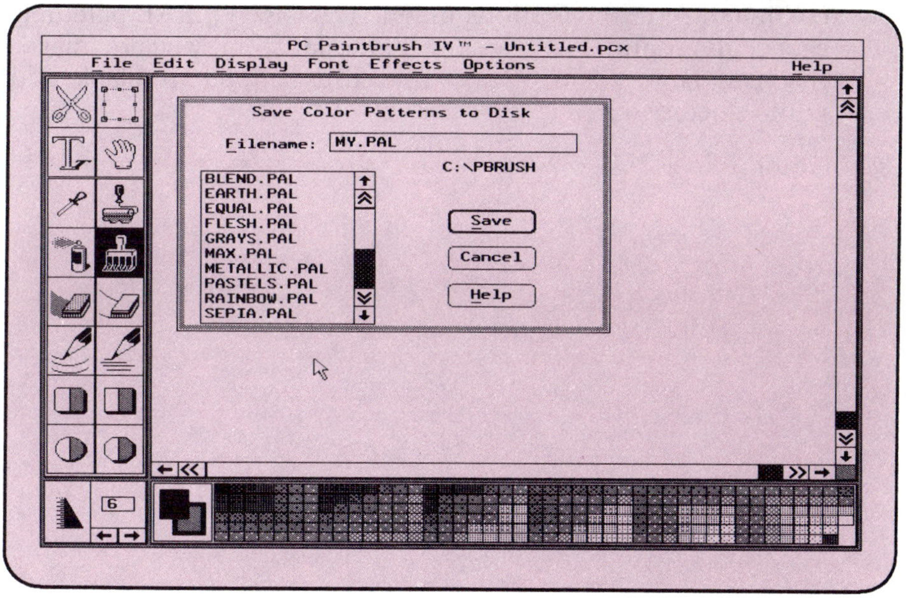

Figure 4.10 The Save Color Patterns to Disk dialog box.

Summary

In this chapter, you've learned:

- Click, right-click, or Shift-click with the Eyedropper tool to select the primary, secondary, or background color from the current painting rather than from the color palette.
- Colors are produced on your monitor by mixing specific intensities of red, green and blue light, known collectively as the additive primary hues.
- The *Color Theory* section of this chapter explains how to mix colors using RGB or HLS values.
- You can edit an individual color pattern by double-clicking on it and then adjusting the controls in the Edit Color Pattern dialog box.
- When you change a true color, you change all occurrences of that color in your painting.
- The easiest way to change your palette is to load one of the .PAL files included with Paintbrush using the Get Palette command from the Options menu. The GRAYS.PAL palette is especially useful for creating high-quality gray-scale images that can be used as figures and illustrations in black and white documents.

Chapter 5

Manipulating Images

What You Will Learn

- *Selecting images with the Scissors and Gadget Box tools*
- *Moving and deleting images*
- *Using the Cut, Copy, and Paste commands*
- *Transforming images or an entire painting*

An image created in Paintbrush is by no means set in stone; it can be moved, duplicated, stretched like a piece of putty, or slanted. This chapter discusses how to manipulate any existing image in your painting to create exciting visual effects. Transformations that would take hours to perform using traditional tools take minutes, even seconds, in Paintbrush.

Selecting an Image

Before you can manipulate an image in Paintbrush, you must first *select* it, that is, define the specific portion of the painting that you want to manipulate.

You can select a portion of the painting with either the Scissors tool or the Gadget Box tool. These are the uppermost tools in the toolbox, appearing as a pair of scissors and a dotted square, respectively. Both tools are used to surround the image that you intend to manipulate with a *selection marquee.*

The Scissors Tool

The Scissors tool allows you to select an image with an irregular outline and to select it precisely so that you do not bring pieces of the background with it. For example, suppose you want to select only the hat on the left side of the painting shown in Figure 5.1. The right brim of the hat slants outward at an angle, extending over a few blades of grass. It is not possible to draw a horizontal or vertical border between the hat and the grass. Using the Scissors tool, however, you can draw at an angle around the hat, just as if you were drawing lines with the Polygon tool. You can therefore use the Scissors tool to create a selection marquee around any irregular image.

Figure 5.1 A perpendicular border cannot be created between the hat and the grass.

4 The Scissors tool in Paintbrush IV has been updated. In earlier versions of Paintbrush, you drew a free-form marquee around an image to select it; now you draw a straight-sided polygon, as described in the following Quick Steps.

Selecting Specific Images

1. Click the Scissors tool.

   Highlights the Scissors tool.

2. Press the mouse button at the point where you want the first straight border of the marquee to begin, then drag. Press the Shift key as you drag to draw borders at 45° angles. Release at the point where you want the border to end.

   The caption bar displays the coordinate of the cursor, the coordinate at which the border begins, the length of the border and its angle, as shown in Figure 5.2.

3. Click to create an additional straight border that begins where the previous border ends. Drag to adjust the angle of the border as you draw it, then release at the point where you want the border to end.

   Creates additional marquee border.

4. Continue clicking and dragging to create a marquee surrounding your image.

   Borders surround the image, as shown in Figure 5.3.

5. Double-click to close the marquee.

   A *gadget box* automatically surrounds the area selected, as shown in Figure 5.4. The cursor appears inside the gadget box as a hand. You can now move or otherwise manipulate the image.

6. To select a different image, move the cursor outside the gadget box and repeat steps 2 through 5.

□

Figure 5.2 Drawing the first border around an image with the Scissors tool.

Figure 5.3 Creating additional borders by clicking and dragging with the Scissors tool.

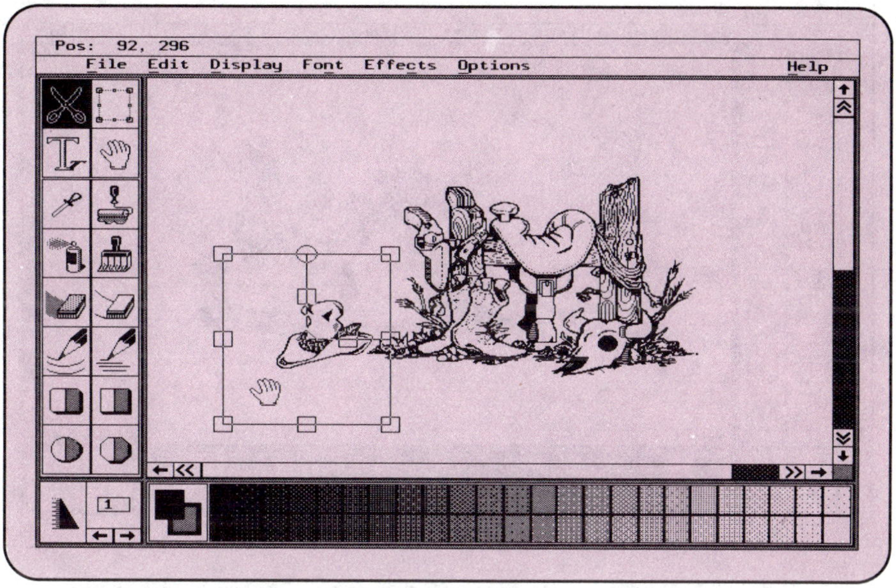

Figure 5.4 A gadget box appears around the image as soon as you close the marquee.

Depending on available memory, you can create up to one hundred straight borders for the marquee, which allows you to select highly complex images. In Figure 5.5, for example, we have selected one of the boots and removed it from its background.

The Gadget Box Tool

Selecting images with the Gadget Box tool is faster and easier than with the Scissors tool. Using the Scissors tool is like drawing a free-form polygon; it requires clicking, dragging, and sometimes Shift-dragging repeatedly. Using the Gadget Box tool is like drawing a simple rectangle; you merely drag around an image, then release.

The trade-off for this ease of use is less accuracy. The Gadget Box tool is capable of selecting only general rectangular areas of a painting. If you try to select a detailed image with the Gadget Box, you will also select unwanted portions of surrounding images. Compare the clean results of selecting the boot from

Figure 5.5 You can select complex images, such as the boot from Figure 5.4, with the Scissors tool.

Figure 5.4 with the Scissors tool, shown in Figure 5.5, with the untidy results of using the Gadget Box tool, shown in Figure 5.6.

Q Selecting General Areas

1. Select the Gadget Box tool.	Highlights the Gadget Box tool.
2. Draw a rectangular marquee around the image you want to select. Press the mouse button to establish the first corner of the marquee, then drag. Press the Shift key while dragging to constrain the marquee to a perfect square.	The caption bar shows the coordinate of the cursor, the coordinate of the first corner, and the width and height of the marquee (labeled "Delta"), as shown in Figure 5.7.

Figure 5.6 The boot from Figure 5.4 after being selected and moved with the Gadget Box tool.

3. Release when the marquee completely surrounds the image.

A gadget box automatically surrounds the area selected, as shown in Figure 5.8. The cursor appears as a hand inside the gadget box. You can now move or otherwise manipulate the image.

4. To select a different image, position the cursor outside the gadget box and repeat steps 2 and 3.

□

> **Tip:** The Gadget Box tool icon can be used for another purpose besides selecting images. If you double-click the Gadget Box icon, you can access the Show Screen... command from the Display menu to display a full-screen view of the current painting. This command is described in the *Full-Screen View* section of Chapter 2. The alert box shown in Figure 2.27 will appear, reminding you how to return to the desktop after the full-screen view.

Figure 5.7 Surrounding an image with the Gadget Box tool.

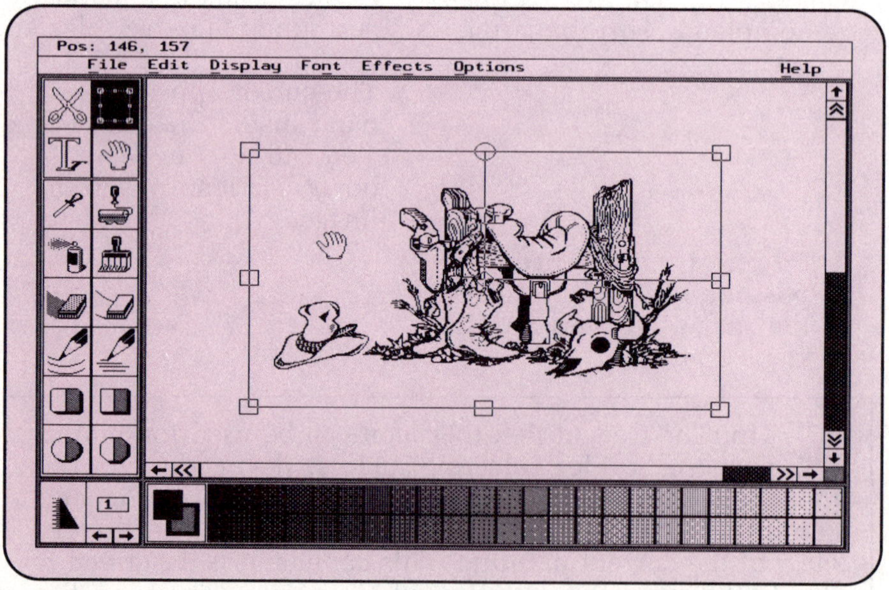

Figure 5.8 A gadget box appears around the selected image.

Moving a Selection

After you select an image, you can manipulate it in a variety of ways which are described throughout the remainder of this chapter. The foremost way to manipulate an image is to move it by positioning the cursor anywhere inside the gadget box and dragging the image to a new location. After moving the image, click outside the gadget box or select a tool to fix the image in its new location.

> **Caution:** When moving an image, be careful not to position the cursor on one of the gadget box handles that appear around the perimeter of the box. You may inadvertently transform the image, as discussed later in this chapter, rather than simply move it. If you accidentally transform an image in an attempt to move it, choose the Undo command from the Edit menu or press Control-U. Then reselect the image and try again to move it.

Overlapping Images

If you move a selected image over another image, the selected image will appear in front of the stationary image. Parts of the selected image will be opaque, covering the image behind them, and parts will be transparent, depending on which tool was used to select the image and whether the image is colored in the background color. Only those portions of the image colored in the background color can be transparent, regardless of the tool used to select the image. All other colors are always opaque.

If you move a shape selected with the Scissors tool, the area in the background color outside the selected shape will be transparent and any enclosed areas in the background color will be opaque. In Figures 5.9, 5.10, and 5.11, white has been selected as the background color, as is common. To produce the results shown in each figure, we selected the image on the left and moved it over a gray rectangle, shown on the right. The image in Figure 5.9 has no breaks in its outline, so when it is moved over the rectangle, its interior appears opaque. The image in Figure 5.10 has breaks in its outline so it appears transparent. In Figure 5.11, the outer shape is enclosed but the inner smaller shape is not; as a result, when the image is moved, the inner shape becomes transparent while the outer shape remains opaque.

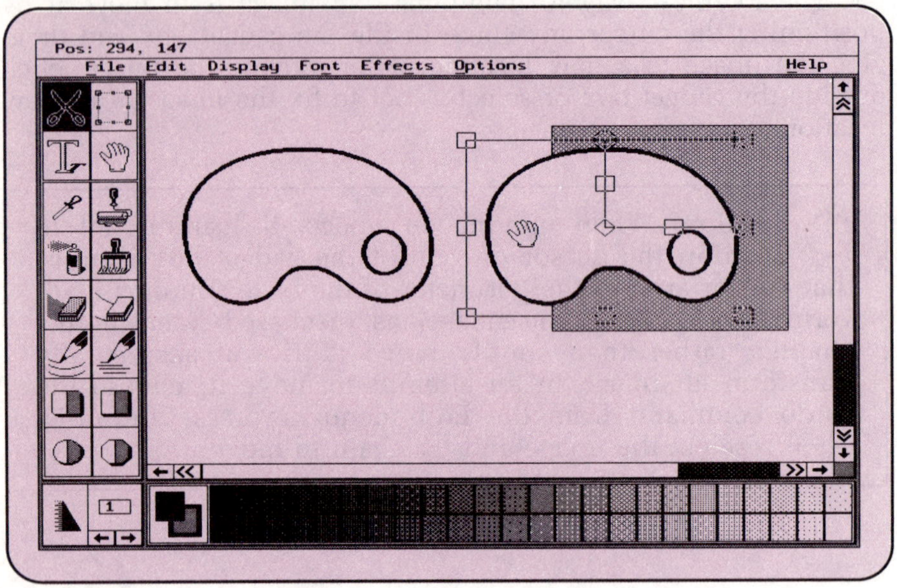

Figure 5.9 Enclosed shapes selected with the Scissors tool are opaque.

If you move an image selected with the Gadget Box tool, the entire area inside the rectangle is opaque, whether or not it is colored in the background color, as shown in Figure 5.12.

Right-Dragging a Selection

The rules about transparency and opacity stated in the previous section apply only when dragging a selected image while pressing the left mouse button. If you right-drag an image to move it, all occurrences of the background color will be transparent, whether the image was selected with the Scissors or Gadget Box tool and whether or not the shapes in the image are enclosed.

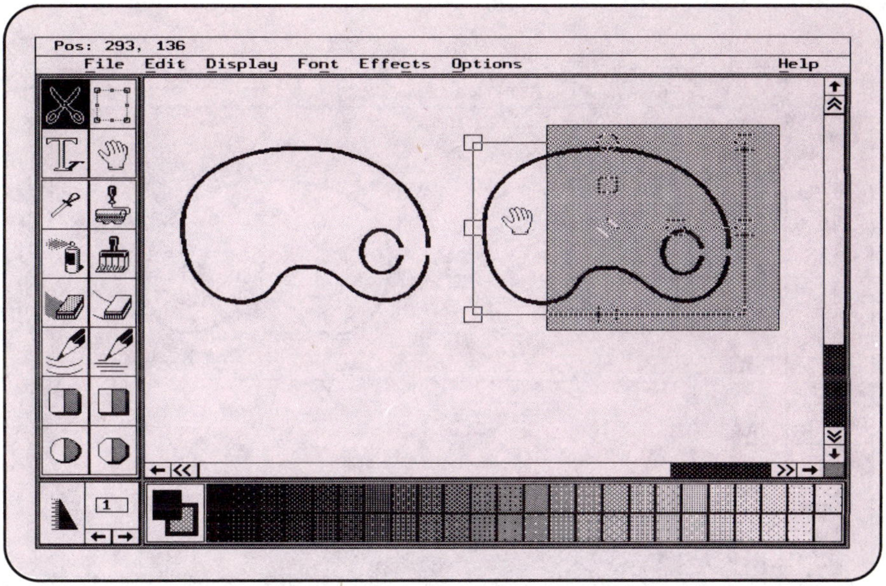

Figure 5.10 If there are breaks in a shape's outline, the shape will be transparent when selected with the Scissors tool.

Erasing a Selection

To delete a selected image from your painting, choose the Cut command from the Edit menu. The image will be deleted from the screen and transferred to the Paintbrush *clipboard*. If you later decide you want to bring the image back, you can restore the image by choosing the Paste command from the Edit menu. Complete information on the Cut command and the clipboard is included in the *Cut, Copy, and Paste* section.

4 The Clear command provided in previous versions of Paintbrush is not available in Paintbrush IV.

Caution: Using the Cut command to delete an image displaces the previous contents of the clipboard. If you want to remove an image from the screen while retaining the clipboard's current contents, use the Eraser tool instead.

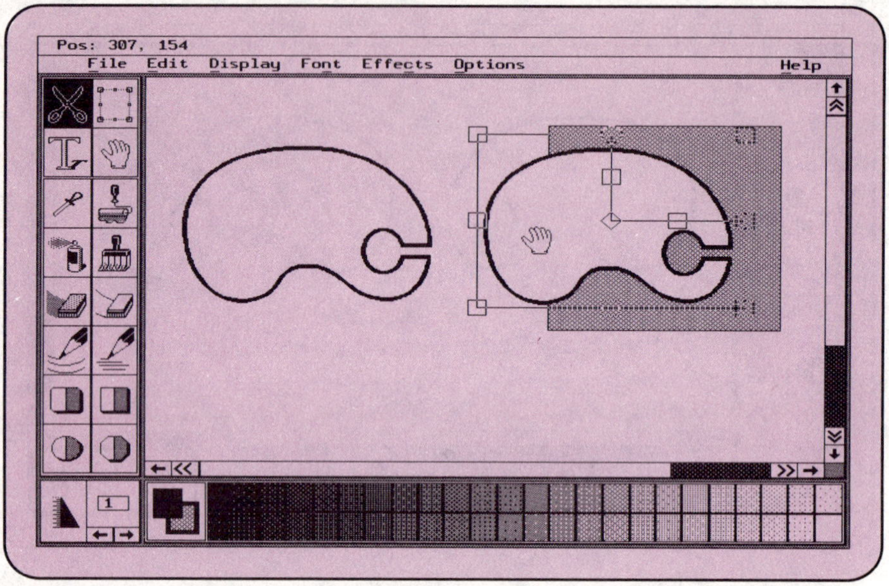

Figure 5.11 The outer shape is enclosed while the inner smaller shape is not; thus, the former is opaque and the latter transparent when the image is selected with the Scissors tool.

Duplicating a Selection

One of Paintbrush's great advantages over the traditional drawing environment is its ability to duplicate a single image over and over without sacrificing the quality of the image in the least. No photocopy machine can replicate this feat!

Duplicating a selection cuts down on drawing time. For example, it takes about ten minutes to draw a small bird like the one in Figure 5.14. Rather than spend ten minutes per bird to draw a whole flock of birds, you can duplicate your first bird, as demonstrated in Figure 5.15. Duplicating an image a hundred times over often takes less time than drawing the image in the first place.

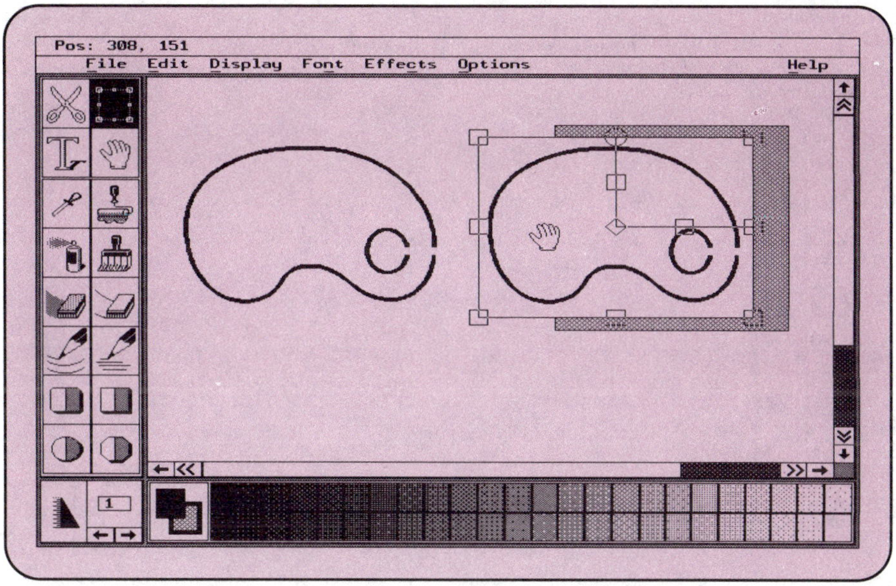

Figure 5.12 The entire rectangular area selected with the Gadget Box tool is always opaque.

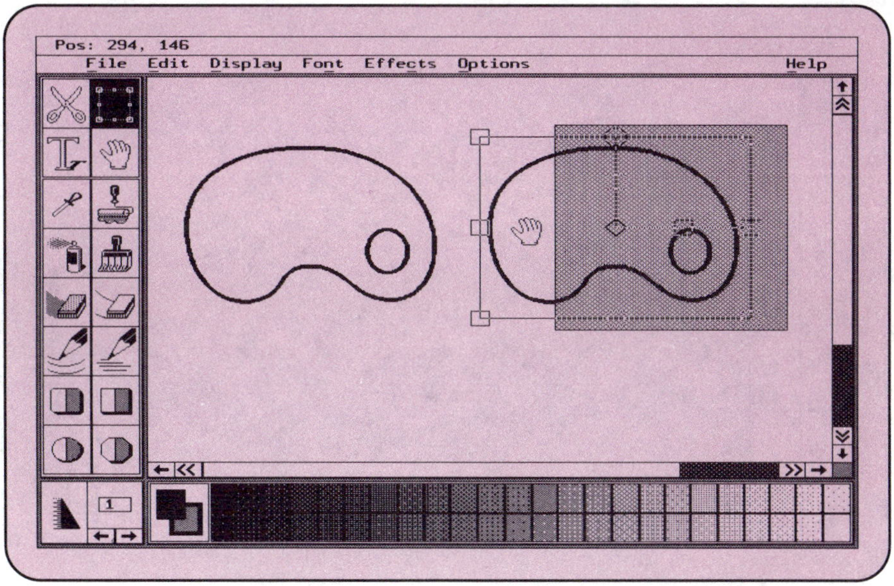

Figure 5.13 Right-drag a selected image to make all occurrences of the background color transparent.

Figure 5.14 To create a single bird, you must draw it from scratch.

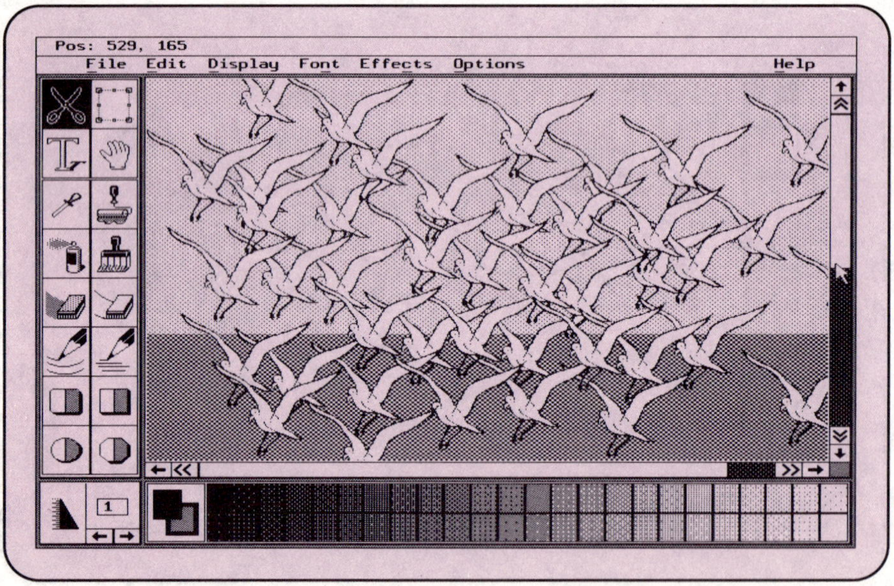

Figure 5.15 To create a flock of birds, you can duplicate the single bird.

Cut, Copy, and Paste

The Cut, Copy, and Paste commands from the Edit menu are the principal means of duplicating images in Paintbrush. Each command utilizes the program's built-in clipboard, which stores a single image at a time for later retrieval.

In tandem, the three commands are useful for creating copies of a selected image. Choose the Cut command to remove the selection from the drawing window and place it on the clipboard, thereby displacing the clipboard's previous contents. Choosing the Copy command also replaces the previous contents of the clipboard but does not remove the selected image from the drawing window.

After you cut or copy an image, the image remains in the clipboard until the next time you choose the Cut or Copy command or until you quit Paintbrush. Thus, you can store an image for as long as you like during a single Paintbrush session.

Choose the Paste command to retrieve the contents of the clipboard. The image will appear in a gadget box in the top, left corner of the drawing window, as shown in Figure 5.16. Whether the image was selected with the Scissors tool or the Gadget Box tool, the entire gadget box holding the clipboard image will be opaque. To make it transparent, right-drag the image to a new location in the painting. Otherwise, simply drag the image to its appropriate location in the current painting.

You can remove the image you just pasted as long as it still appears in the gadget box by choosing the Undo command. After you fix the image in place by clicking outside the gadget box or by selecting a new tool, you can no longer undo the paste.

The Cut, Copy, and Paste commands are thus useful for storing an image that you intend to apply to the drawing window several times during a single Paintbrush session. But their primary function is to transfer images from one painting to another, a process described in the following Quick Steps.

Q Transferring Images between Paintings

1. Open the painting containing the image you want to transfer.
2. Select the image with the Scissors tool or the Gadget Box tool. — A gadget box surrounds the selected image.

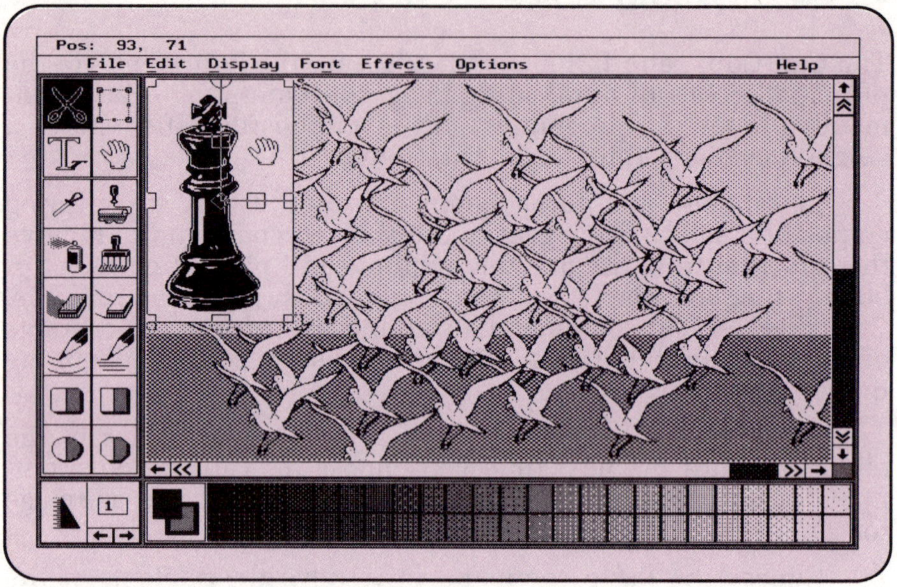

Figure 5.16 Choose the Paste command to retrieve the contents of the clipboard, in this example, a chess piece.

3. Choose the Copy command from the Edit menu.

   The image is stored on the clipboard.

4. If you've made any changes to the current painting that you want to keep, save the painting before opening a new one. Otherwise, open the painting to which you will transfer the image.

5. Choose the Paste command from the Edit menu.

   The clipboard image appears inside a gadget box in the painting just opened. □

Cloning

Cut, Copy, and Paste are powerful duplication commands, but they are not the only means to duplicate images. In fact, if you just want to create a few duplicates that you intend to use immediately, there is a much quicker duplication method known as *cloning*. Cloning creates a quick copy of an image without using the clipboard or displacing its current contents. Clones are extremely simple to create, as demonstrated in the following Quick Steps.

Q Cloning an Image

1. Select an image with the Scissors or Gadget Box tool.	A gadget box surrounds the selected image.
2. Press the Shift key and drag the image to a new location. Left-drag to create an opaque clone, right-drag to make the clone transparent.	Creates a copy of the selected image at the new location, leaves the original at the old location.
3. Repeat step 2 to create additional clones.	In Figure 5.17, we cloned the cowboy hat by Shift-dragging after selecting the hat with the Scissors tool.

Drawing with an Image

Shift-dragging creates one clone each time that you drag and release the mouse button. You can create a constant stream of clones that will follow the course of your drag by pressing the Control key as you drag. In Figure 5.18, we created a border of hats around the painting by Control-dragging the cowboy hat. Note that the cloned hats are opaque.

The number of clones created by Control-dragging depends on how fast you drag. When you Control-drag slowly, you create more clones than if you Control-drag quickly.

> **Tip:** For the best results, Control-drag images selected with the Scissors tool. Otherwise, a large white area will appear around each clone, obscuring the clone before it.

Figure 5.17 Shift-drag a selected image to create a quick copy of it.

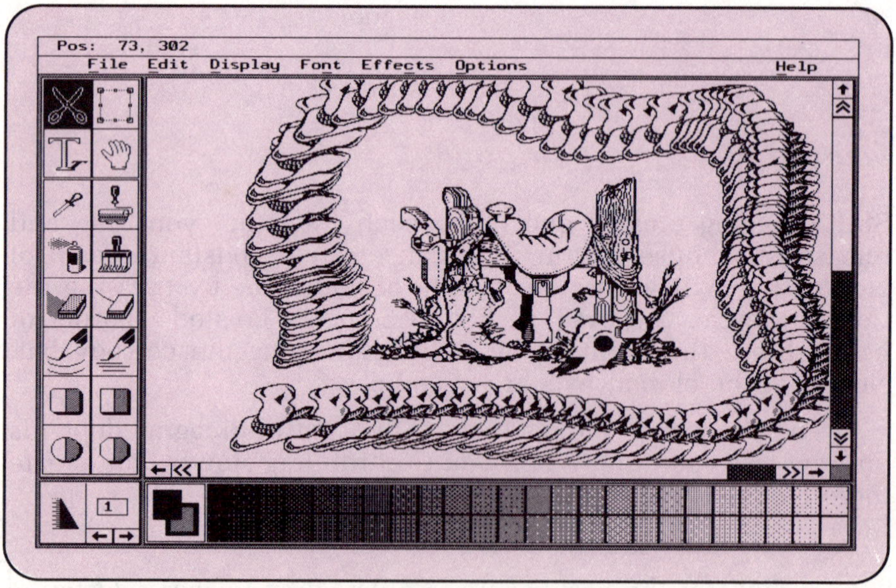

Figure 5.18 Control-drag a selection to create multiple opaque clones.

You can create a stream of transparent clones, as shown in Figure 5.19, by Control-right-dragging. Also notice in this figure that we have created two streams of cowboy hats, one on each side of the painting. The method for creating multiple streams of clones is described in the following Quick Steps.

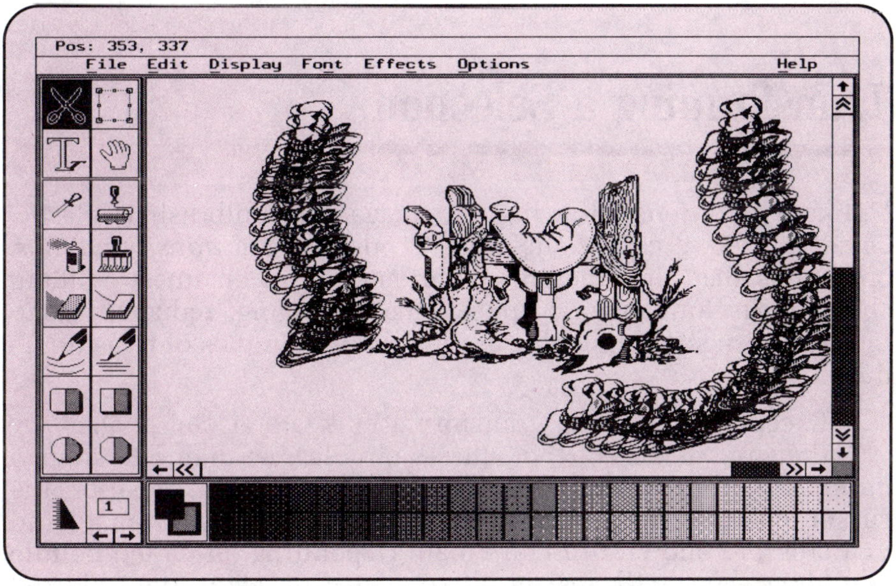

Figure 5.19 Control-right-dragging to create multiple transparent clones.

Creating Multiple Clones

1. Select an image with the Scissors tool.

   A gadget box surrounds the selected image.

2. Press the Control key and drag the image to a new location. Left-drag to create opaque clones, right-drag to make the clones transparent.

   Creates a stream of opaque or transparent clones.

3. Release the Control key but do not release the mouse button.

   Dragging the selection no longer produces a stream of clones.

4. Drag the selected image to the point where you want to start the next stream of clones.

5. Press the Control key and left-drag or right-drag the selection.	Creates an additional stream of opaque or transparent clones.
6. Release both the Control key and the mouse button.	Completes the cloning process. □

Transforming a Selection

Unlike a traditional drawing, an image in Paintbrush is elastic. Once selected, it can be subjected to one or more *transformations*, operations that alter the size or orientation of an image without changing its fundamental appearance. Enlarging, reducing, rotating, and even simply moving an image are examples of transformations.

4 Except for moving, transformations are accomplished by dragging at one of the square, circular, or diamond-shaped *handles* that appear on the gadget box. When you position the cursor over one of these handles, the cursor changes from a hand to a cross, as shown in Figure 5.20. Depending on which handle you drag, you will resize, flip, rotate, or slant the selected opaque image.

> ▶ **Tip:** Dragging a gadget box handle transforms an opaque image. Right-dragging a gadget box handle transforms a transparent image.

Resizing an Image

4 To resize a selected image, drag on one of the square handles around the perimeter of the gadget box. The handle that you drag and the manner in which you drag it will determine how Paintbrush resizes the image.

You can resize the width of an image without affecting its height by dragging one of the two side handles. If you drag toward the image, you make it narrower, as shown in Figure

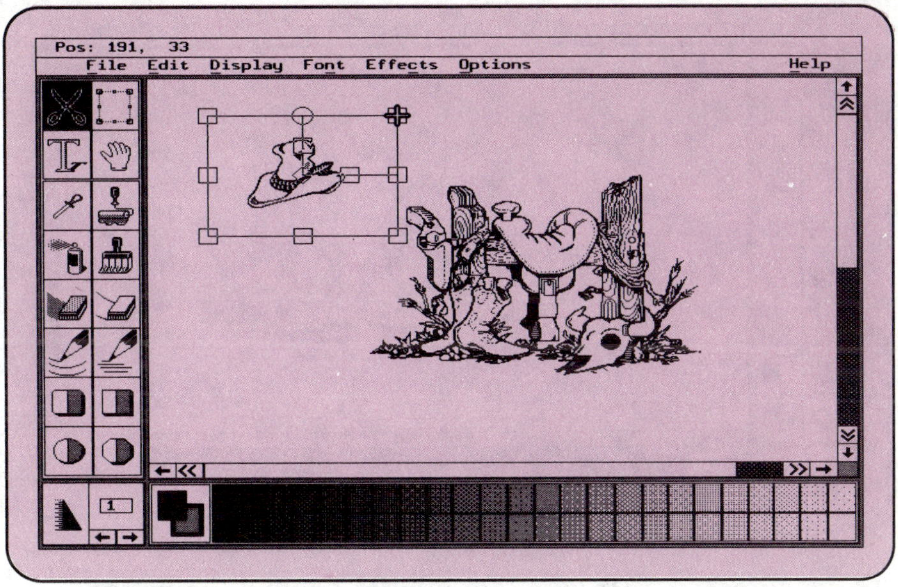

Figure 5.20 The cursor appears as a cross when positioned over a gadget box handle.

5.21. If you drag away from the image, you make it wider, as shown in Figure 5.22.

To resize the height of an image without affecting its width, drag the handle at the bottom of the gadget box. If you drag toward the image, you make it shorter, as shown in Figure 5.23. If you drag away from the image, you make it taller, as shown in Figure 5.24.

To resize the width and height of an image at the same time, drag one of the four corner handles. If you drag toward the image, you reduce it. If you drag away from the image, you enlarge it. If you press the Shift key while dragging a corner handle, you will reduce or enlarge the image proportionally, as shown in Figures 5.25 and 5.26, respectively. The height and width of the image will be changed by the same percentage.

When you reduce an image, you decrease the number of pixels Paintbrush uses to represent the image. This means that the program has to eliminate some details. Figures 5.21, 5.23, and 5.25 demonstrate this loss of detail in a reduced image. In contrast, when you enlarge an image, the number of pixels used to represent an image increases, so the image takes on a more

Figure 5.21 Drag a side handle toward the image to reduce it horizontally.

Figure 5.22 Drag a side handle away from the image to enlarge it horizontally.

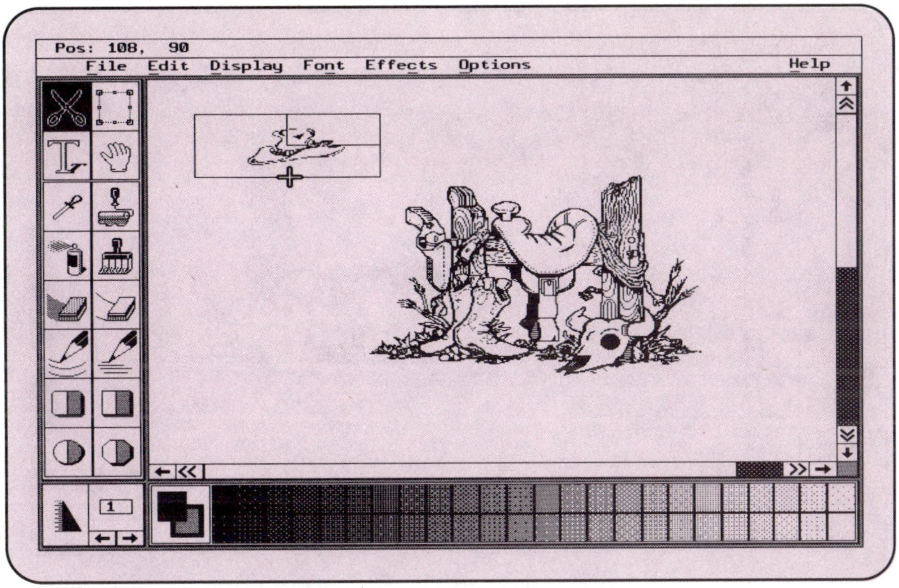

Figure 5.23 Drag the bottom handle toward the image to reduce it vertically.

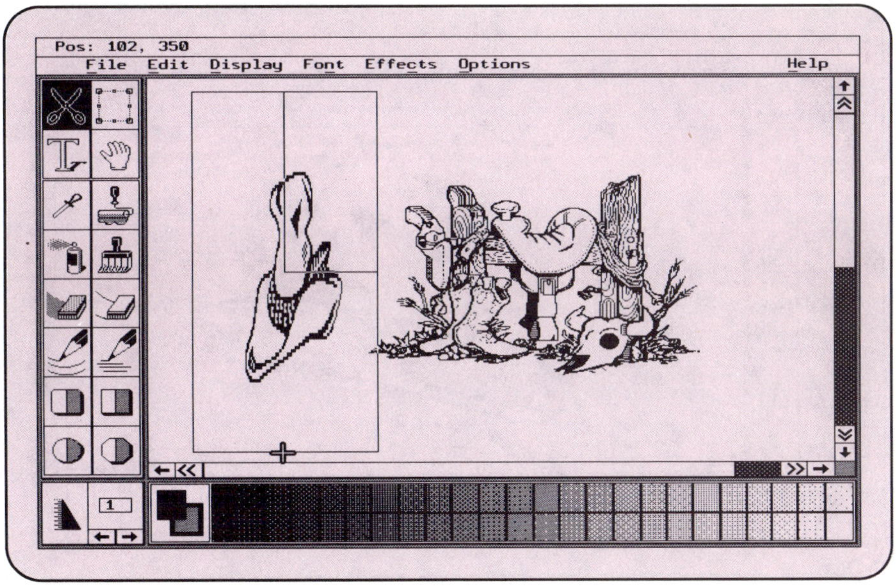

Figure 5.24 Drag the bottom handle away from the image to enlarge it vertically.

Figure 5.25 Shift-drag a corner handle toward the image to reduce it proportionally.

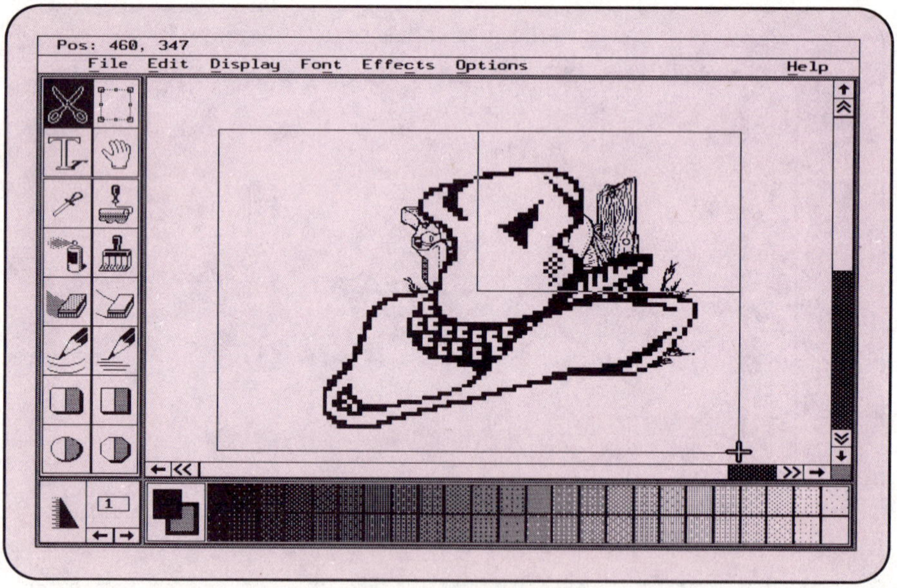

Figure 5.26 Shift-drag a corner handle away from the image to enlarge it proportionally.

jagged appearance, as shown in Figures 5.22, 5.24, and 5.26. In either case, you will probably have to redraw portions of the scaled image to maintain the quality of its appearance. Figure 5.27 shows the image in Figure 5.26 after being redrawn.

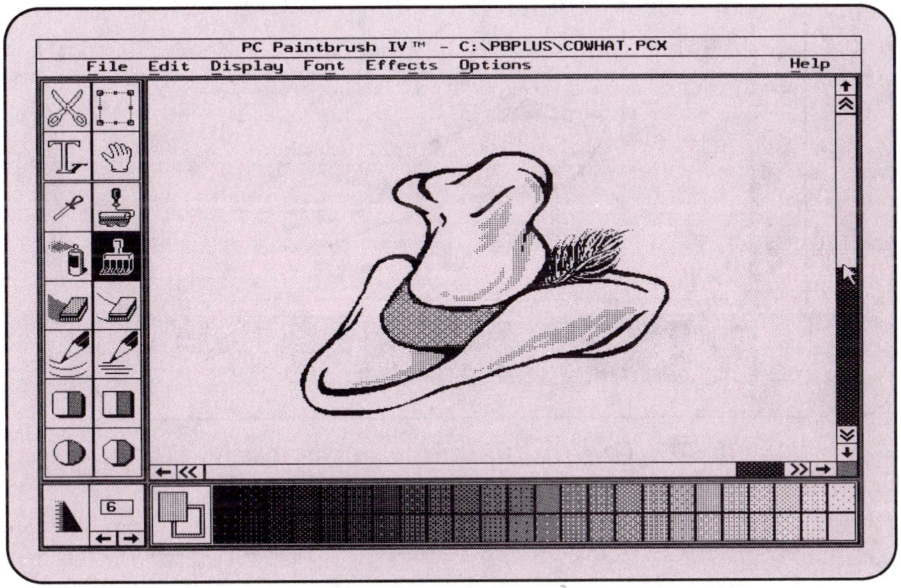

Figure 5.27 It took about 45 minutes to clean up the enlarged image shown in Figure 5.26.

Flipping an Image

4 To flip a selection, click one of the square handles inside the gadget box. Each handle flips the image in a different direction. Click the square handle above the diamond-shaped handle to flip the selection horizontally, as shown in Figure 5.28.

Click the square handle to the right of the diamond-shaped handle to flip the selection vertically, as shown in Figure 5.29.

Click both square handles inside the gadget box to flip the selection upside down, as shown in Figure 5.30.

If you drag one of the square handles inside the gadget box, the selection will flip and then move with your drag. Flip an image horizontally to create a mirror image and flip it vertically to create shadows and reflections.

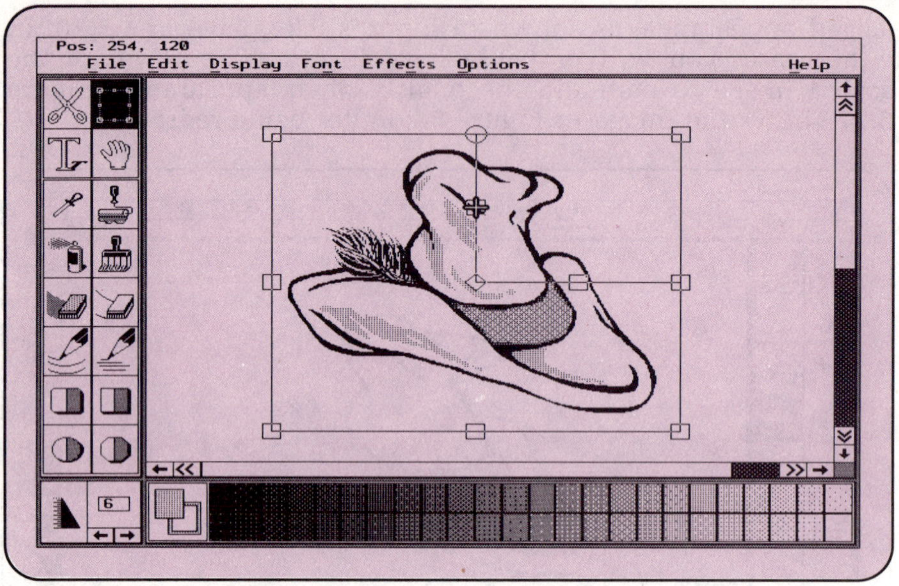

Figure 5.28 To flip the image horizontally, click the handle where the cursor is positioned.

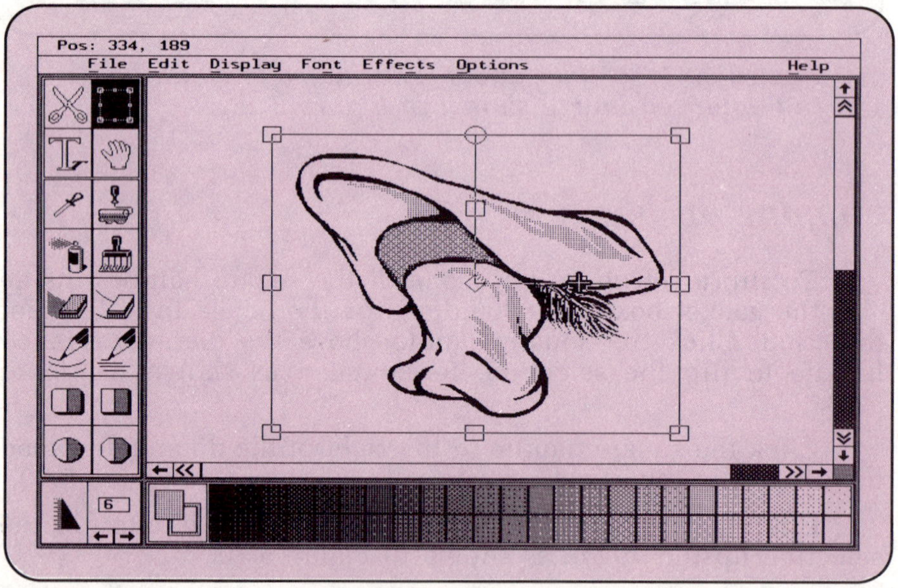

Figure 5.29 To flip the image vertically, click the handle where the cursor is positioned.

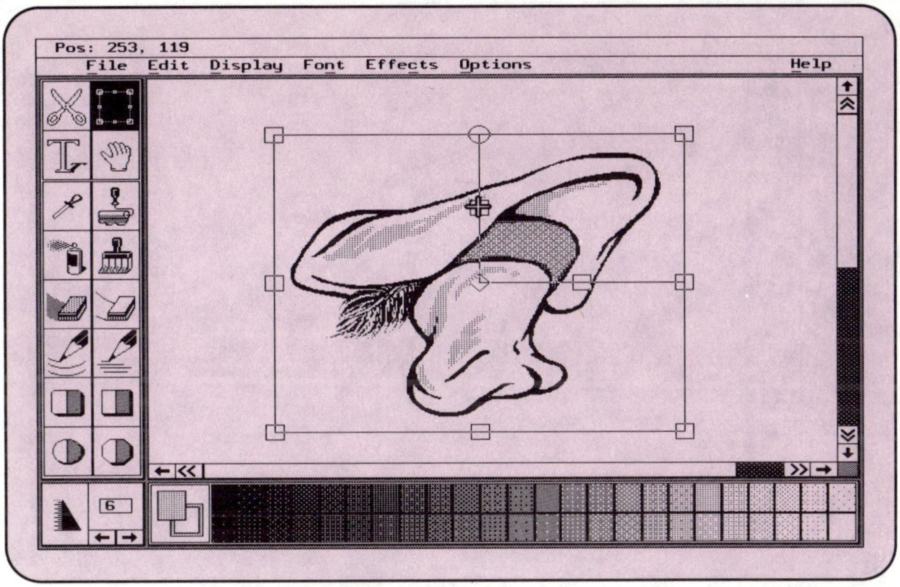

Figure 5.30 To flip the image upside down, first click one of the handles inside the gadget box, then the other.

Rotating an Image

4 To rotate a selection, click the diamond-shaped handle in the center of the gadget box. The selection will rotate clockwise 90°, or one quarter circle, every time you click, as shown in Figure 5.31. To rotate an image 180°, or upside down, click the diamond-shaped handle twice. To rotate an image 90° counterclockwise, click the handle three times. If you drag the diamond-shaped handle, the selection will rotate 90° and then move with your drag.

Slanting an Image

4 To slant a selection, drag the circular handle at the top of the gadget box. The direction that you drag the handle determines the direction of the slant. By dragging the top handle to the right, you slant the selected image forward, as shown in Figure 5.32. By dragging the top handle to the left, you slant the selected image backward, as shown in Figure 5.33.

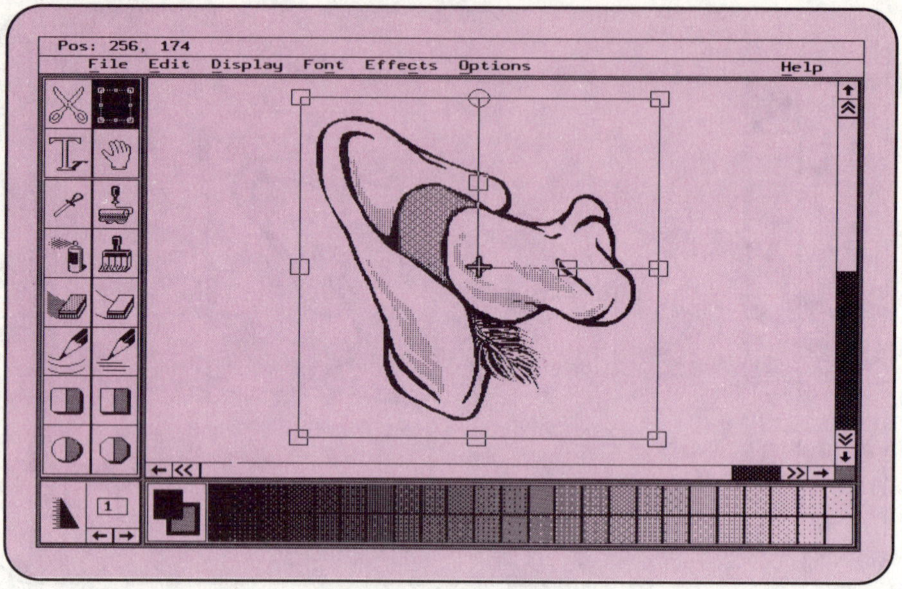

Figure 5.31 Clicking the diamond-shaped handle rotates the selection 90° clockwise.

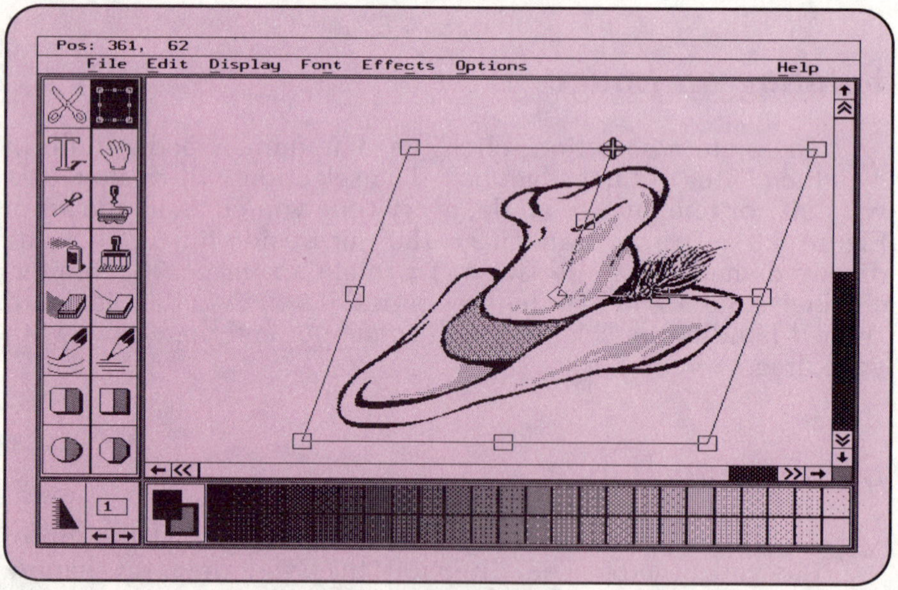

Figure 5.32 Slant the selection forward by dragging the circular handle to the right.

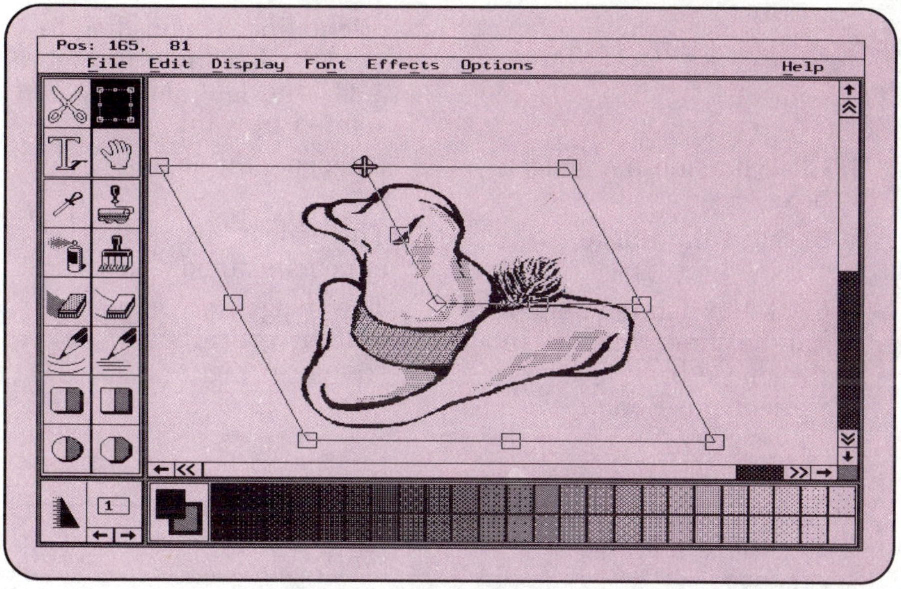

Figure 5.33 Slant the selection backward by dragging the circular handle to the left.

Unfortunately, you can only use the gadget box to slant an image horizontally and not vertically. You can get past this limitation by combining slanting with rotating. The following Quick Steps explain how to combine these two types of transformations to slant an image vertically.

Q Slanting an Image Vertically

1. Select the image you want to slant using the Scissors or Gadget Box tool. — A gadget box appears around the selected image.
2. Click the diamond-shaped handle in the center of the gadget box to rotate the image 90°. — Swaps the height and width of the image. The circular handle now affects the selection's previously vertical attributes.
3. Drag the circular handle to slant the image. — If you drag to the right, what used to be the left side of the image appears slanted upward when the image is returned to its original

orientation. If you drag to the left, as shown in Figure 5.34, the right side appears slanted upward.

4. Click outside the gadget box.

   Deselects the image.

5. Reselect the image.

   The gadget box no longer appears slanted.

6. Click the diamond-shaped handle three times to rotate the image back to an upright position.

   The image now appears with a vertical slant, as shown in Figure 5.35. □

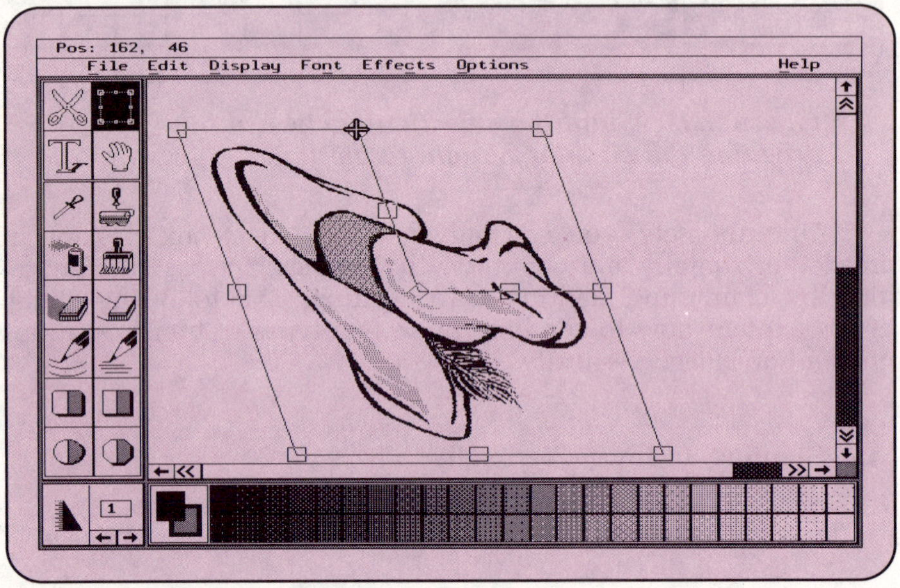

Figure 5.34 Drag to slant the vertical attributes of the rotated image.

▶ **Note:** If your transformations don't appear to work correctly, it is probably because Paintbrush is running low on memory. Choose the Undo command, select a smaller image to use less memory, and try again.

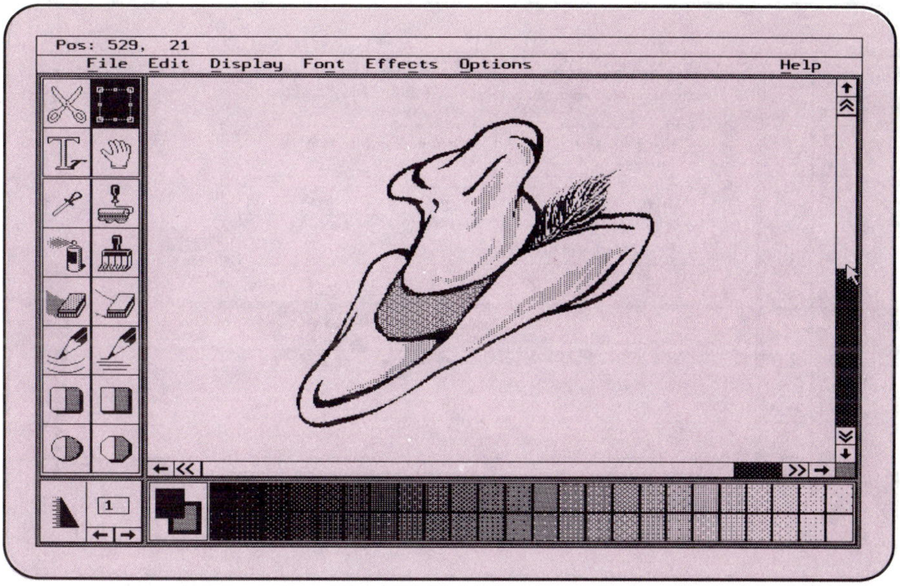

Figure 5.35 The final, vertically slanted image.

Transforming an Entire Painting

Paintbrush Plus provides an additional feature, the Change Entire Image... command, that allows you to transform an entire painting. This command is especially useful if you can't select an entire image because the image extends beyond the scroll bars. It is also useful if you want to enlarge an image to a size that's too large to fit in the drawing area.

Choose the Change Entire Image... command from the Edit menu to display the Change Entire Image dialog box, shown in Figure 5.36. This dialog box contains options for flipping, rotating, and resizing the current painting. There is no slanting option.

Since Paintbrush Plus cannot undo the effects of the Change Entire Image... command, be sure to save the current painting before you apply the changes! If you're unhappy with your results, you'll then be able to start over by reopening the painting.

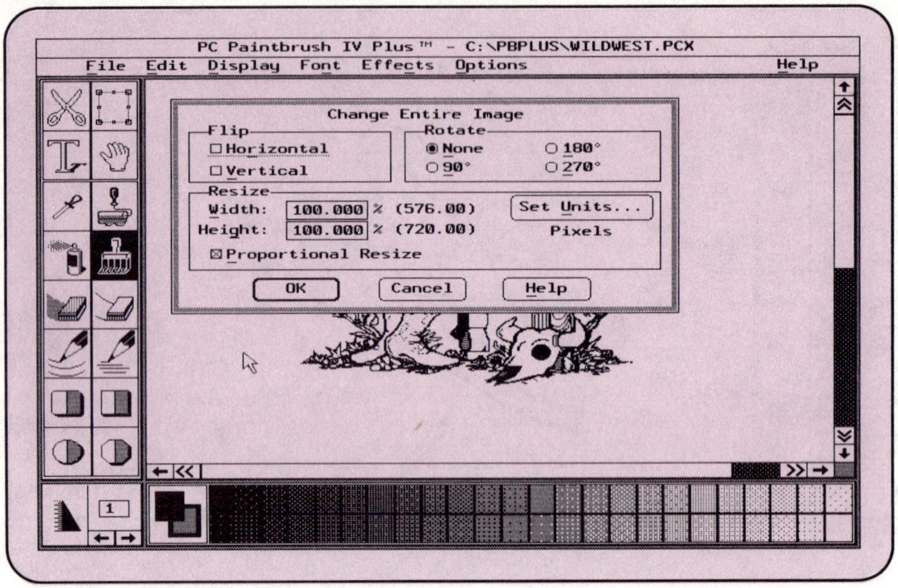

Figure 5.36 The Change Entire Image dialog box available only in PC Paintbrush IV Plus.

Q Flipping, Rotating, or Resizing an Entire Painting

1. Save your painting.
2. Press Alt-E followed by the E key. — The Change Entire Image dialog box displays.
3. Press Alt-R or Alt-V or both to flip the painting. — Alt-R flips a painting horizontally (Figure 5.28) and Alt-V flips a painting vertically (Figure 5.29). Selecting both options flips the painting upside down.
4. Press Alt-9, Alt-1, or Alt-2 to rotate the painting in 90° increments. Press Alt-N if you do not want to rotate the painting. — Rotates the painting 90°, 180°, or 270° in a clockwise direction.

5. Press Alt-W and enter a percentage by which to resize the painting horizontally.	A value less than 100 narrows the painting, a value greater than 100 widens the painting. The number to the right of the Width option reflects the new width of the painting in the current unit of measure.
6. If you want the height of the painting to be resized to a different percentage than the width, press Alt-P. Otherwise, skip to step 8.	Deselects the Proportional Resize option, which resizes the height in proportion to the width.
7. Press Alt-G and enter a percentage by which to resize the painting vertically.	A value less than 100 makes the painting shorter, a value greater than 100 makes the painting taller. The number to the right of the Height option reflects the new height of the painting in the current unit of measure.
8. Press Enter to transform the painting.	An hourglass displays on the screen. If you made extensive alterations, Paintbrush may take a few minutes to complete the transformation. □

Figure 5.37 shows the result of enlarging the Wild West image by 300% proportionally and rotating the image 90°. We chose the Zoom Out command to better display the transformed painting. This command shows the painting at one-third its normal size in the left window, so you are able to see the effect of the transformation on the entire painting. Because the right half of the window displays the painting at its actual size, there is only room enough for the image under the cursor, which is the hat on the post.

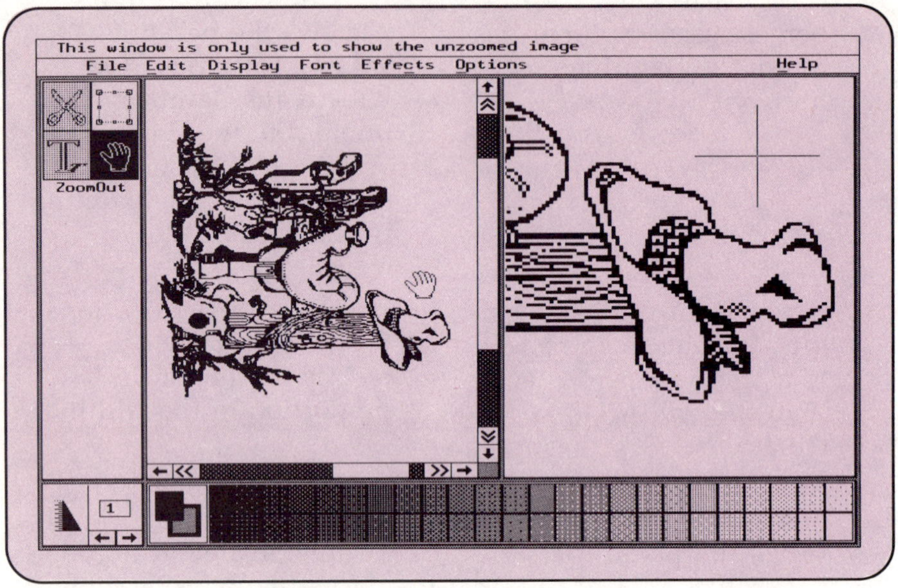

Figure 5.37 A greatly resized and rotated painting.

> **Note:** Transforming a painting also changes the size of your document. The degree to which you can enlarge a painting will depend on the amount of memory available to Paintbrush.

Inverting and Outlining

Paintbrush provides two additional methods for manipulating selected images: inverting and outlining. Both actually change the appearance of an image, creating what is termed a *special effect*. For examples of more complicated special effects, see Chapter 7, *Special Effects*.

Inverting an Image

Inverting an image is one of only two manipulations that actually change the colors of pixels in an image. If a selected image is black and white, choosing the Invert command from the Edit menu will change all selected black pixels to white and all selected white pixels to black, as shown in Figure 5.38. Choosing the Invert command twice in a row returns an image to its original appearance.

Figure 5.38 An inverted black and white image.

If the selected image contains additional colors, the Invert command replaces each color with its opposite, the color halfway around the color wheel from it. Red pixels become cyan, chartreuse pixels become violet, and so on. For a complete explanation of opposite colors, refer to *The Color Wheel* and *Changing the Entire Palette* sections of Chapter 4.

The Invert command is useful for creating photographic negatives of a selected image. It is also useful when you want to create images in reverse.

Outlining an Image

4 Choosing the Outline command from the Edit menu draws a thin outline around the perimeter of colored areas in the selected image. The outline is drawn in the same color as the

area it surrounds. The colored pixels inside the outlines are changed to the current background color, generally white. The result is a delicate outlined image, as shown in Figure 5.39. Choosing the Outline command twice in a row produces no effect. Paintbrush will *not* draw outlines around outlines.

Figure 5.39 An outlined image.

Exporting and Importing

Exporting an image saves an isolated portion of a painting to disk. *Importing* an image retrieves the saved image from disk and places it in the drawing window. These techniques are similar to copying and pasting, except that the Copy and Paste commands utilize the clipboard, a temporary storage site in the computer's memory. Although it takes more time to write or read an image on disk than to access the same image in memory, exporting and importing offer a versatility and permanence that copying and pasting do not.

For example, unlike copying, which allows you to store only one selection at a time in your computer's memory, exporting allows you to save as many images as you like to disk. You can also export an image during one Paintbrush session and import it during another.

Exporting an Image

You can export the current selection by choosing the Copy To... command from the Edit menu. The selected image can be saved in the PCX or TIF format, just like a standard painting, and can be retrieved using the Paste From... command or opened as a standard Paintbrush file. (For more information on the PCX or TIF format, review the *Saving a Painting in PCX or TIF Format* section of Chapter 2.)

Q Copying to Disk

1. Select the image you want to export using the Scissors or Gadget Box tool.	A gadget box surrounds the selected image.
2. Choose the Copy To... command from the Edit menu.	The Copy a Picture to Disk dialog box displays, as shown in Figure 5.40.
3. Press Alt-P, Alt-T, or Alt-U.	Selects the PCX, TIF, or TIF Uncompressed Image Format option.
4. Enter a file name in the Filename option box. The file name is limited to eight characters and must have a .PCX or .TIF extension.	
5. Press Enter or click Copy.	Saves the image to disk. If you are copying over an existing export, an alert box appears asking if you want to save over the previous copy of the image.
6. Press the Y key or the N key.	The Y key saves over the old file and the N key cancels the Copy To... command. □

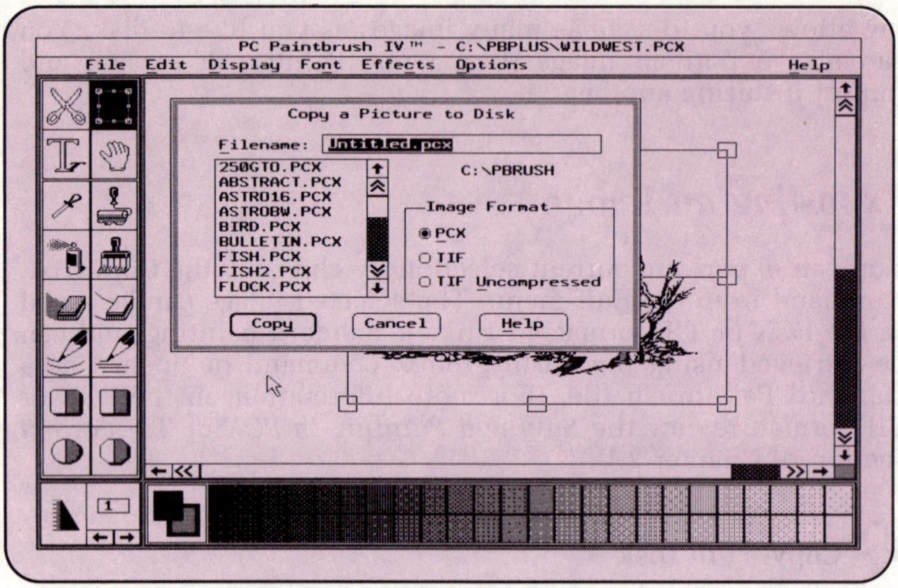

Figure 5.40 The Copy a Picture to Disk dialog box.

Importing an Image

Whether exported to disk with the Copy To... command or saved to disk with the Save command, an image can be imported into the current painting using the Paste From... command from the Edit menu. If the image is too large to fit in the current painting, the painting will be enlarged to accommodate it.

Q Pasting from Disk

1. Choose the Paste From... command from the Edit menu.	The Paste a Picture from Disk dialog box displays, as shown in Figure 5.41.
2. Press Alt-P or Alt-T.	Selects the PCX or TIF Image Format option.
3. Select an image from the scrolling field of file names. (Change to a different drive or directory to change the display of file names.)	Highlights the selected file.

4. Press Enter or click Paste. — Opens the highlighted file. The image appears in a gadget box in the top-left corner of the drawing window, as shown in Figure 5.42. □

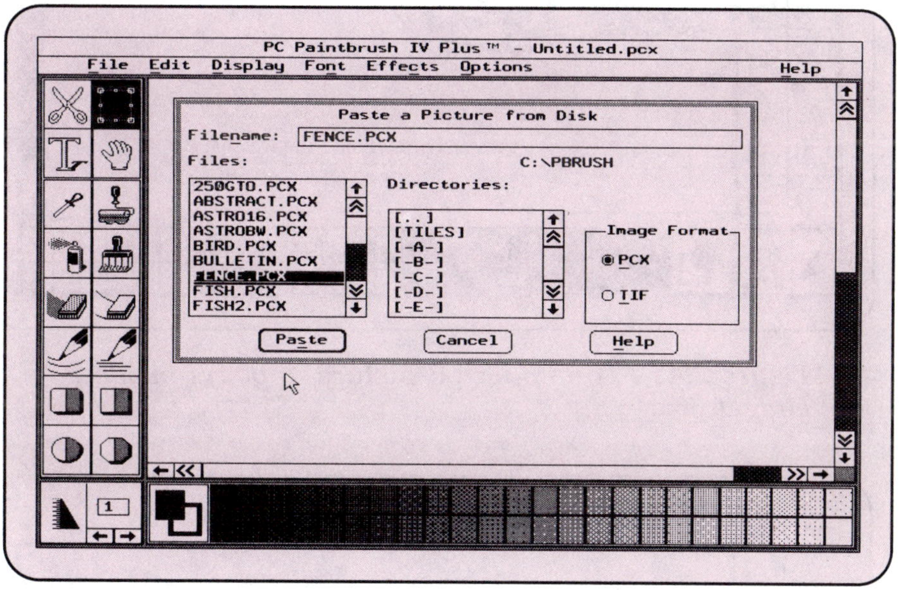

Figure 5.41 The Paste a Picture from Disk dialog box.

You can also load an exported image using the Open... command from the File menu. The image will appear inside a drawing window the same size as the original gadget box, as shown in Figure 5.43.

Figure 5.42 The imported picture appears inside a gadget box.

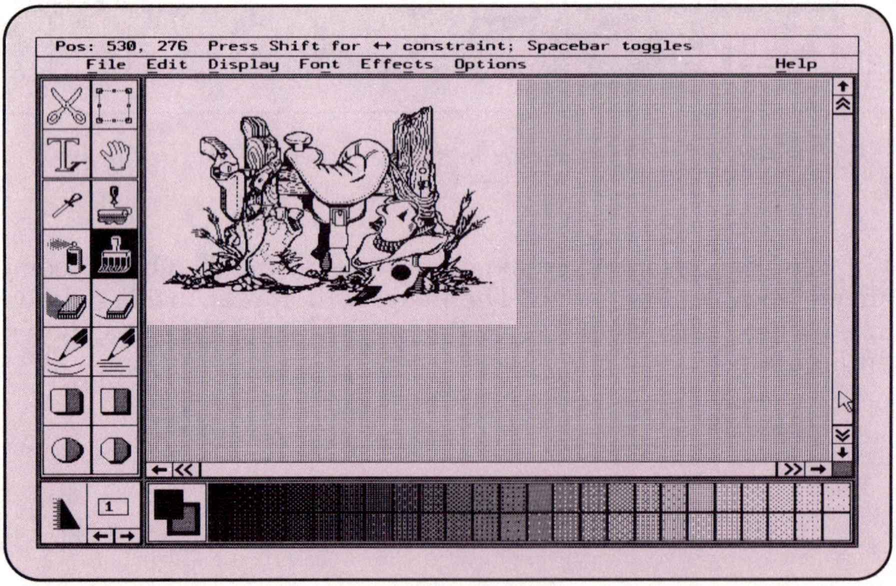

Figure 5.43 Opening an exported image as a standard painting.

Summary

In this chapter, you've learned:

- You can manipulate any image created in Paintbrush by selecting it and applying commands, such as Cut, Paste, and Copy To ..., or by performing mouse operations, such as left-dragging and Shift-dragging to clone an image.
- Selecting an image with either the Scissors or Gadget Box tool surrounds the image with a gadget box.
- You can move a selected image to a new location in the painting by dragging the gadget box.
- Right-dragging a selection makes it transparent.
- You can clone a selected image by pressing the Shift key while dragging the image. Control-dragging creates multiple clones.
- You can resize a selection by dragging at one of the square handles around the perimeter of the gadget box. Shift-dragging a square handle resizes the image proportionally.
- Clicking one of the square handles inside the gadget box flips a selection.
- Clicking the diamond-shaped handle in the center of the gadget box rotates a selection 90°.
- Dragging the circular handle at the top of the gadget box slants a selection horizontally.

Chapter 6

Adding Text

What You Will Learn

- ▶ *Creating type with the Text tool*
- ▶ *Choosing a font*
- ▶ *Specifying type size and spacing*
- ▶ *Enhancing the appearance of type*
- ▶ *Creating special effects*

A picture is worth a thousand words. But a picture without words may leave too much to viewer imagination. Headlines, labels, and captions may be needed to fill in the gaps in your visual message. In this chapter, you will learn how to add text to your paintings and how to enhance the text so that it is both legible and impressive.

Type Limitations

Before you can learn how to create type using the Text tool and its associated commands, you must understand the manner in which text is treated in Paintbrush. Type is just another graphic element, like an image. Once created, it can be entirely or partially erased, it can be enhanced by drawing on it with the Paintbrush tool, it can be filled with the Paint Roller, or it can be transformed using any of the gadget box handles.

The advantage of being able to manipulate text like an image is obvious—many interesting and unusual textual effects can be achieved easily, such as those shown in Figure 6.1.

Figure 6.1 Type in PC Paintbrush can be manipulated like an image.

Printing Problems

There are certain limitations to treating text as an image. First and foremost, the number of pixels in a character of type is fixed. Since the resolution of your printer is generally higher than that of your screen, the printed page contains more pixels per square inch than the screen display. This means that Paintbrush must shrink your text during the printing process so that it doesn't look jagged when printed. A letter that appears about one-inch tall on your 640-by-480-pixel monitor will print less than one quarter-inch tall on a standard 300-dots-per-inch laser printer. In contrast, text created in a word processor will print smoothly because each character is defined geometrically. Rather than shrinking the text to make it smooth, your printer increases the number of pixels assigned to the text so that it prints at the same size as it appears on the screen.

The printing resolution problem is slightly different if you place your paintings in a desktop publishing program like PageMaker PC. Your graphic will not reduce automatically when printed. If you do not resize the painting by hand in PageMaker, your text will print with noticeable jagged edges.

Editing Problems

Unlike text in a word processing program, type in Paintbrush is not *editable*. After you have created a block of text, you cannot go back later and fix a typo or change the type size or italicize a word. If you want to reformat a block of text, you must change the formatting settings and reapply the text, as discussed later in this chapter.

For these reasons, you may not want to create type in Paintbrush. You may prefer to create only the graphics in Paintbrush and then add smooth, editable type in a program like PageMaker that can combine text and imported graphics on the same page.

On the other hand, only a painting program like Paintbrush allows you to manipulate type by drawing and erasing over it. If you're willing to spend a little extra time, you can create special type effects that would be impossible to create in a word processing, desktop publishing, or drawing program.

Creating Type

4 Creating type in Paintbrush IV is not a complicated process, but it does involve a number of steps in which you must choose from several different options. The basic steps required to create a block of text are described in the following Quick Steps. The tools, commands, and dialog box options referred to in these Quick Steps are described in detail in later sections of this chapter. If you prefer to experiment now and learn the details later, the

Creating a Block of Text Quick Steps will be enough to get you started.

Creating a Block of Text

1. Select the Text tool.	The Enter Text dialog box appears.
2. Enter text from the keyboard and edit text as needed.	The text appears in the text entry field.
3. Press Enter to accept what you have typed or click OK.	The dialog box disappears and the cursor appears as an I-beam.
4. Select the primary, secondary, and background colors.	Type is created in the secondary color, outlines in the primary color, shadows and gradients in the background color.
5. Specify font, type specifications, and type styles using commands from the Font menu.	
6. Draw a text frame by dragging with the I-beam cursor.	A text frame with handles appears around the text.
7. Drag the frame to move it and drag at the handles to resize the frame.	
8. If final results are not what you want, choose the Undo command to redo steps 5, 6, and 7. When satisfied, select a different tool to fix the text in place.	You can now manipulate the text with other tools.

The Text Tool

4 Click the Text tool, the second tool down on the left in the toolbox, to display the Enter Text dialog box. If you are creat-

ing text for the first time in this Paintbrush session, a blinking *insertion marker* will appear in the *text entry field*, as shown in Figure 6.2. If you have already created text during this session, the text will appear highlighted in the text entry area, as shown in Figure 6.3.

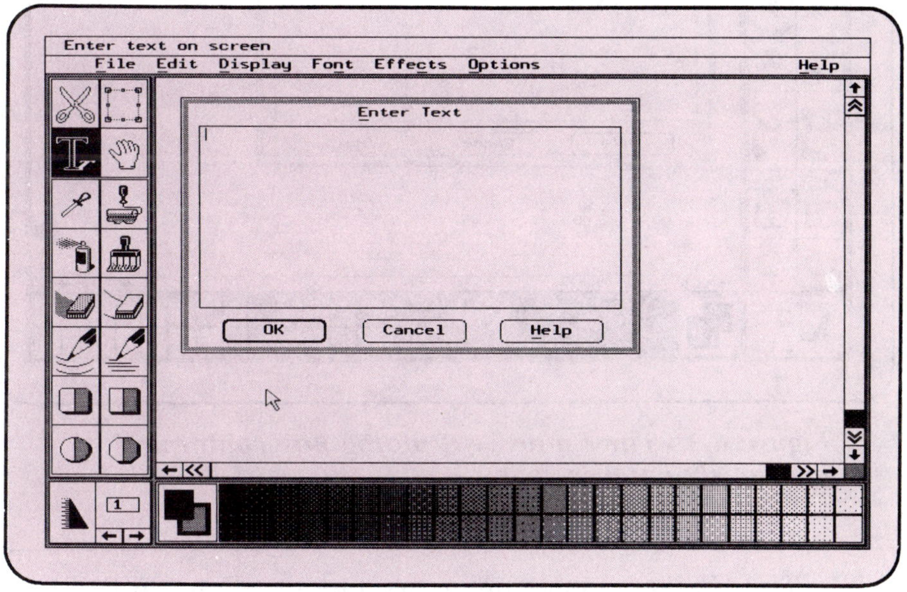

Figure 6.2 The Enter Text dialog box with an empty text entry area.

To enter text into this dialog box or to replace highlighted text, simply begin typing. If you don't want to replace the highlighted text, click after the last letter highlighted or press End to remove the highlight from the text, then enter additional text. After you fill up the length of the text entry field with type, the insertion marker drops down to the next line. You can enter up to 400 characters in the Enter Text dialog box, enough to create a standard paragraph.

Rather than dropping the insertion marker down to the next line of type in the text entry area, pressing Control-Enter inserts a line return character ↵, displayed as highlighted in Figure 6.4. When you later apply the text in the drawing window, text appearing after the line return character will start on a new line.

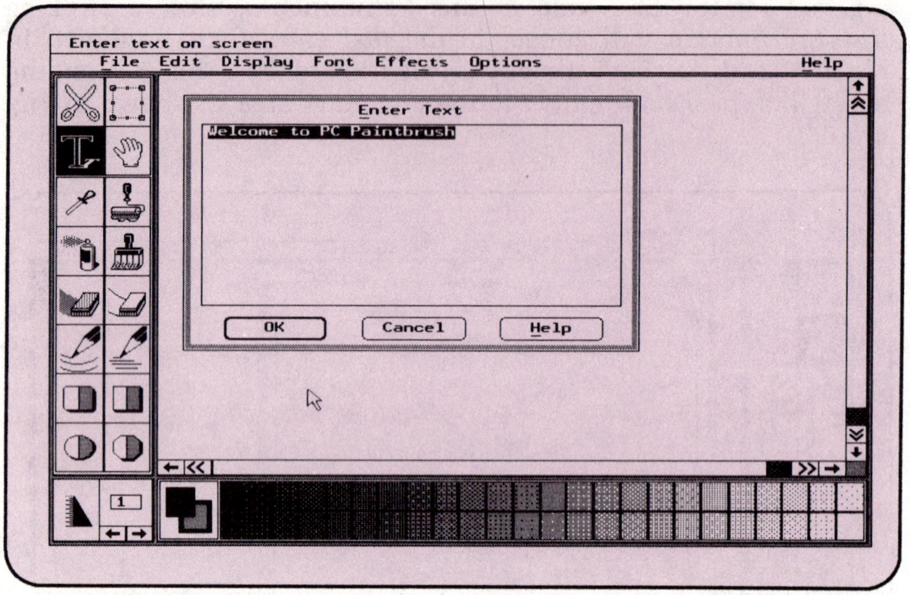

Figure 6.3 The Enter Text dialog box containing previously entered text.

> **Tip:** Unlike in some programs, pressing Enter in Paintbrush does not drop the insertion marker down to the next line of type; it selects the OK button. To insert a line return, the Paintbrush equivalent of starting a new line of type, you must press Control-Enter.

You can edit text in the text entry field by pressing the keys and key combinations listed in Table 6.1. You can also click in the text entry area to move the insertion marker or drag over a section of text to highlight it.

Table 6.1 Keys Used to Edit Type in the Text Entry Field

Key	Function
Right Arrow	Moves the insertion marker forward one letter
Left Arrow	Moves the insertion marker backward one letter
Home	Moves the insertion marker to the beginning of the text

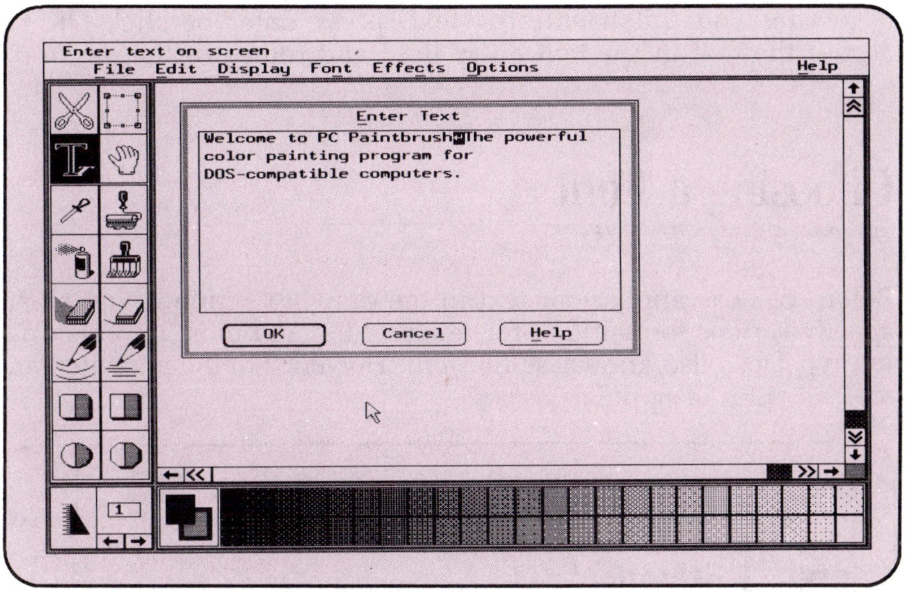

Figure 6.4 The line return symbol is produced by pressing Control-Enter.

Key	Function
End	Moves the insertion marker to the end of the text
Up Arrow	Moves the insertion marker up one line
Down Arrow	Moves the insertion marker down one line
Backspace	Deletes the character to the left of the insertion marker
Delete	Deletes the character to the right of the insertion marker
Control-Right Arrow	Deletes all characters to the right of the insertion marker
Alt-E	Highlights all text in text entry field
Alt-H	Displays the Help System dialog box
Control-Enter	Inserts a line return character ←
Escape	Cancels the text entering process
Enter	Accepts the text and returns you to the desktop

After you finish entering text, press Enter or click OK to accept the text in the text entry field and return to the desktop.

Choosing a Font

Before you can apply your text in the drawing window, you must specify various formatting preferences. First and most important is the typeface, also known as the *font*. Helvetica and Times Roman are examples of popular fonts.

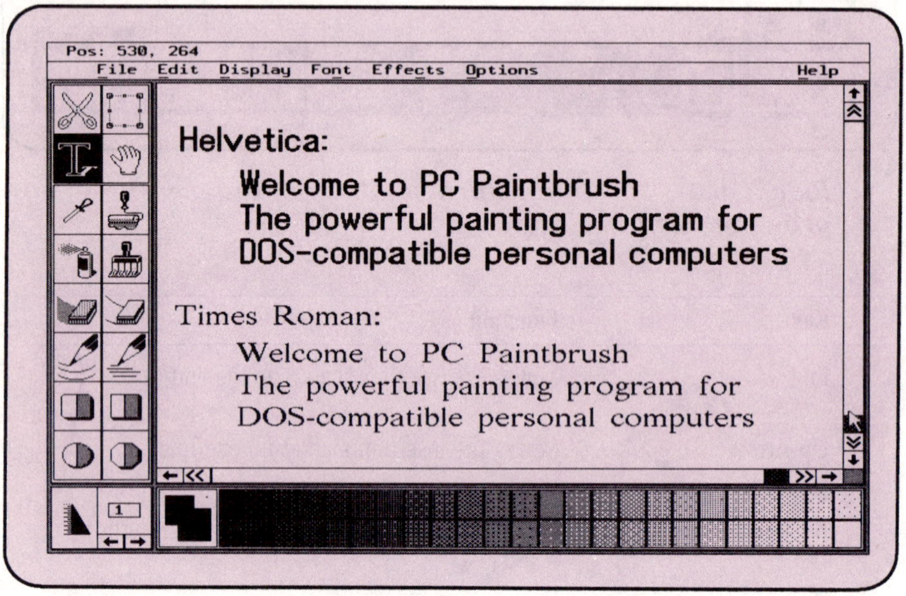

Figure 6.5 The popular fonts Helvetica and Times Roman.

Two kinds of fonts are provided with Paintbrush: *bit-mapped fonts* and *outline fonts*. Both fonts print the same; i.e., they appear smaller on the printed page than on the screen, but they behave differently when scaled to different sizes on the screen.

Bit-mapped Fonts

Bit-mapped fonts are defined as a collection of pixels; hence, they are designed to be displayed at a specific size and style. For example, the Helvetica and Times Roman fonts shown in Figure 6.5 are the bit-mapped fonts Helv8 and Tms6. If you want to reduce or enlarge the text, you must select a different bit-mapped font, such as Helv6 or Tms10. If you want to create bold or italic type, you must also select a separate font, such as Tms14b (*b* for bold) or Tms8i (*i* for italic).

Generally, bit-mapped fonts are most useful when creating small to moderately sized type, such as labels and captions. The bit-mapped fonts included with Paintbrush are shown in Figure 6.6. Table 6.2 lists the available bit-mapped fonts along with their full typeface names and their approximate type size in pixels. Type Size is measured from the top of a capital letter to the bottom of a lowercase descender, like *g* or *p*.

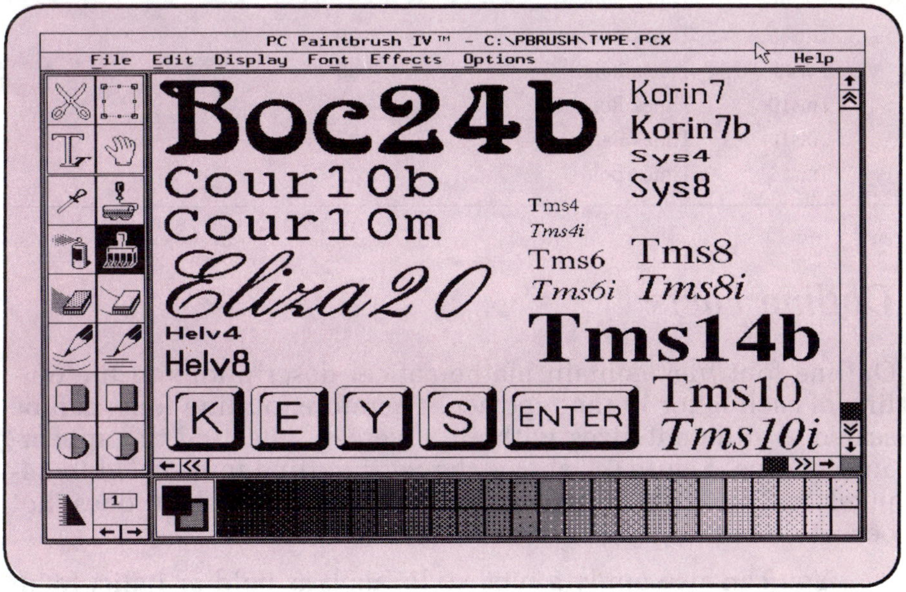

Figure 6.6 The bit-mapped fonts included with PC Paintbrush.

Table 6.2 Bit-mapped Font Statistics

Font Name	Typeface Name	Type Size in Pixels
Boc24b	Arnold Böcklin Bold	90
Cour10b	Courier Bold	37
Cour10m	Courier Medium	37
Eliza20	Elizabeth Script	75
Helv4	Helvetica	15
Helv8	Helvetica	30
Keys	Keys	61
Korin7	Korina	26
Korin7b	Korina Bold	26
Sys4	System Font	15
Sys8	System Font	30
Tms4	Times Roman	15
Tms4i	Times Italic	15
Tms6	Times Roman	22
Tms6i	Times Italic	22
Tms8	Times Roman	30
Tms8i	Times Italic	30
Tms10	Times Roman	37
Tms10i	Times Italic	37
Tms14	Times Bold	52

Outline Fonts

Outline font files contain mathematical descriptions of the outline of each letter in the typeface. Therefore, outline fonts can be scaled to different sizes without adversely affecting the appearance of type. Figure 6.7 shows the Serif outline font scaled to 24-pixel and 48-pixel type sizes. Notice that the text does not become more jagged as it is enlarged.

You can also apply a type style, such as bold or italic, to an outline font without making the type appear awkward or jagged.

So why not always use outline fonts if they're so versatile? First, Paintbrush only comes with four outline fonts: Serif, Serif Italic, Sans Serif, and Sans Serif Italic, shown in Figure 6.8 at a 60-pixel type size. The outline fonts are generic typefaces, useful

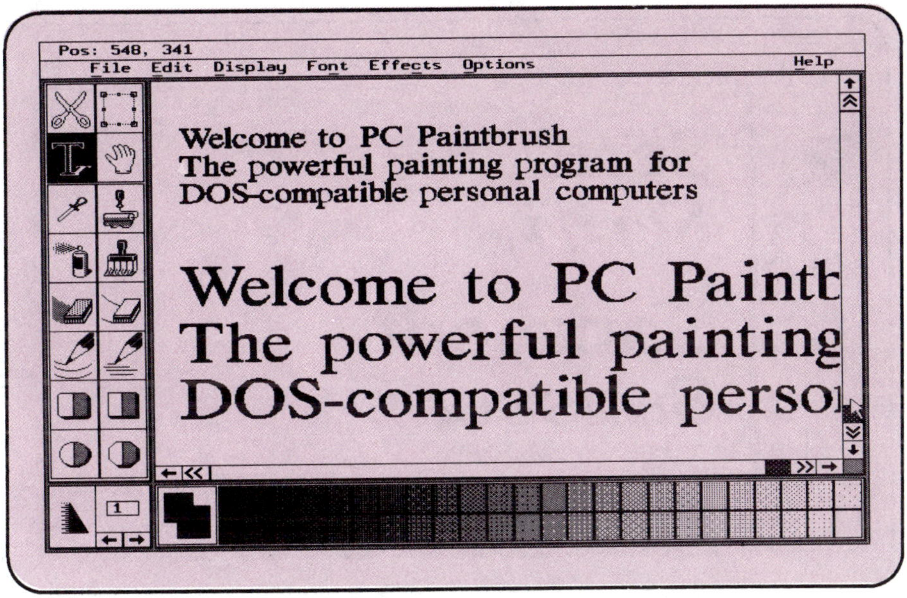

Figure 6.7 The Serif outline font scaled to two different type sizes.

for everyday applications but not for special applications. The outline fonts do not have the elegance of the bit-mapped font Eliza20 or the impact of Arnold Böcklin Bold. Second, as you can see by comparing the outline fonts in Figure 6.7 with the bit-mapped fonts in Figure 6.5, outline fonts look strange at small and moderate sizes. They perform best at large sizes, such as in headlines.

Selecting a Font File

To specify a font, you must choose a font name from the Font menu. Press Alt-N or click on the Font menu name to display the menu. There are four numbered slots for font names at the top of the Font menu. When you start Paintbrush, only one of the slots is filled, as shown in Figure 6.9. You can add additional font names to the Font menu using the Select Font File... command.

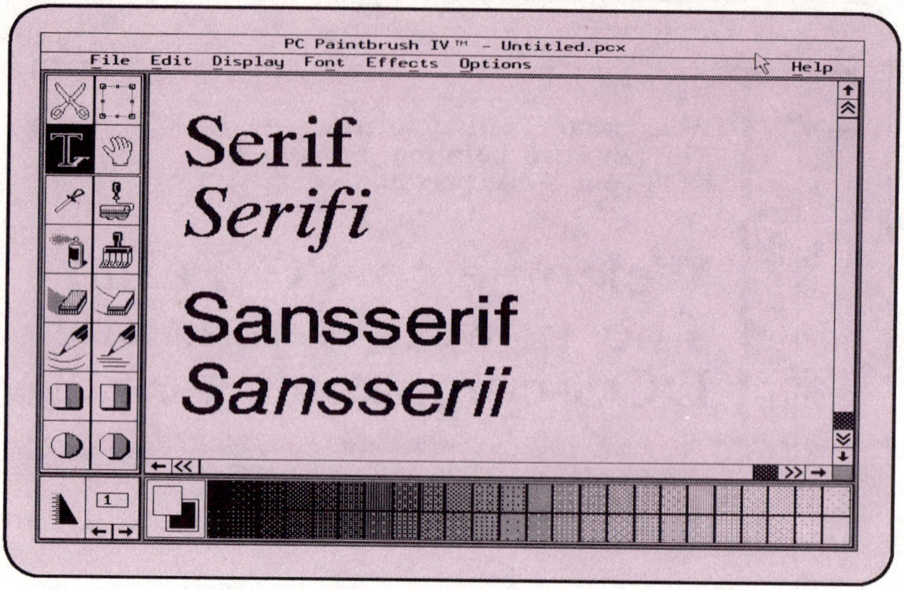

Figure 6.8 The outline fonts included with PC Paintbrush.

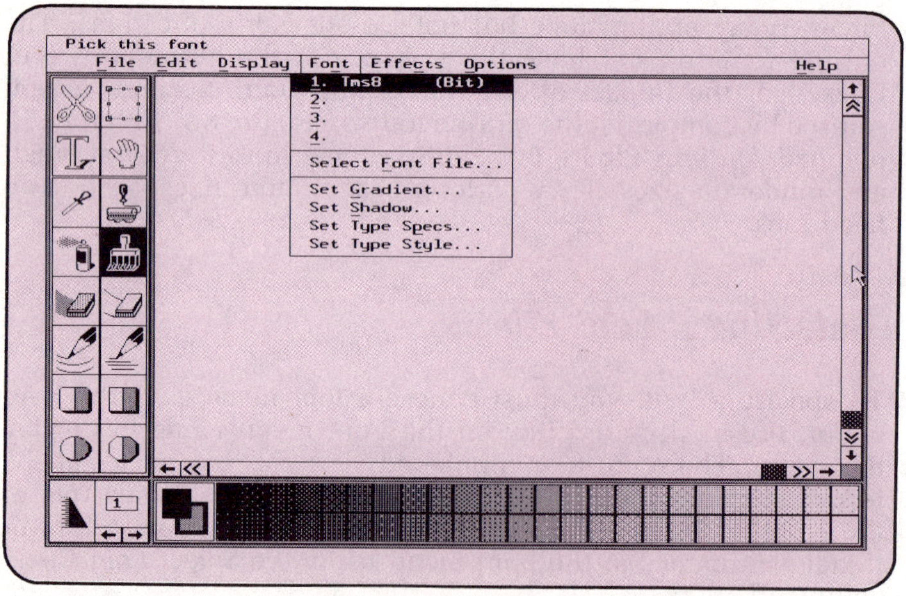

Figure 6.9 The Font menu displaying a single font name.

Adding Fonts to the Font Menu

1. Choose Select Font File... from the Font menu or press Alt-N followed by the F key.	The Load a Font from Disk dialog box shown in Figure 6.10 appears. (The Paintbrush Plus dialog box is slightly different.)
2. Press Alt-B or Alt-L or click the Bitmap or Outline Font Format option.	Bitmap displays bit-mapped font names with .XFR extensions. Outline displays outline font names with .OTL extensions.
3. Select a font from the scrolling Filename field using Figures 6.6 and 6.8 as a guide to the appearance of each font.	Highlights the selected font name.
4. Press Enter or click Open.	The font name appears in first slot of the Font menu preceded by a check mark, indicating that text applied in the drawing window will appear in this font. ☐

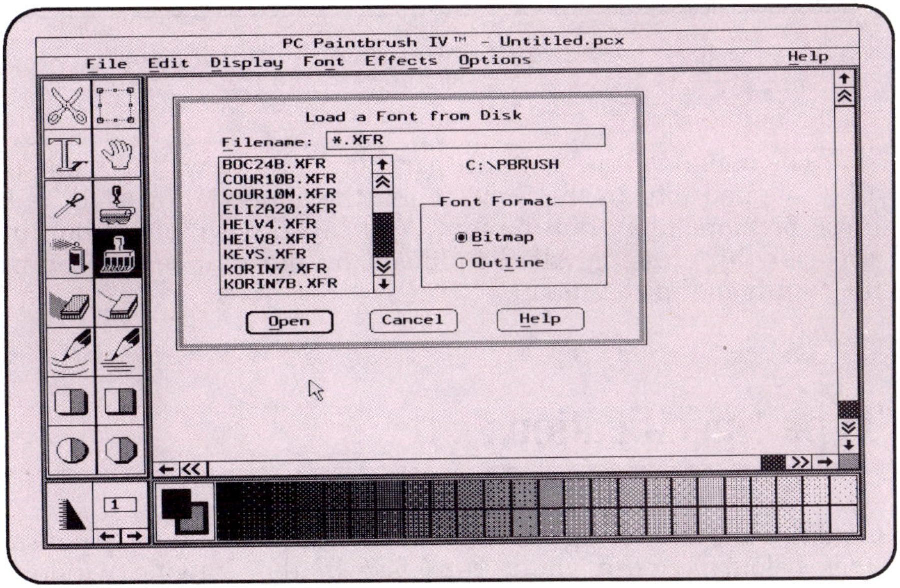

Figure 6.10 The Load a Font from Disk dialog box in PC Paintbrush.

Figure 6.11 shows how the Font menu appears when all four slots are full. Adding another font at this point will bump the fourth font off the menu since each font is moved down a slot to make room for the new font.

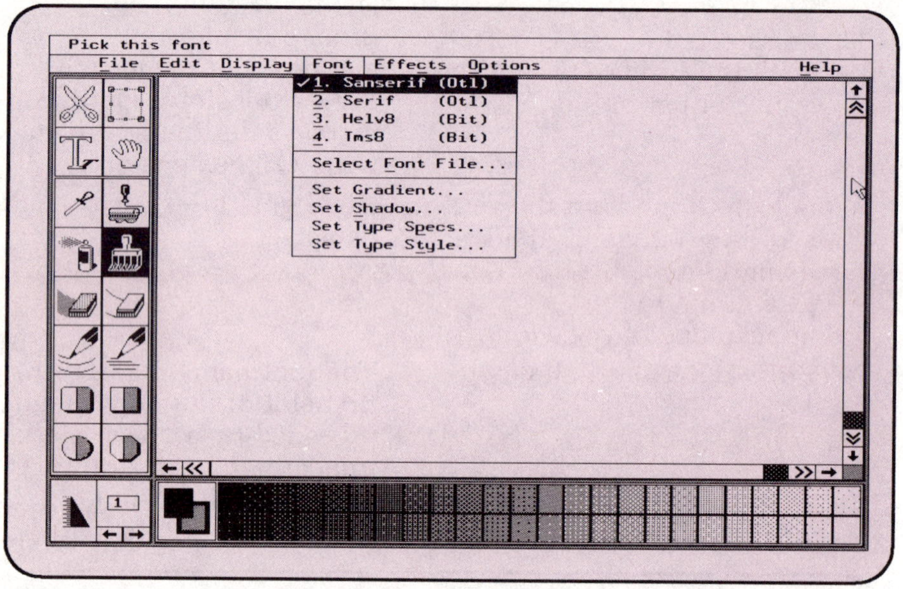

Figure 6.11 The Font menu displaying four font names.

The abbreviation "Bit" (in parenthesis) follows the name of a bit-mapped font in the Font menu; the abbreviation "Otl" follows the name of an outline font. You can choose fonts from the keyboard by pressing Alt-N followed by the number preceding the font name in the menu.

Type Specifications

In addition to specifying a font, you will need to set *type specifications* before you can apply your text in the drawing window. Choose the Set Type Specs... command from the Font menu to display the Adjust Font and Type Specifications dialog box, shown in Figure 6.12. This dialog box contains options for altering such formatting characteristics as type size, leading, and letter spacing. You can return all options in the dialog box to their original values at any time by selecting the Default button.

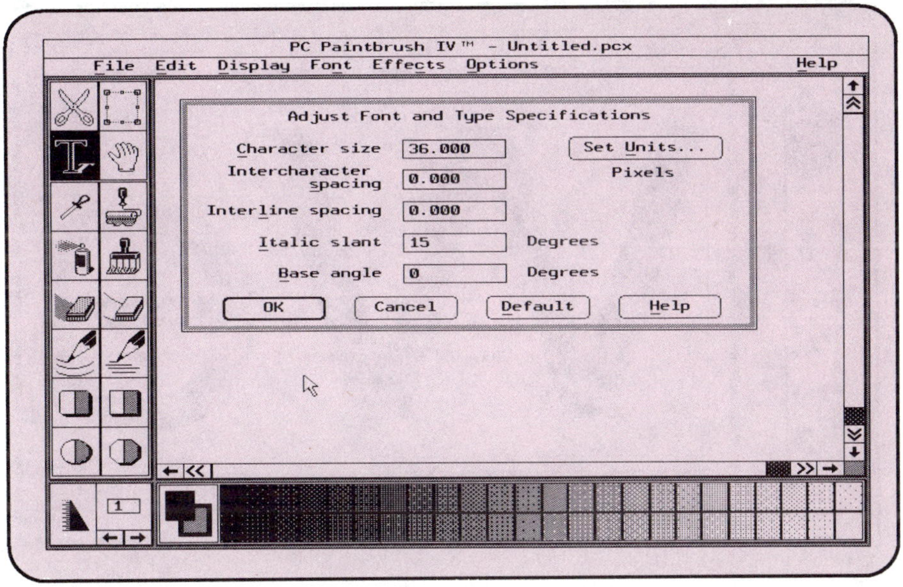

Figure 6.12 The Adjust Font and Type Specifications dialog box.

Type Size

Character size, the first option in the Adjust Font and Type Specifications dialog box, controls the type size. If a bit-mapped font is currently selected, this option will be dimmed. You can only change the type size when using an outline font. (You change the type size of a bit-mapped font by changing fonts; for example, by changing from Tms4 to Tms6.)

You can enter any type size between 0 and the largest size of character that will fit on your screen, generally around 360 pixels, as shown in Figure 6.13. 360 pixels represents the standard VGA display adapter limit; there are screens larger than 360 pixels but they are not as common. (If you have problems creating type this large on a 640-by-480-pixel display, you have probably reached the limits of available memory. Create a smaller painting and try again.) Theoretically, Paintbrush can create type up to 300 points (a point is 1/72 of an inch) in size. 300 points is equivalent to about 1250 pixels if you're printing to a standard 300-dots-per-inch laser printer.

Figure 6.13 Text created in the 360-pixel type size.

Letter Spacing

Intercharacter spacing, the second option in the Adjust Font and Type Specifications dialog box, determines the amount of *letter spacing*—horizontal space between individual characters of type—assigned to a block of text. A negative value brings letters closer together, a positive value spreads them farther apart. Figure 6.14 shows letter spacings of -5 pixels and 5 pixels combined with a 60-pixel type size.

Leading

4 Interline spacing, the third option in the Adjust Font and Type Specifications dialog box, determines the amount of *leading*—vertical spacing between lines of type—assigned to a block of text. A negative value brings lines closer together, a pos

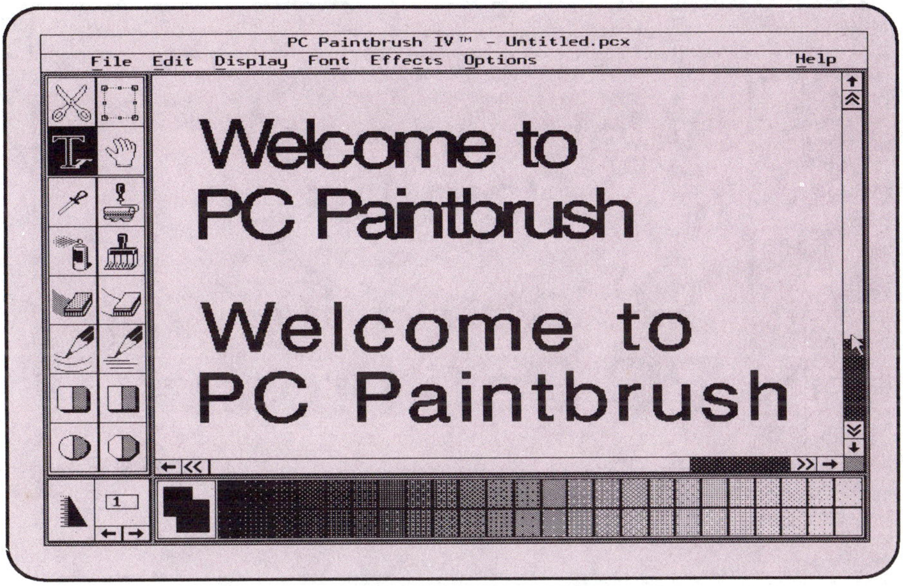

Figure 6.14 Text created with negative and positive letter spacing.

itive value spreads them farther apart. Figure 6.15 shows leadings of -10 pixels and 10 pixels combined with a 60-pixel type size.

> **Caution:** When using negative leading, make sure that tall characters, like *A* and *f*, don't overlap descending characters, like *g* and *p*.

Slanted Type

4 The Italic slant option in the Adjust Font and Type Specifications dialog box determines the degree to which text is slanted when italicized. (Italic type is selected in the Select Type Style dialog box, discussed later in this chapter.) Standard italic type, such as Tms8i or Serifi, is not affected by this option.

You can enter any value between -45 and 45 for the Italic slant option. A negative value slants type backward, a positive

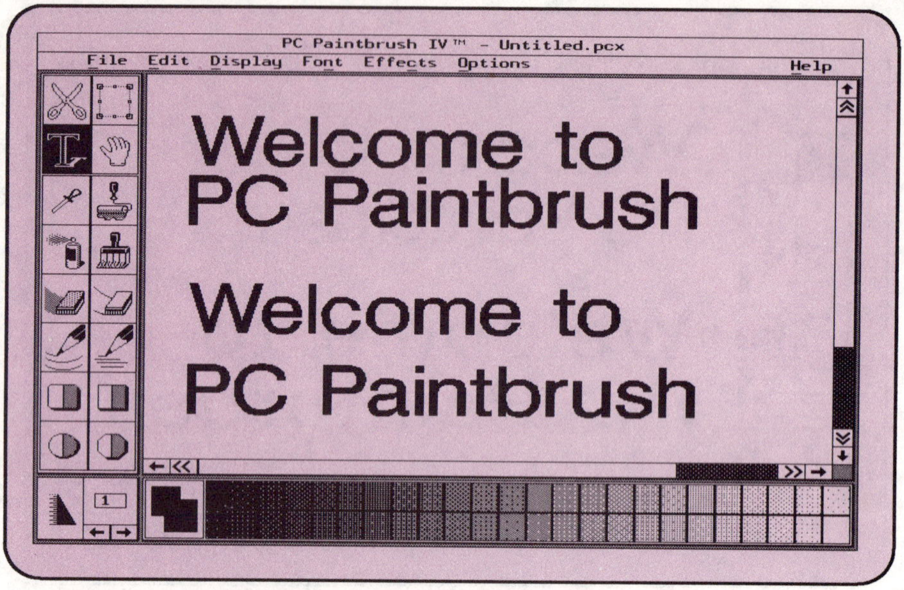

Figure 6.15 Text created with negative and positive leading.

value slants type forward. Figure 6.16 shows text slanted 30° forward, -30° backward, and a line of italicized text created using the San serifi outline font.

Rotated Type

4 Base angle, the last option in the Adjust Font and Type Specifications dialog box, controls the orientation of a text block. You can rotate text in one-degree increments. Thus, you have more control over the rotation of text than you have over the rotation of images, which you can rotate only in ninety-degree increments. However, you can only rotate text created with an outline font.

Once again, both negative and positive values are acceptable. A negative value rotates type clockwise, a positive value rotates type counterclockwise. Figure 6.17 shows text rotated 20° and -20°.

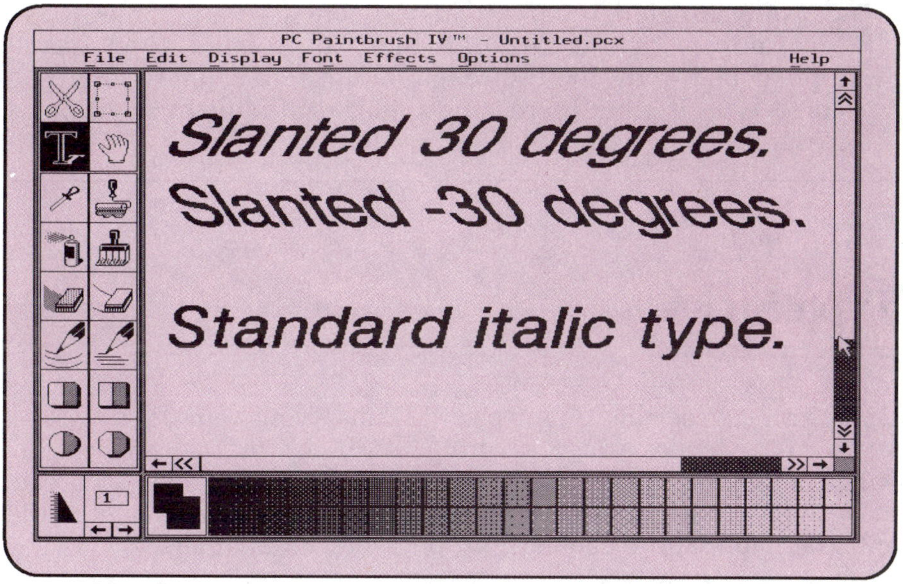

Figure 6.16 Two lines of italicized text with altered slants and a line of type in an italic font.

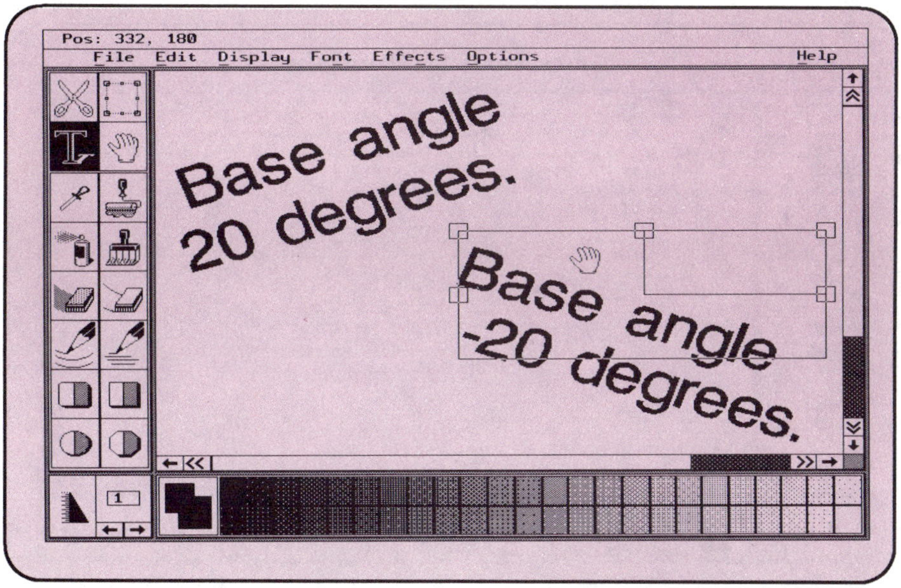

Figure 6.17 Two blocks of rotated type.

> **Note:** Rotated type extends beyond its text frame; for example, in Figure 6.17 the -20° rotated type has dropped below the bottom edge of the frame. Increasingly rotated type is thus increasingly more difficult to position in your painting.

Type Styles

Once you've set the type specifications, you can choose *type styles*. Type styles are formatting attributes that allow you to enhance the appearance of a typeface (font). For example, you can make type bolder, underline text, add shadows, and create gradients that fade within letters from one color to another.

Choose the Set Type Style... command from the Font menu to display the Select Type Style dialog box shown in Figure 6.18. This dialog box contains options for stylizing text and determining its alignment.

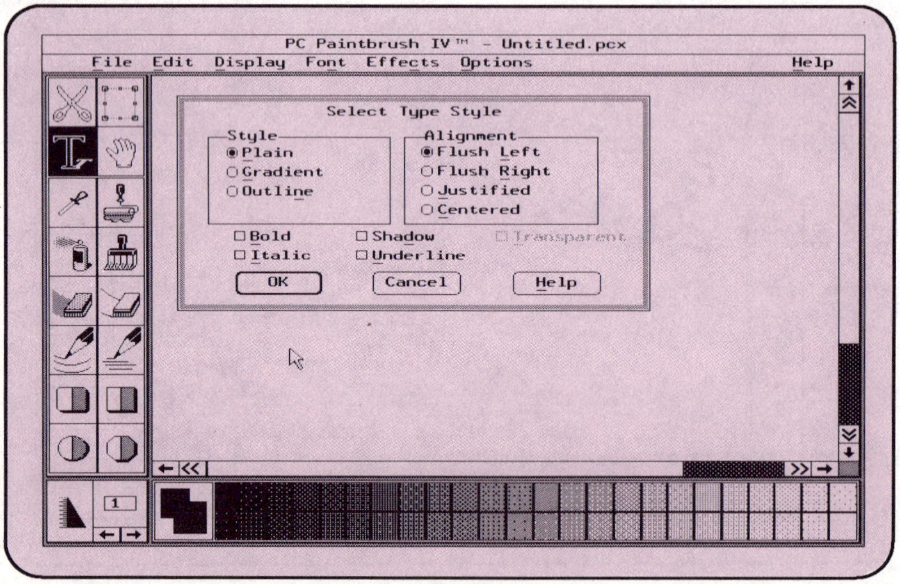

Figure 6.18 The Select Type Style dialog box.

Basic Type Styles

4 You can apply one of three mutually exclusive Style options to a block of text: *Plain, Gradient,* or *Outline.* An example of each type style is shown in Figure 6.19. Note that we selected a lighter color as the secondary color in the last example to better demonstrate the appearance of outlined type.

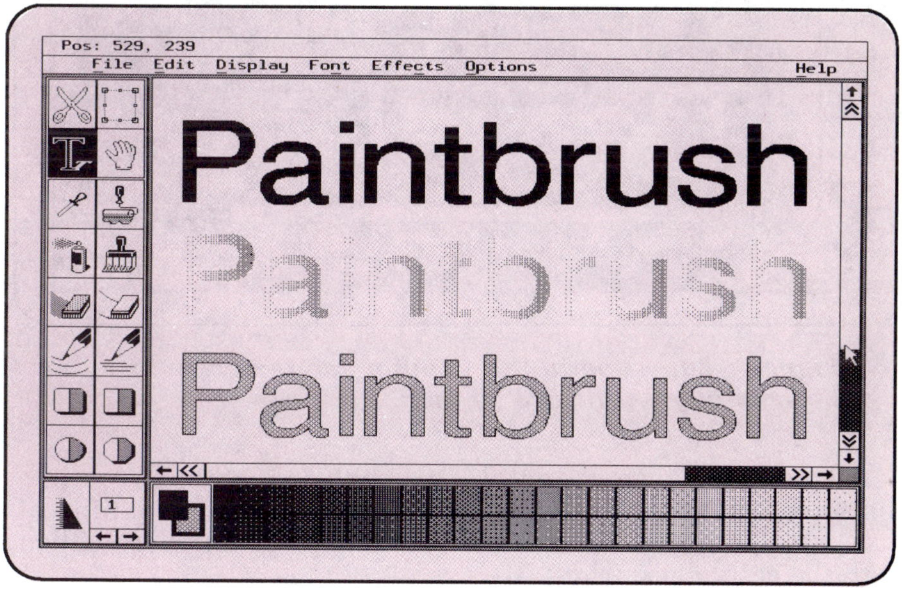

Figure 6.19 Plain, Gradient, and Outline type styles.

The Plain option creates type in the normal font without any enhancement and in the secondary color. Plain type was used in most of the figures shown earlier in this chapter.

The Gradient option creates multicolored letters, beginning in the background color and fading into the secondary color. Gradient type can fade horizontally, vertically, or radially, as shown in Figure 6.20. As this figure demonstrates, gradient type is most effective against a differently colored background. You specify the direction of the gradation by choosing the Set Gradient command from the Font menu, which is described later in this chapter.

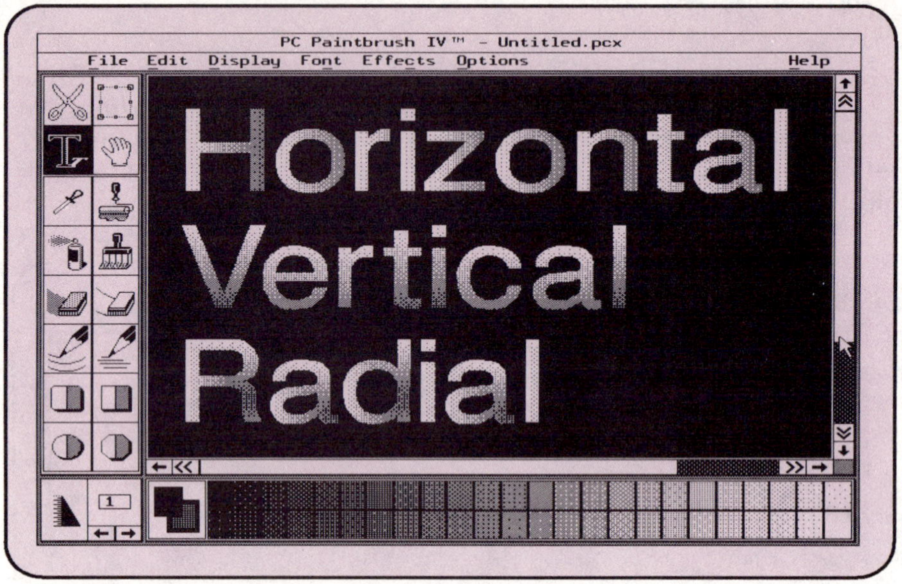

Figure 6.20 Type in the Gradient style can fade horizontally, vertically, or radially.

- The Outline style—not to be confused with an outline font—creates a thin outline around each letter. The outline of each letter is drawn in the primary color and the interior is filled with the secondary color.

Alignment

4 The Select Type Style dialog box also offers four mutually exclusive Alignment options: *Flush Left*, *Flush Right*, *Justified*, and *Centered*. *Alignment* determines the relative positioning of each line of type in a block of text. Type is aligned with respect to the text frame.

The Flush Left option aligns every line of text against the left side of the frame, as shown in Figure 6.21. This option is the default setting and provides the most legible alignment for paragraphs of small type.

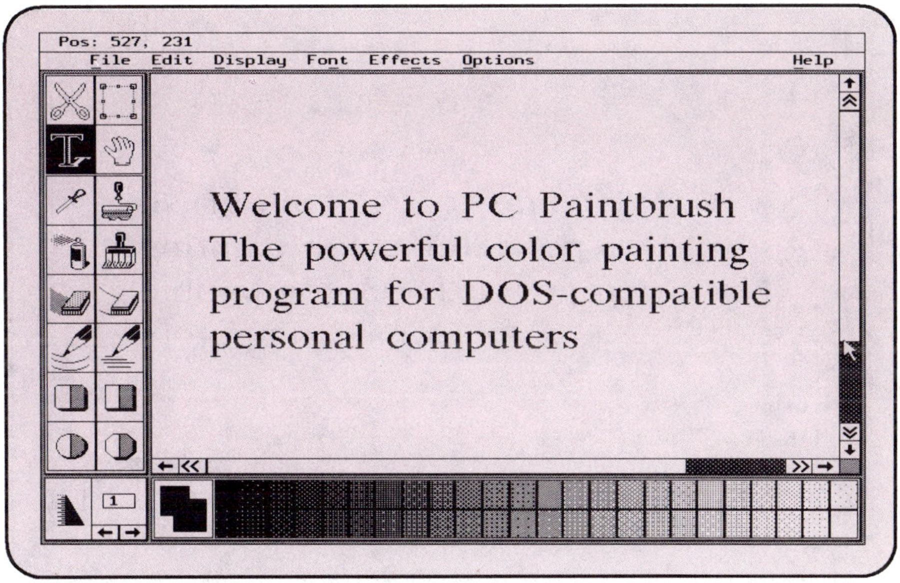

Figure 6.21 Four lines of flush left text.

The Flush Right option aligns every line of text against the right side of the frame, as shown in Figure 6.22. This alignment is not particularly legible. However, flush right type can make headlines or other special text appear distinctive.

The Justified option adjusts the letter spacing in every line of text so that both edges align with the sides of the text frame, as shown in Figure 6.23. You commonly see justified type in books and newspaper articles. However, unlike standard justified type, the Paintbrush Justified option justifies the last line of type. If you want your last line to appear flush left, you must apply it as a separate block of text and then select the Flush Left option. Justified type is most commonly applied to long blocks of text.

The Centered option centers every line of text between the left and right sides of the frame, as shown in Figure 6.24. This setting is most commonly applied to headlines and captions.

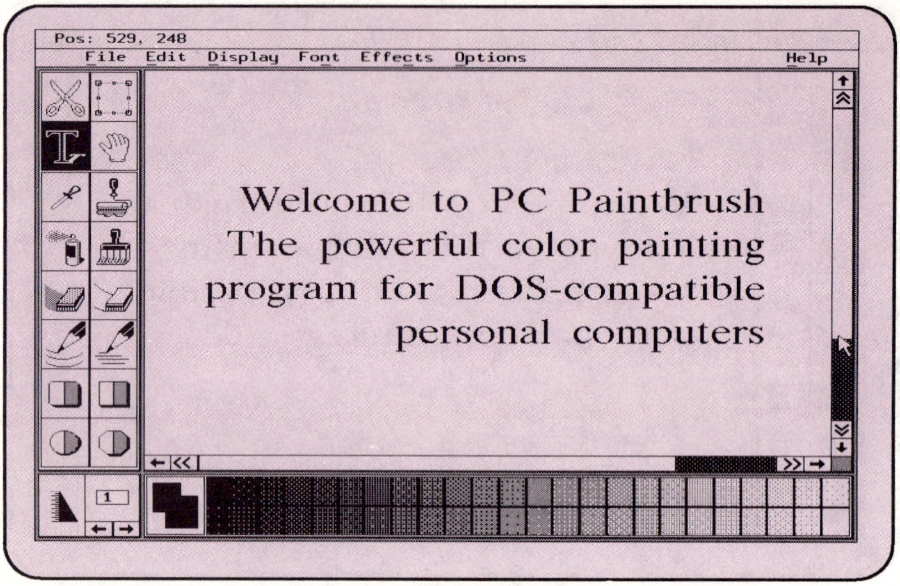

Figure 6.22 Four lines of flush right text.

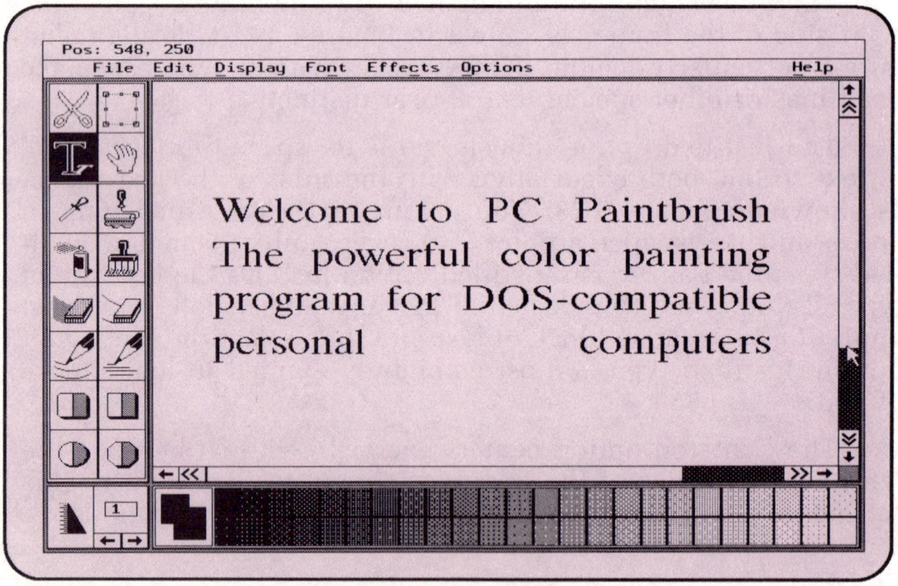

Figure 6.23 Four lines of justified text.

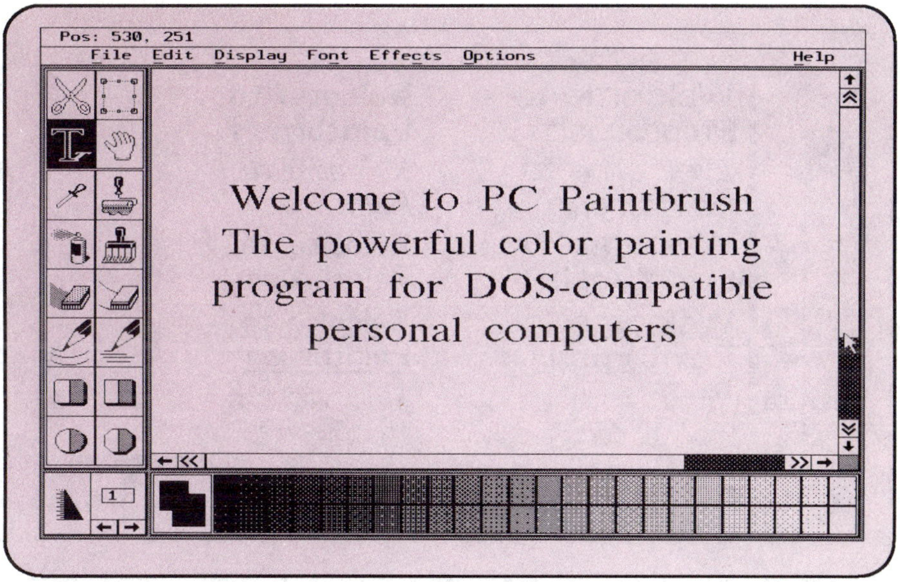

Figure 6.24 Four lines of centered text.

Other Type Styles

Paintbrush supplies five additional style options at the bottom of the Select Type Style dialog box: *Bold*, *Italic*, *Shadow*, *Underline*, and *Transparent*. Each style is shown applied to an outline font and to a bit-mapped font in Figure 6.25.

The Bold option to make a text block bold. The bold style is more noticeable when applied to a bit-mapped font than to an outline font. You can see this difference in the first example in Figure 6.25.

The Italic option to slant the letters in a text block at the angle specified by the Italic Slant option in the Adjust Font and Type Specifications dialog box, which is discussed earlier in this chapter.

The Shadow option creates a drop shadow in back of the text block. The shadow appears in the background color, and the text appears in the secondary color. You can specify how far the shadow is offset from the text by choosing the Set Shadow command from the Font menu, which is discussed later in this chapter.

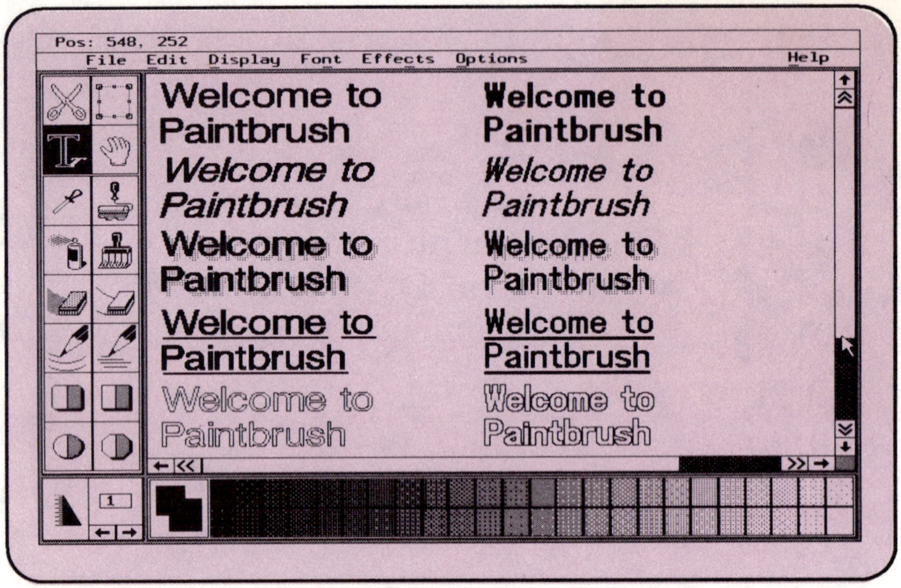

Figure 6.25 Bold, italic, shadow, underlined, and transparent styles applied to an outline font (left) and a bit-mapped font (right).

The Underline option underlines each word in a text block. The thickness of the underline is proportional to the size of the type.

The Transparent option is only available when Outline is selected from the Style options. Select the Transparent option to make the interior of outlined text transparent rather than filled with the secondary color.

Since each additional style can be selected independently of the others, more than one style can be applied to a block of text. For example, Figure 6.26 shows a block of type with all five additional styles applied at once.

Type Effects

4 Two of the type styles provided by Paintbrush IV go beyond the traditional definition of type style into the realm of spe-

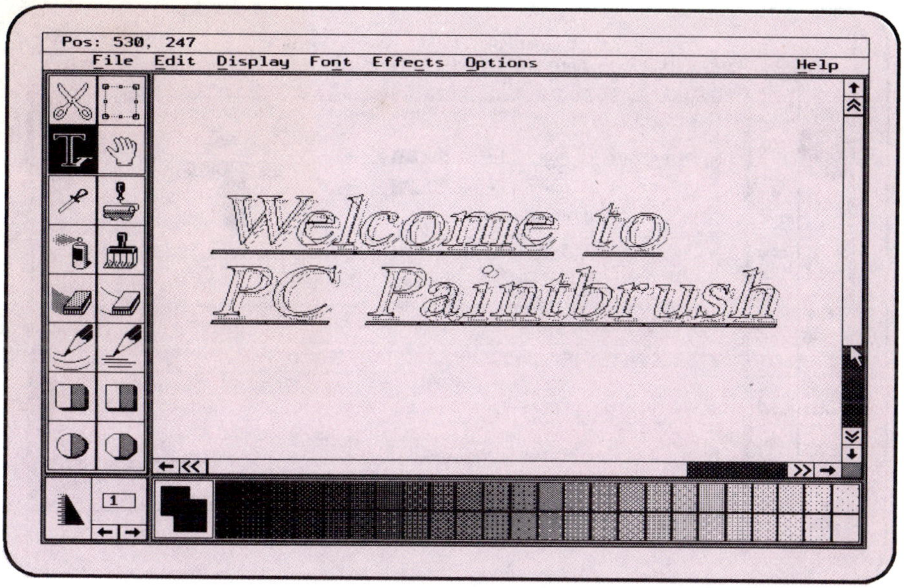

Figure 6.26 A block of bold, italic, shadow, underlined, and transparent text.

cial effects. You can do more than just apply these styles to a block of text; you can also customize each style to fit your specific graphic requirements. For example, if you are creating a text block using the shadow type style (one of the "additional" type styles), you can specify the exact distance between shadow and text. And if you are creating gradient text (a "basic" style), you can determine the direction at which one color fades into another.

The Shadow Effect

To alter the particulars of the shadow style, first select the Shadow option in the Select Type Style dialog box, then choose the Set Shadow... command from the Font menu. The Set the Type Shadow dialog box, shown in Figure 6.27, will appear. The dialog box offers three options for customizing shadow type: *X offset*, *Y offset*, and *3D shadow*.

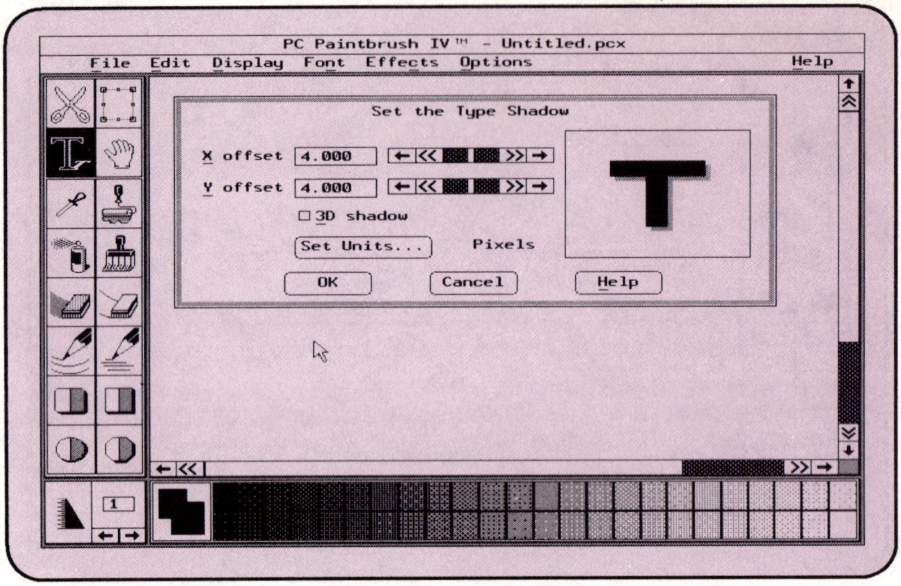

Figure 6.27 The Set Type Shadow dialog box.

The X offset value determines the horizontal distance between a letter and its shadow. Adjust the scroll bars to change this value or enter a new value between -500 and 500 pixels. A negative value places the shadow to the left of the text, a positive value places the shadow to the right.

The Y offset value determines the vertical distance between a letter and its shadow. Adjust the scroll bars to change this value or enter a new value between -500 and 500 pixels. A negative value places the shadow above the text, a positive value places the shadow below.

The 3D shadow option creates a three-dimensional shadow instead of a drop shadow.

Figure 6.28 shows a few modifications of shadow type. All of the shadows in the left column are drop shadows; that is, the 3D shadow option was not selected. The 3D shadow option was turned on to create all shadows in the right column. The X and Y offset values were both 4 for the first row of text blocks, 8 for the second, and -16 for the third.

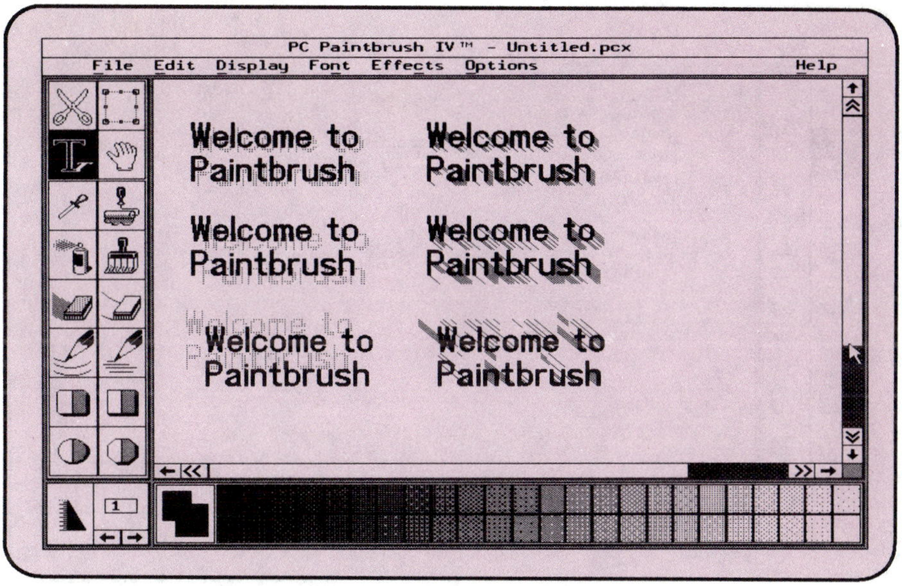

Figure 6.28 Different examples of shadow type.

> **Tip:** When creating shadow type, be sure to change the background color to a different color than the current background or you won't be able to see the shadow.

The Gradient Effect

Choosing the Set Gradient... command from the Font menu displays the Select a Gradient Effect dialog box, shown in Figure 6.29. This dialog box offers three mutually exclusive Style options—*Horizontal*, *Vertical*, and *Radial*—and the *Solid Colors Only* check box in Paintbrush or the Set Halftones... button in Paintbrush Plus. The Gradient option in the Select Type Style dialog box must be selected to apply your changes to the Set a Gradient Effect dialog box.

The Horizontal Style option fades the color gradient from the background color on the left to the secondary color on the right in Paintbrush; in Paintbrush Plus, this option fades the color gradient from the background color on the right to the sec-

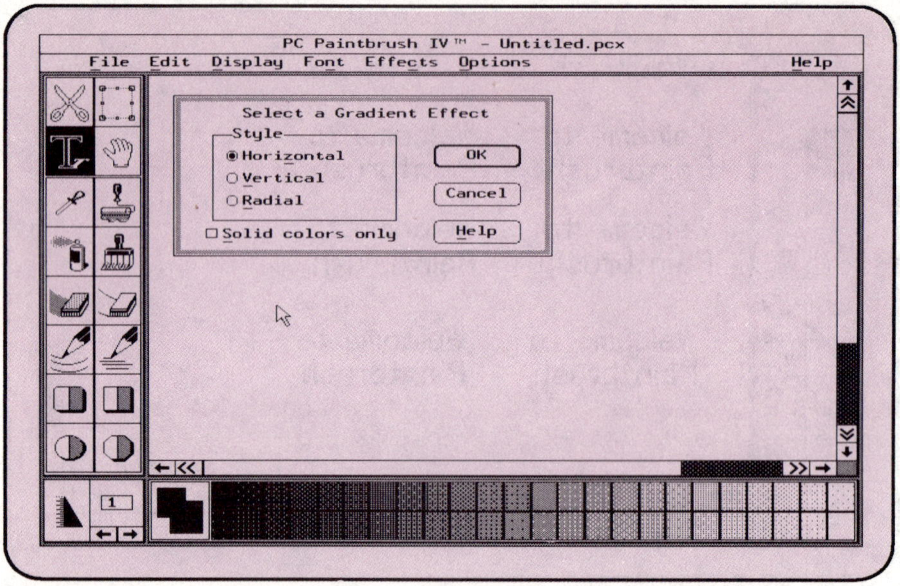

Figure 6.29 The Select a Gradient Effect dialog box.

ondary color on the left. The horizontal gradient is applied to each letter individually rather than to the text block as a whole, as shown in Figure 6.30.

The Vertical Style option fades the color gradient from the background color at the top to the secondary color at the bottom in Paintbrush; in Paintbrush Plus, this option fades the color gradient from the background color at the bottom to the secondary color at the top. The vertical gradient is applied to each line of type individually rather than to the text block as a whole, as shown in Figure 6.31.

The Radial Style option fades the color gradient from the secondary color in the center of a letter to the background color at its perimeter in Paintbrush. In Paintbrush Plus, this option fades the color gradient from the secondary color at the perimeter of a letter to the background color at its center. The radial gradient is applied to each letter individually rather than to the text block as a whole, as shown in Figure 6.32.

The Solid Colors Only option creates a color gradient using solid colors only rather than blended colors. For best results, only select this option if you are working in the 256-color mode.

Figure 6.30 The horizontal gradient effect.

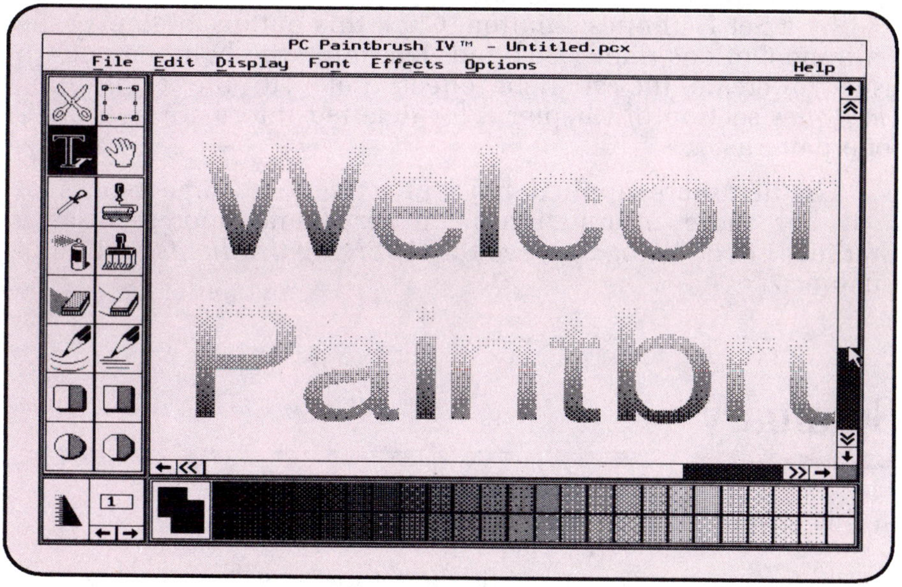

Figure 6.31 The vertical gradient effect.

Figure 6.32 The radial gradient effect.

In Paintbrush Plus, the Solid Colors Only option is replaced by a Set Halftones... button. Click this button to display the Halftone Options dialog box and determine the halftone pattern used to create the gradient effect. Refer to the *Controlling Halftones* section of Chapter 2 for detailed information on halftone patterns.

Gradients are applied most effectively to large blocks of text. For more information about gradients and the Set a Gradient Effect dialog box, see the *Applying Gradients* section of Chapter 7.

Summary

In this chapter, you've learned:

- Selecting the Text tool displays the Enter Text dialog box, into which you enter type from the keyboard.
- Pressing Control-Enter inserts a line return character in the text entry field.

- Pressing Alt-E highlights all text in the text entry field.
- Bit-mapped fonts are designed to be used at a specific size. The type size of outline fonts can be changed without affecting their smoothness.
- Bit-mapped fonts work best when creating small type; outline fonts are preferable for creating large type.
- You can alter the type size, letter spacing, and leading, or even rotate a text block, by choosing the Set Type Specs... command from the Font menu.
- The Set Type Style... command allows you to adjust the type style and alignment.
- After entering text and specifying a font, style, and other formatting options, you apply text to your painting by drawing a text frame in the drawing area.
- By dragging the text frame you can move text in the drawing window, by dragging the side handles you can adjust the column width.

Chapter 7

Special Effects

What You Will Learn

- *Using commands from the Effects menu*
- *Using drawing tools in different painting modes*
- *Blending, smudging, and tinting images*
- *Creating gradient fills*
- *Painting with pattern*

The Effects Menu

You probably don't think of the colors you lay down on the screen as being like real paint. Sure, you lay the colors down with various artist's tools, but once the colors are in the drawing area, you manipulate them differently than you would on a traditional canvas. On a real canvas, you blend colors, smear brush strokes, and tint images by painting with diluted washes. In Paintbrush, you select images, then move, duplicate, or transform them. This isn't painting, this is surgery!

For those who feel the urge to paint—to create brilliant images by moulding and manipulating colors—Paintbrush provides the set of commands available from the Effects menu. If you want to blend colors on screen, choose the Blend command. If you want to smear colors around, choose Smudge. If you want to apply diluted washes, choose the Tint command. If you want to paint, a world of options are open to you, and in Paintbrush, you don't have to worry about the paint going dry.

4 The Effects menu and all commands and features discussed in this chapter are new to Paintbrush IV.

The Standard Command

If you display the Effects menu by pressing Alt-C or by clicking on the menu name, you will notice that the Standard command has a check mark in front of it. The check mark indicates that you are currently in the standard *painting mode*. With the exception of the background color, all colors that you apply are treated as opaque. All existing colors in the drawing window are treated like dry paints so that no blending or smearing occurs.

All tools are available in the standard painting mode. But if you select one of the other commands from the Effects menu, such as the Gradient command, your toolbox changes. Many tools become dimmed, others disappear. Only those tools which appear in the toolbox and which are not dimmed are available, such as the Hand tool, Paint Roller, and Paintbrush shown in Figure 7.1. To return to the standard mode at any time, choose Standard from the Effects menu or press Alt-C followed by the S key.

Painting Modes

Here are some facts you should know about painting modes:

- The name of the current painting mode is displayed in the toolbox beneath the Hand tool, except in the standard painting mode, in which case no name is displayed.
- You can change the line width, but you cannot alter the brush shape when working in a painting mode other than standard.
- The Hand tool is available in all modes. The Scissors, Gadget Box, and Text tools are available only in the standard painting mode.

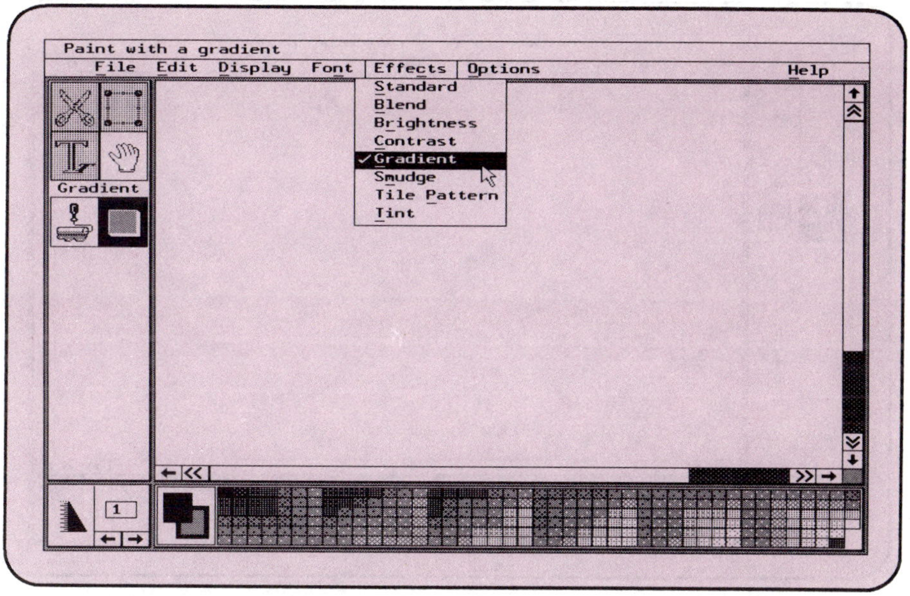

Figure 7.1 Choosing a command other than the Standard command from the Effects menu reduces the number of available tools.

- Changing painting modes nullifies the Undo command. In other words, after you choose a command from the Effects menu, you can no longer undo the results of the previous tool operation.
- The standard painting mode was used to create every figure in this book except those in this chapter.

Blending Images

Choose the Blend command from the Effects menu to enter the blend painting mode. This command is only available when your monitor is configured to display 4 or more colors. Your toolbox and color palette will change, as shown in Figure 7.2. Only the Hand tool, the Paintbrush, and the Filled Rectangle tool can be used in this mode.

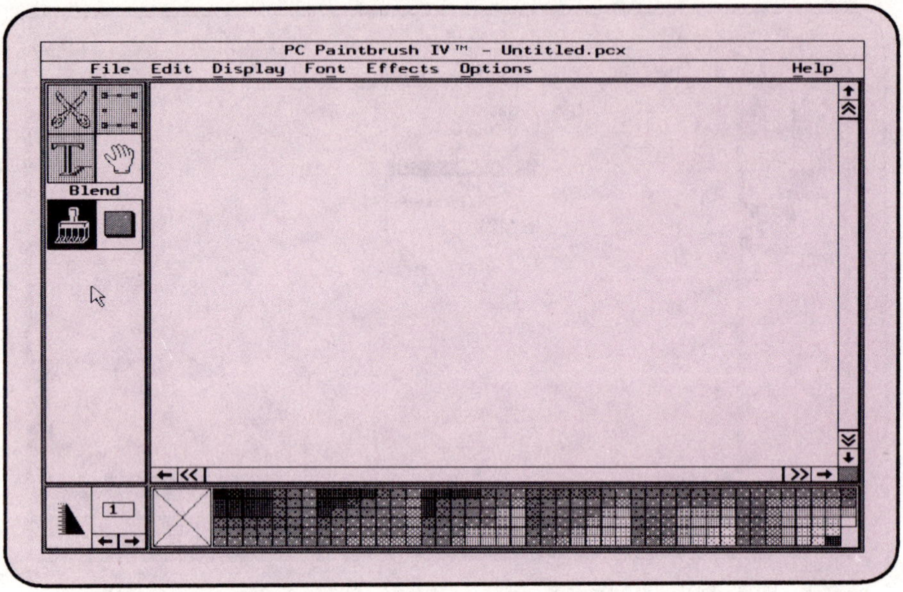

Figure 7.2 The blend painting mode.

In the blend mode, painting in the drawing window will cause the colors of adjacent pixels to blend. For example, suppose an area of white pixels borders an area of red pixels. If you drag over the border with the Paintbrush tool, a series of pink pixels will be created between the red and white pixels. The result is a more gradual and naturalistic border.

Figure 7.3 shows a magnified view of the rose painting included with Paintbrush. Notice the border between light and dark areas to the left of the Paintbrush cursor. After we drew over this border with the Paintbrush tool in a 10-pixel line width, the border became much softer and less focused, as shown in Figure 7.4.

Note the large X in the color palette in both Figures 7.3 and 7.4. It indicates that the current primary, secondary, and background colors have no effect in this mode.

If you want to soften borders between colors, use the Paintbrush tool following the instructions in the *Blending Borders* Quick Steps. If you want to make large areas appear less focused or jagged, use the Filled Rectangle tool, which is described in the *Blending Large Areas* Quick Steps.

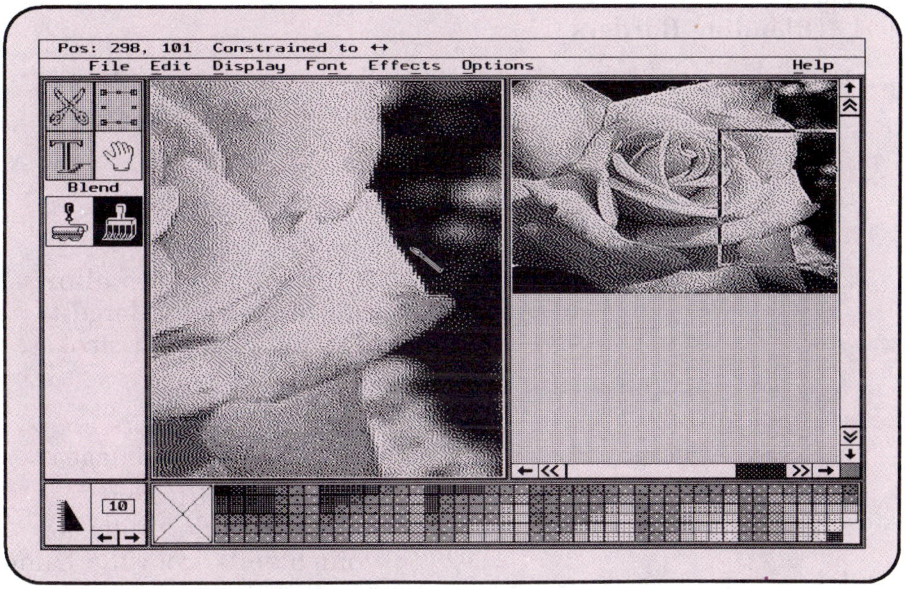

***Figure 7.3** A sharp border between light and dark pixels.*

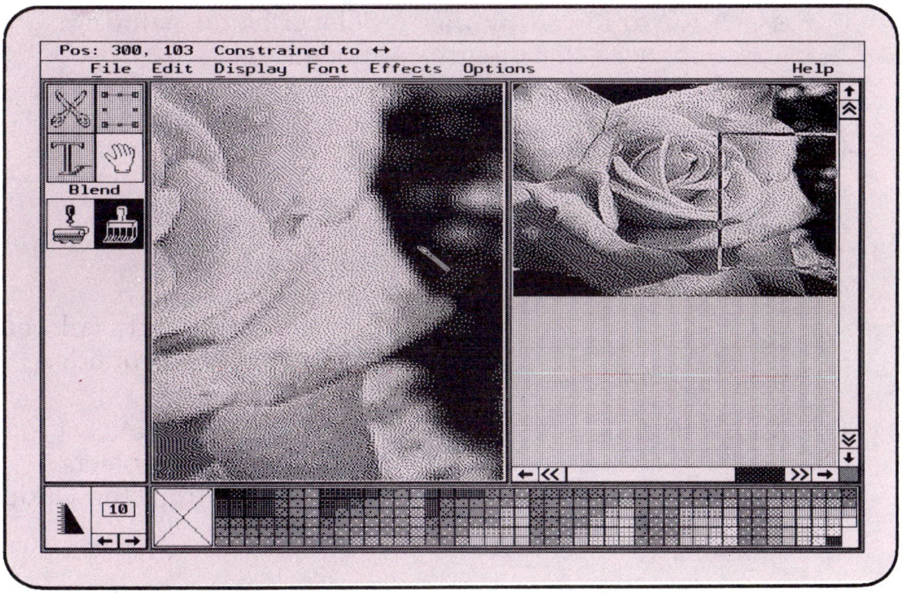

***Figure 7.4** A soft border created with the Paintbrush tool in the blend painting mode.*

Blending Borders

1. With a painting in the drawing window, press Alt-C followed by the B key to choose the Blend command from the Effects menu. — Selects blend painting mode.
2. Select a line width. — A thick line width allows you to cover the largest area in the fewest strokes.
3. Select the Paintbrush tool.
4. Drag along the borders you want to blend. — Intermediary colors are created between images.
5. Press Alt-C followed by the S key. — Selecting a different painting mode protects your blends from the Undo command. □

Blending Large Areas

1. Press Alt-C followed by the B key to choose the Blend command from the Effects menu. — Selects blend painting mode.
2. Select the Filled Rectangle tool.
3. Draw a rectangle around the area you want to blend. — After you release, Paintbrush creates intermediary colors between differently colored pixels in the surrounded area.
4. Press Alt-C followed by the S key. — Selecting a different painting mode protects your blends from the Undo command. □

Adjusting the Brightness of an Image

Choose the Brightness command from the Effects menu to enter the brightness painting mode. The Brightness command is only available when your monitor is configured to display 4 or more colors. Your toolbox and color palette will change, as shown in Figure 7.5. Only the Hand tool, the Paintbrush, and the Filled Rectangle tool can be used in this mode. The color palette changes to display 40 brightness *values* from black to white. The currently selected brightness value appears on the left side of the palette.

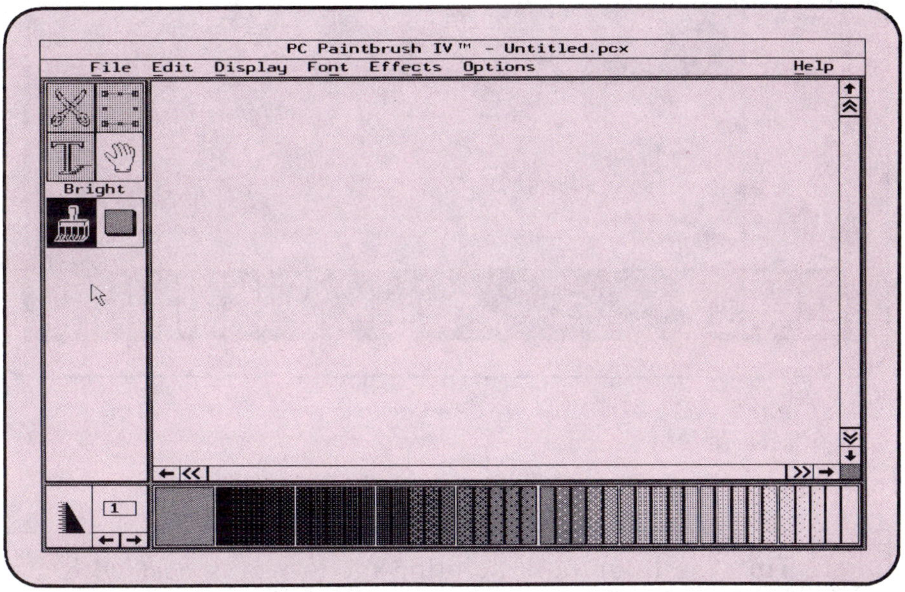

Figure 7.5 The brightness painting mode.

In the brightness mode, painting in the drawing window will lighten or darken the colors of pixels, depending on the brightness value you select in the palette. If the current brightness value is lighter than medium gray, you will lighten the colors in the painting. If the brightness value is darker than medium gray, you will darken the colors in the painting. Solid white or black brightness values produce the most dramatic results.

For example, in Figure 7.6, we drew four straight lines across the rose picture with the Paintbrush tool in a 10-pixel line width. Two of the lines were created with the black value (the darkest brightness value) and two with the white value (the lightest brightness value). In Figure 7.7, we used the paintbrush tool more selectively, lightening the background around the rose without affecting the rose itself.

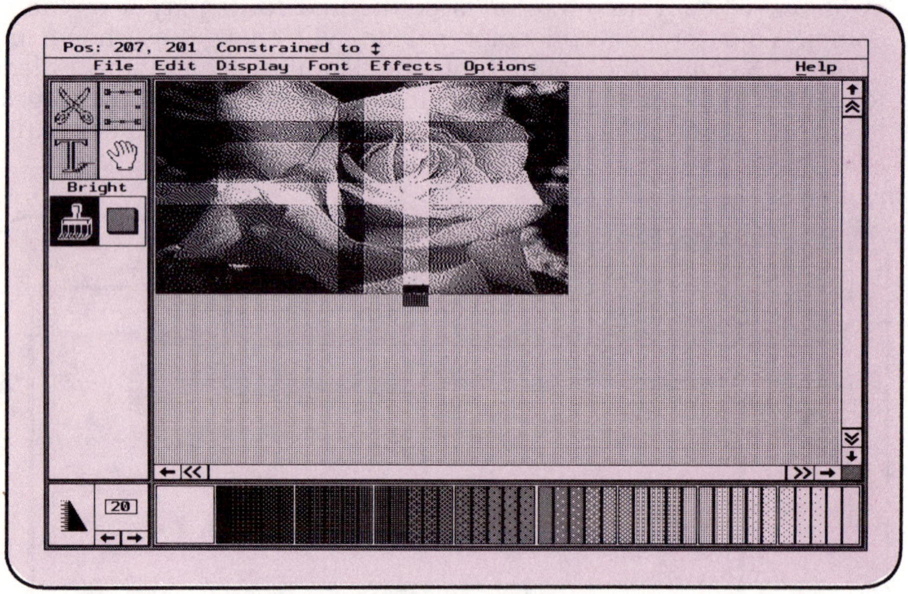

Figure 7.6 Straight lines created with black and white brightness values.

> **Tip:** The brightness painting mode works best with a palette of 256 true colors. However, if your monitor is set to display 16 or fewer colors, load the GRAYS.PAL color palette before entering this mode by choosing the Get Palette... command from the Options menu. The gray palette offers lighter and darker shades of the same hue, whereas other 16-color palettes only offer different hues (red, green, blue, yellow, etc.).

The Paintbrush and Filled Rectangle tools, which function similarly in the blend modes, function dissimilarly in the brightness mode. Drawing with the Paintbrush lightens or darkens an area uniformly. If you draw over an area more than once, it will

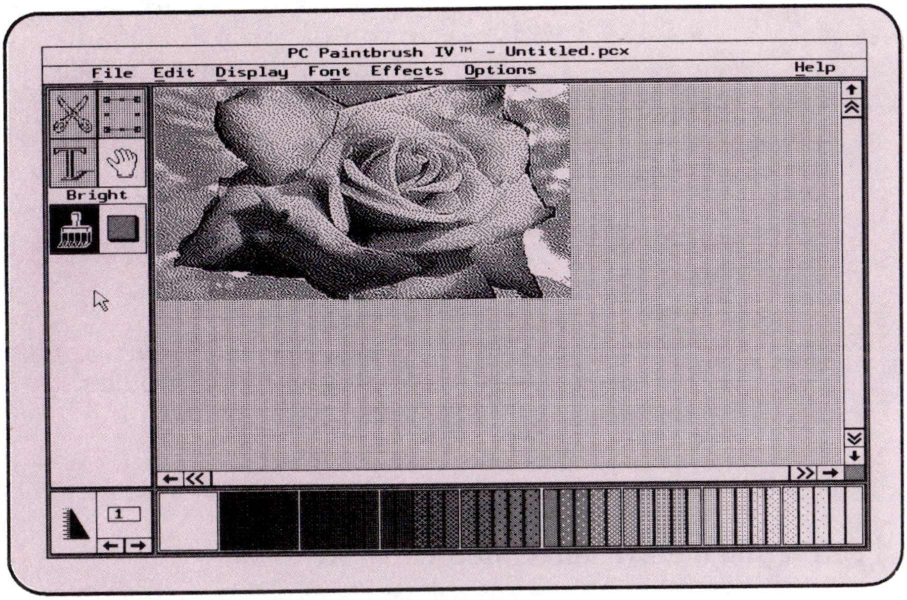

Figure 7.7 Using a white brightness value to lighten the area behind the rose.

not become increasingly lighter or darker unless you reselect the tool or select a new color value. Repeated applications of the Filled Rectangle tool, however, will lighten or darken colors additionally, whether or not you reselected the tool.

The Quick Steps, *Altering the Brightness of a Small Area*, describe how to use the Paintbrush tool in the brightness mode; *Altering the Brightness of a Large Area* explains how to use the Filled Rectangle tool in the brightness mode.

Q Altering the Brightness of a Small Area

1. Press Alt-C followed by the R key to choose the Brightness command from the Effects menu. — Selects brightness painting mode.
2. Select a color value in the palette. — Dark color values darken an area, light color values make an area lighter. The default medium color generally produces no effect.

3. Select a line width.	A thick line width allows you to cover the largest area in the fewest strokes.
4. Select the Paintbrush tool, then paint over the area you want to affect.	The area dragged over becomes lighter or darker depending on the selected value.
5. Select a different value or reselect the Paintbrush.	Allows you to lighten or darken an area additionally.
6. Press Alt-C followed by the S key.	Selecting a different painting mode protects your changes from the Undo command.

212 **Q** Altering the Brightness of a Large Area

1. Press Alt-C followed by the R key to choose the Brightness command from the Effects menu.	Selects brightness painting mode.
2. Select a value in the color palette.	Dark values darken an area, light values make an area lighter. The default medium value generally produces no effect.
3. Select the Filled Rectangle tool, then draw a rectangle around the area you want to affect.	After you release, the area becomes lighter or darker depending on the selected value.
4. Continue drawing with the Filled Rectangle tool.	Repeated applications of the tool lighten or darken the painting additionally.
5. Press Alt-C followed by the S key.	Selecting a different painting mode protects your changes from the Undo command.

Adjusting the Contrast of an Image

Choose the Contrast command from the Effects menu to enter the contrast painting mode. The Contrast command is only available when your monitor is configured to display 4 or more colors. Your toolbox and color palette will change, as shown in Figure 7.8. Only the Hand tool, the Paintbrush, and the Filled Rectangle tool can be used in this mode. The color palette changes to display 40 *contrast levels* from gray over gray (no contrast) to white over black (high contrast). The currently selected contrast level appears on the left side of the palette.

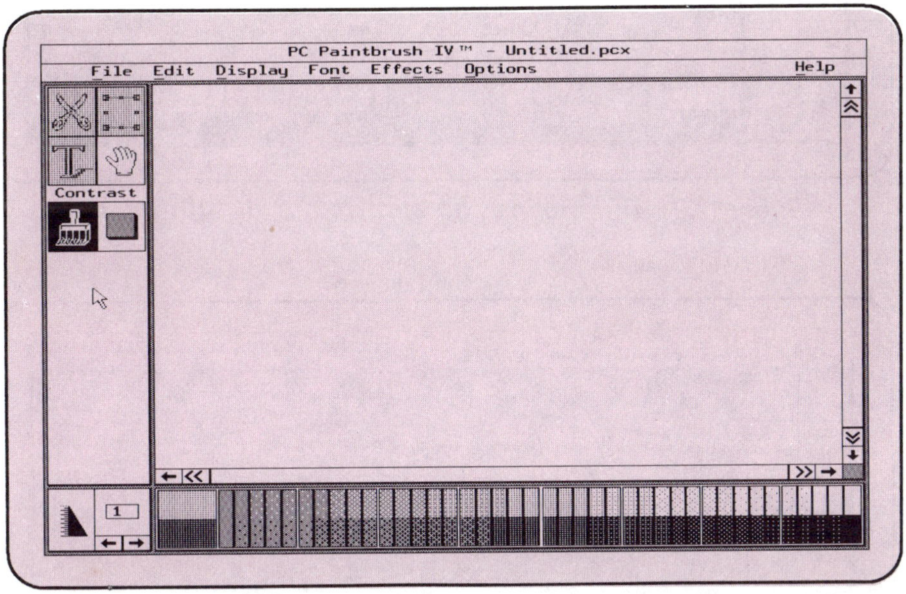

Figure 7.8 The contrast painting mode.

In the contrast mode, painting in the drawing window will boost or diminish the contrast between pixels in a painting, depending on the contrast level you select in the palette. If the current level comes from the right half of the palette, you will increase the contrast between pixels in a painting, making light pixels lighter and dark pixels darker, as shown in Figure 7.9. If the current level comes from the left half of the palette, you will decrease the contrast between pixels in a painting, making light pixels darker and dark pixels lighter so that the entire image appears gray, as shown in Figure 7.10.

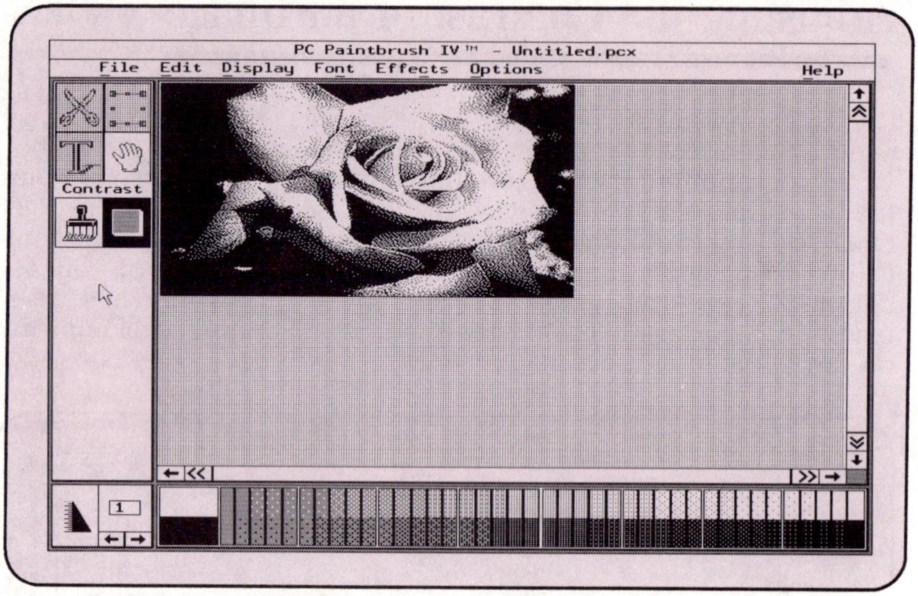

Figure 7.9 Increasing the contrast of a painting.

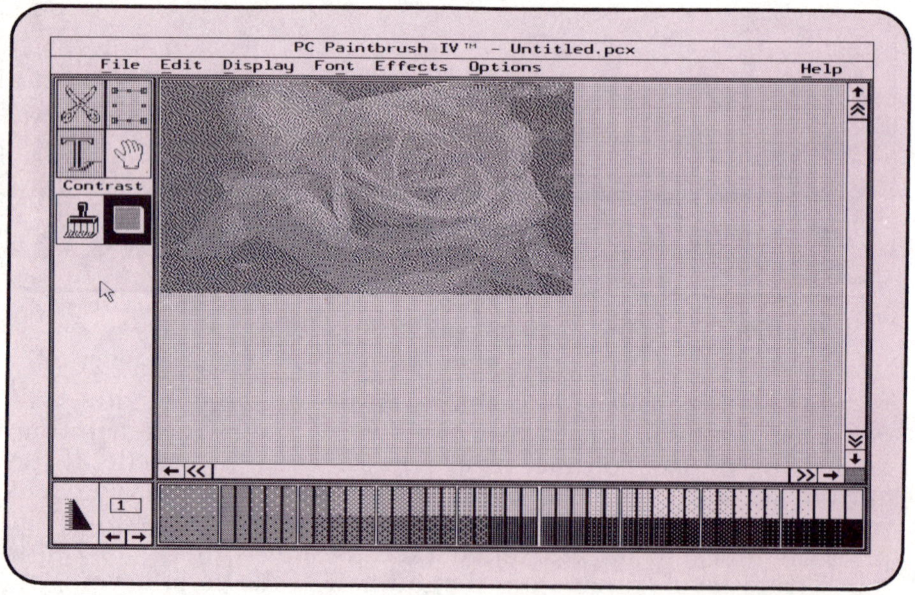

Figure 7.10 Decreasing the contrast of a painting.

> **Tip:** The contrast painting mode works best with a palette of 256 true colors. However, if your monitor is set to display 16 or fewer colors, load the GRAYS.PAL color palette before entering this mode by choosing the Get Palette... command from the Options menu. The gray palette offers lighter and darker shades of the same hue, whereas other 16-color palettes only offer different hues (red, green, blue, yellow, etc.).

The Paintbrush and Filled Rectangle tools function dissimilarly in the contrast mode. Drawing with the Paintbrush changes the contrast of an area uniformly. If you draw over an area more than once, its contrast will not be affected additionally unless you reselect the tool or select a new contrast level. Repeated applications of the Filled Rectangle tool, however, will boost or diminish the contrast additionally, whether or not you reselected the tool.

The Quick Steps, *Altering the Contrast of a Small Area*, describe how to use the Paintbrush tool in contrast mode; *Altering the Contrast of a Large Area* explains how to use the Filled Rectangle tool in contrast mode.

Q Altering the Contrast of a Small Area

1. Press Alt-C followed by the C key to choose the Contrast command from the Effects menu.	Selects contrast painting mode.
2. Select a contrast level in the color palette.	Levels on the left lessen contrast, levels on the right heighten contrast. The default middle level generally produces no effect.
3. Select a line width.	A thick line width allows you to cover the largest area in the fewest strokes.
4. Select the Paintbrush tool, then paint over the area you want to affect.	As you drag, the area becomes grayer or more black and white depending on the selected level.

5. Select a different contrast level or reselect the Paintbrush.	Allows you to boost or diminish the contrast additionally.
6. Press Alt-C followed by the S key.	Selecting a different painting mode protects your changes from the Undo command. ☐

Q Altering the Contrast of a Large Area

1. Press Alt-C followed by the C key to choose the Contrast command from the Effects menu.	Selects contrast painting mode.
2. Select a contrast level in the color palette.	Levels on the left lessen contrast, levels on the right heighten contrast. The default middle level generally produces no effect.
3. Select the Filled Rectangle tool, then draw a rectangle around the area you want to change.	After you release, the surrounded area becomes grayer or more black and white depending on the selected level.
4. Continue drawing with the Filled Rectangle tool.	Repeated applications of the tool additionally boost or diminish the contrast.
5. Press Alt-C followed by the S key.	Selecting a different painting mode protects your changes from the Undo command. ☐

Applying Gradients

Choose the Gradient command from the Effects menu to enter the gradient painting mode. Your toolbox will change, but your color palette will remain the same, as shown in Figure 7.11. Only the

Hand tool, the Paint Roller, and the Filled Rectangle tool can be used in this mode.

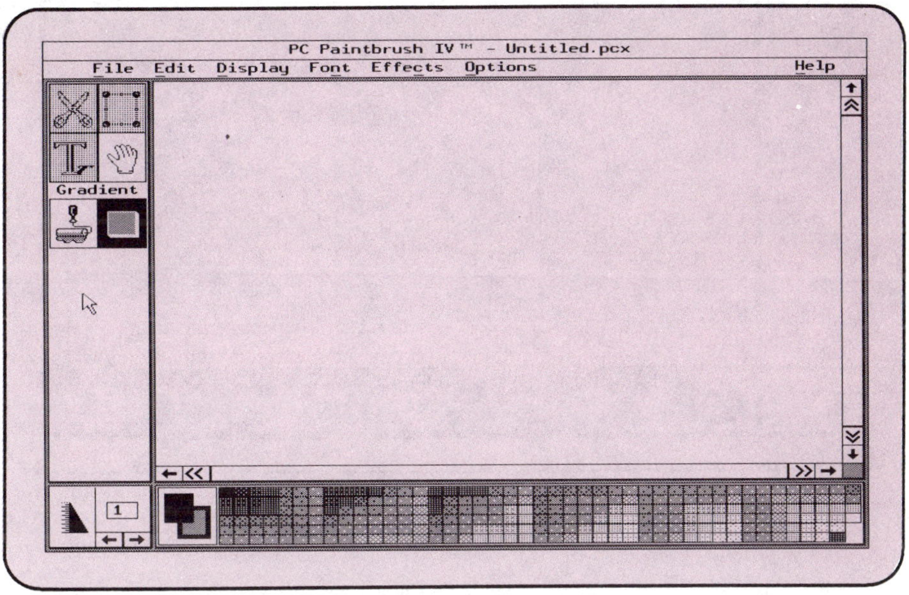

Figure 7.11 The gradient painting mode.

In the gradient mode, you can create multicolored fills that begin in the background color and fade into the secondary color (or from secondary to background in Paintbrush Plus). Gradient fills can fade horizontally, vertically, or radially, as shown in Figure 7.12.

You specify the direction of the gradation by choosing the Set Gradient... command from the Options menu. This displays the Select a Gradient Effect dialog box, shown in Figure 7.13, which offers three mutually exclusive Style options—*Horizontal*, *Vertical*, and *Radial*—and the *Solid Colors Only* check box in Paintbrush or the Set Halftones... button in Paintbrush Plus.

The Horizontal option fades the gradient from the background color on the left to the secondary color on the right, or vice versa in Paintbrush Plus. The Vertical option fades the gradient from the background color at the top to the secondary color at the bottom, or vice versa in Paintbrush Plus. The Radial option fades the gradient from the secondary color in the center of a letter to the background color at its perimeter, or vice versa in Paintbrush Plus.

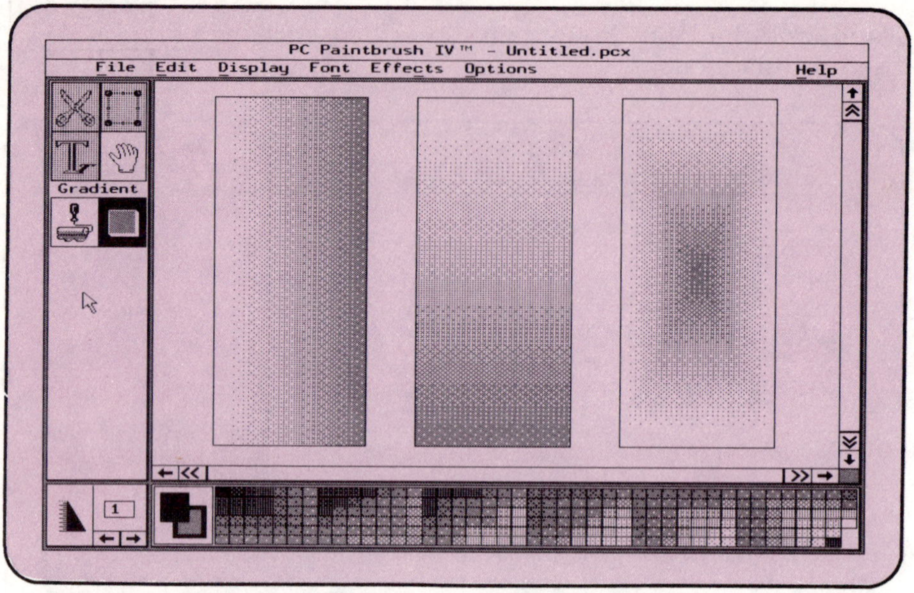

Figure 7.12 Horizontal, vertical, and radial gradient fills.

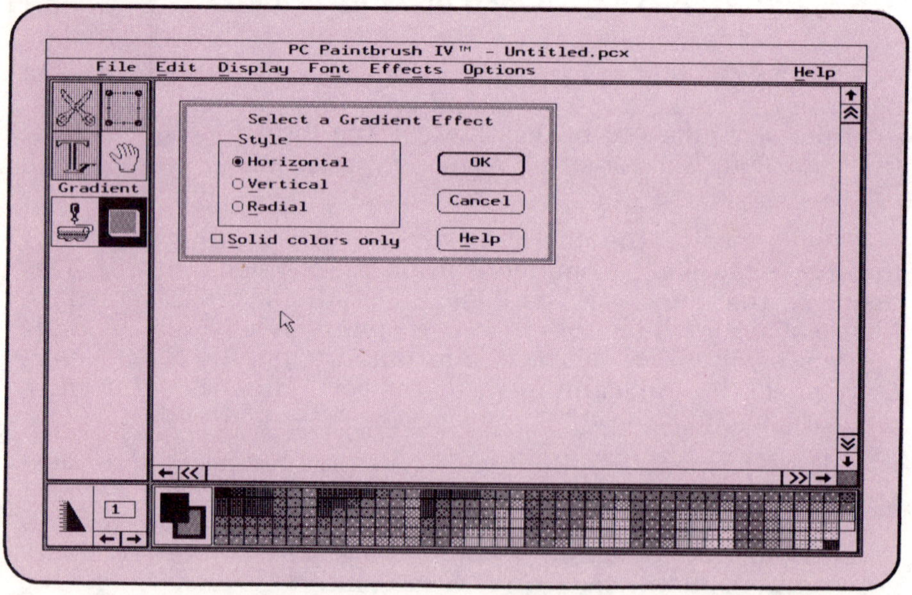

Figure 7.13 The Select a Gradient Effect dialog box in PC Paintbrush.

If you select the Solid Colors Only option, Paintbrush uses solid colors rather than blended colors to create your gradient fill. For best results, only select this option if you are working in the 256-color mode.

In Paintbrush Plus, the Solid Colors Only option is replaced by a Set Halftones... button, as shown in Figure 7.14. Click this button to display the Halftone Options dialog box shown in Figure 7.15. The options in this dialog box determine the halftone pattern used in the gradient effect. Refer to the *Controlling Halftones* section of Chapter 2 for detailed information on the Halftone options.

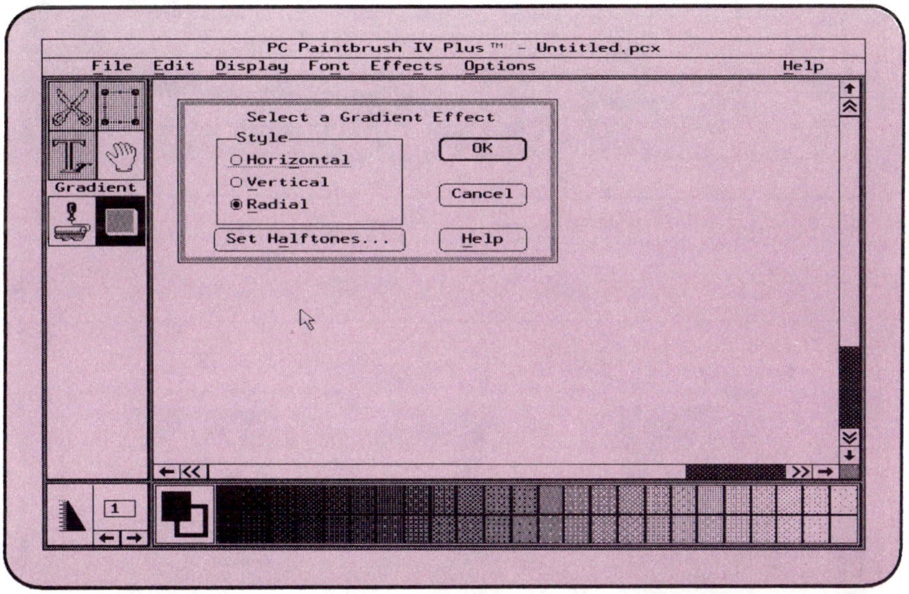

Figure 7.14 The Select a Gradient Effect dialog box in PC Paintbrush Plus.

The six halftone patterns available when opening a painting with an incompatible color palette are also available for creating a gradient fill. You can choose from None, Bayer, Diffused, Enhanced, Fatting, and Hex Bayer. Examples of each halftone pattern applied to horizontal gradient fills are shown in Figure 7.16; vertical and radial gradient fills are shown in Figures 7.17 and 7.18, respectively.

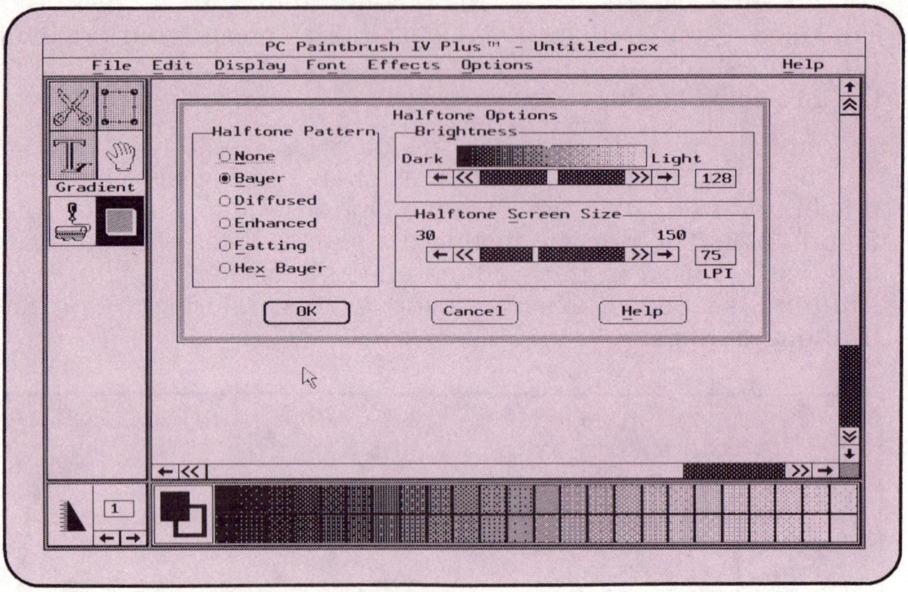

Figure 7.15 The Halftone Options dialog box.

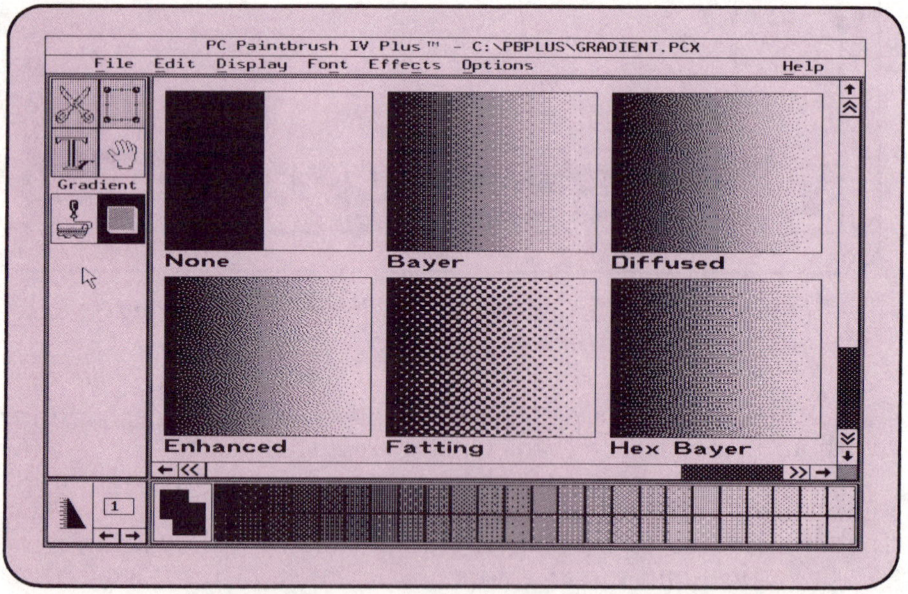

Figure 7.16 Horizontal gradient fills using each of the six halftone patterns.

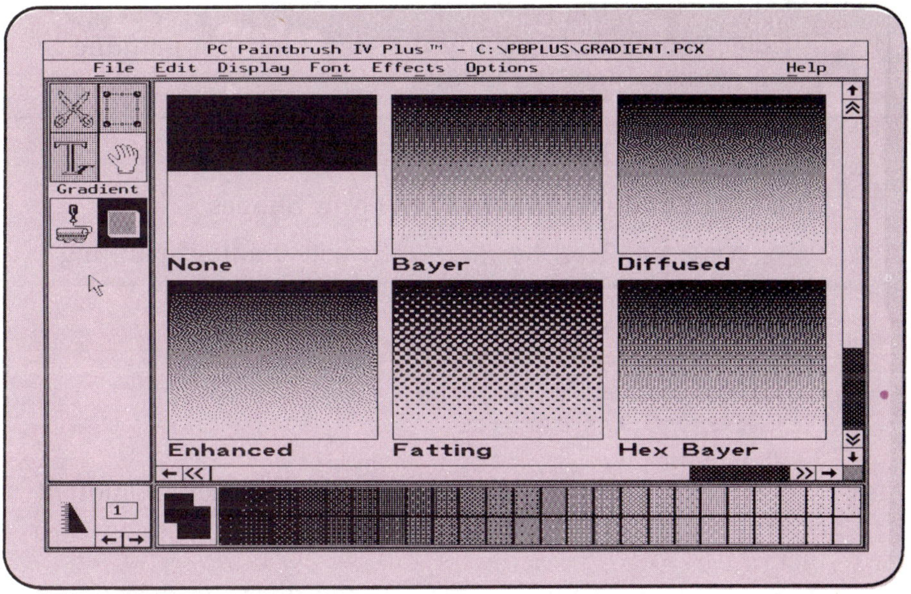

Figure 7.17 Vertical gradient fills using each of the six halftone patterns.

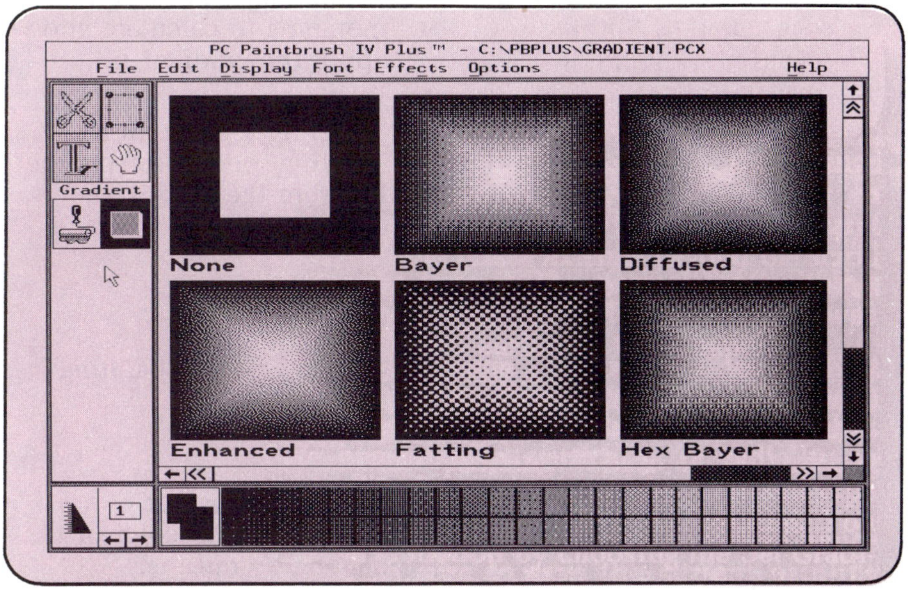

Figure 7.18 Radial gradient fills using each of the six halftone patterns.

> **Note:** You cannot magnify the view size of a painting in the gradient painting mode.

Applying Gradient Fills to Free-Form Shapes

1. Press Alt-C followed by the G key to choose the Gradient command from the Effects menu.	Selects gradient painting mode.
2. Select the secondary and background colors from the color palette.	
3. Select the Set Gradient... command from the Options menu.	Displays Select a Gradient Effect dialog box.
4. Select the Horizontal, Vertical, or Radial Style and, optionally, Solid Colors Only.	Determines the direction of the gradient fill and whether patterns or solid colors are used in the fill.
5. Select the Paint Roller tool, then click inside the enclosed or solid area you want to fill.	Paintbrush takes a few moments to calculate and apply the gradient fill.
6. Press Alt-C followed by the S key.	Selecting a different painting mode protects the fill from the Undo command.

Applying Gradient Fills to Rectangles

1. Press Alt-C followed by the G key to choose the Gradient command from the Effects menu.	Selects gradient painting mode.
2. Select the primary, secondary, and background colors from the color palette.	The primary color determines the color of the rectangle's outline.
3. Select the Set Gradient... command from the Options menu.	Displays Select a Gradient Effect dialog box.

4. Select the Horizontal, Vertical, or Radial Style and, optionally, Solid Colors Only.	Determines the direction of the gradient fill and whether patterns or solid colors are used in the fill.
5. Select a line width.	The line width determines the thickness of the rectangle's outline.
6. Select the Filled Rectangle tool, then draw your rectangle.	After you release, Paintbrush takes a few moments to calculate and apply the gradient fill.
7. Press Alt-C followed by the S key.	Selecting a different painting mode protects the fill from the Undo command. □

Smudging Images

Choose the Smudge command from the Effects menu to enter the smudge painting mode. Your toolbox and color palette will change, as shown in Figure 7.19. Only the Hand tool, the Spraycan, and the Filled Rectangle tool can be used in this mode.

In the smudge mode, painting in the drawing window will randomly mix the colors of adjacent pixels. For example, suppose an area of white pixels borders an area of red pixels. If you drag over the border with the Spraycan tool, white pixels will diffuse into the red area and red pixels will diffuse into the white area. The result is a smeared borderline, like the one shown in Figure 7.20.

Suppose we use the Filled Rectangle tool to smudge the entire rose painting. All the pixels in the image will become jumbled, as shown in Figure 7.21. The result is like a mosaic or an impressionist painting. You can also use the smudge mode to make an image appear as if behind a panel of textured glass.

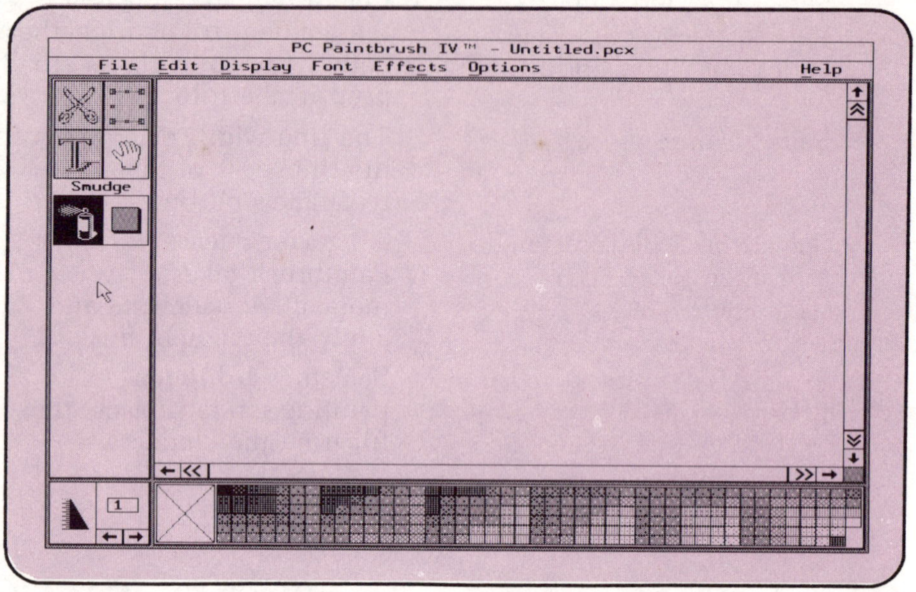

Figure 7.19 The smudge painting mode.

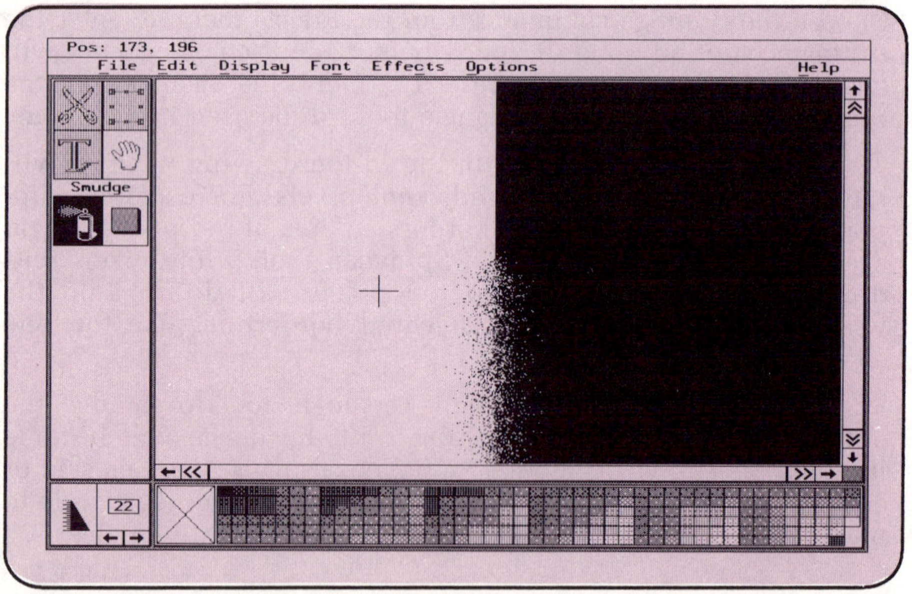

Figure 7.20 The lower half of the border has been smudged.

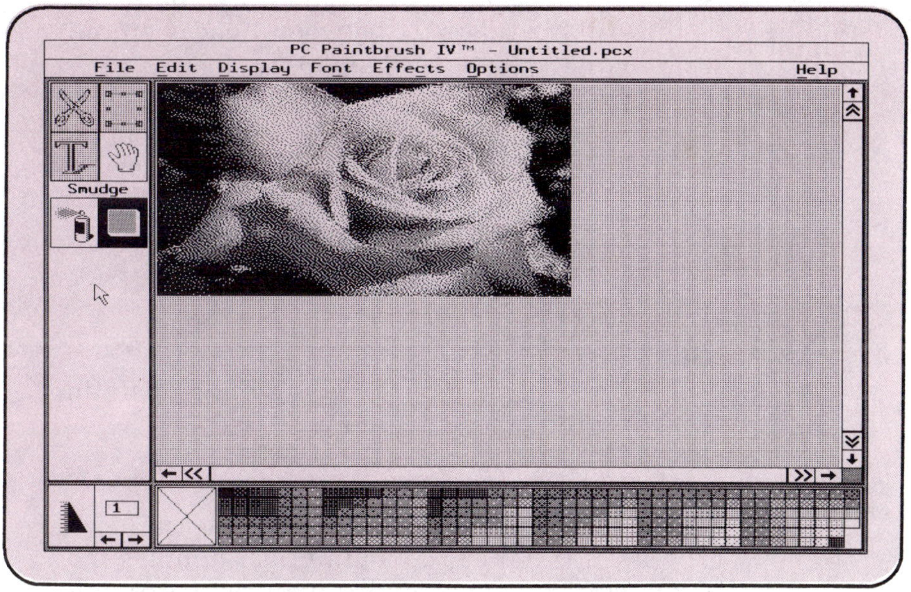

Figure 7.21 The smudged rose painting.

The primary, secondary, and background colors have no effect in this mode, as indicated by the large X in the color palette.

If you want to smudge borders between colors, use the Spraycan tool following the directions in the *Smudging Borders* Quick Steps. If you want to make large areas appear textured or jumbled, use the Filled Rectangle tool as described in *Smudging Large Areas*.

> **Note:** You cannot magnify the view size of a painting in the smudge painting mode.

Q Smudging Borders

1. Press Alt-C followed by the M key to choose the Smudge command from the Effects menu.	Selects smudge painting mode.
2. Select a line width.	Thick line widths smudge larger areas, thin line weights allow finer control.

3. Select the Spraycan tool, then drag along the borders you want to blend. — As you drag, the pixels between images are mixed randomly.
4. Press Alt-C followed by the S key. — Selecting a different painting mode protects your jumbled pixels from being righted by the Undo command. □

Q Smudging Large Areas

1. Press Alt-C followed by the M key to choose the Smudge command from the Effects menu. — Selects smudge painting mode.
2. Select the Filled Rectangle tool, then draw a rectangle around the area you want to smudge. — After you release, Paintbrush jumbles the pixels in the surrounded area.
3. Press Alt-C followed by the S key. — Selecting a different painting mode protects your jumbled pixels from being righted by the Undo command. □

Using Patterns

Choose the Tile Pattern command from the Effects menu to enter the pattern painting mode. Your toolbox and color palette will change, as shown in Figure 7.22. Only the Hand tool, the Straight Line tool, and the Filled Rectangle tool can be used in this mode. In the pattern mode, you can draw with any image copied to the clipboard or exported to disk. The image is referred to as a *tile*.

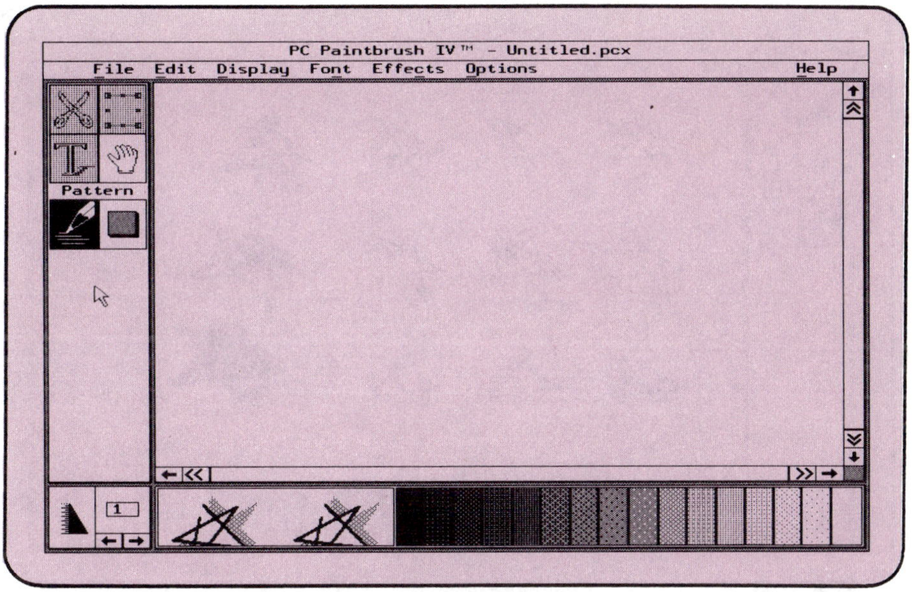

Figure 7.22 The pattern painting mode when a tile has been loaded.

When you draw with the Filled Rectangle tool, you create a repeating pattern of tiles, as shown in the left image in Figure 7.23. When you draw with the Straight Line tool, you create overlapping tiles, almost as if you were creating clones by Control-dragging a selection (described in Chapter 5). Three short lines of varying lengths have been drawn in the right half of Figure 7.23.

To specify the contents of a tile, first copy an image to the clipboard or export it to disk using the Copy To... command from the Edit menu. Then choose the Set Tile Pattern... command from the Options menu. The Load a Tile Pattern from Disk dialog box shown in Figure 7.24 will display. This dialog box looks slightly different in Paintbrush Plus.

Select the Load From Clipboard button to paste the contents of the clipboard into the current tile. You can also load a tile from disk by selecting a tile name from the scrolling field and pressing Enter. Paintbrush includes several sample tile pattern files, which are stored in the Tiles directory.

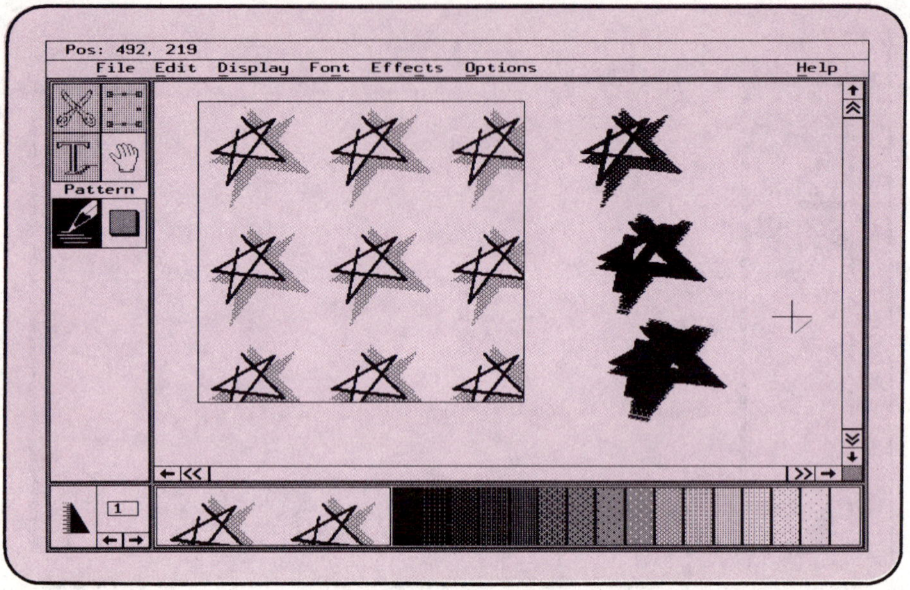

Figure 7.23 Drawing in the pattern painting mode.

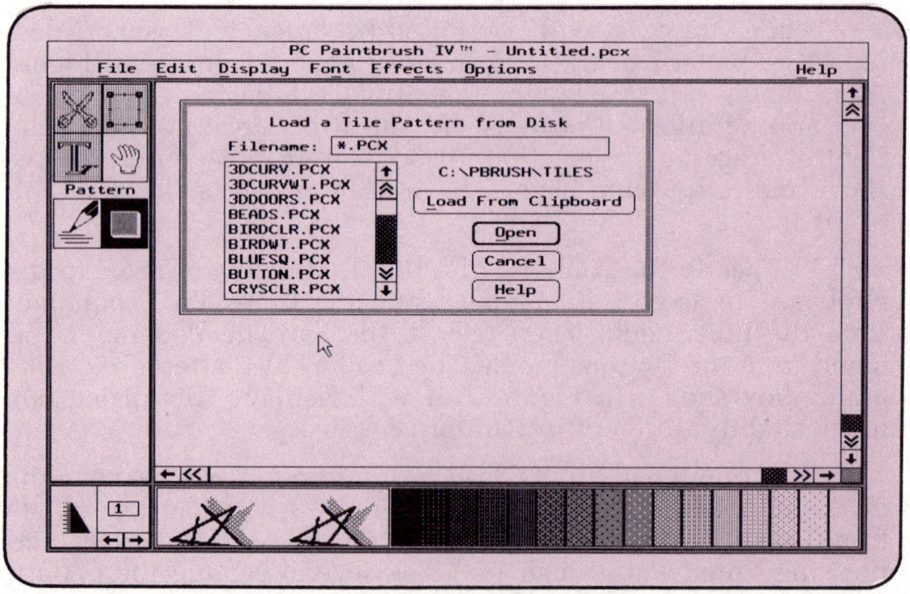

Figure 7.24 The Load a Tile Pattern from Disk dialog box in PC Paintbrush.

After you load the tile, it appears on the left side of the color palette, provided you are in the pattern mode. The color palette serves no other function in the pattern mode than to display the tile. Clicking the pattern box or any of the true color boxes, for example, will produce no effect.

The Quick Steps, *Applying Tiles in a Straight Line*, describe how to use the Straight Line tool in the pattern painting mode; *Applying a Repeating Pattern of Tiles* explains the use of the Filled Rectangle tool in the pattern painting mode.

> **Note:** You cannot magnify the view size of a painting in the pattern painting mode.

Q Applying Tiles in a Straight Line

1. Select and copy the tile image to the clipboard or to disk. Skip this step if you intend to use an image previously exported to disk.
2. Select the Tile Pattern command from the Effects menu by pressing Alt-C followed by the P key.
   Selects pattern painting mode.
3. Use the Set Tile Pattern... command from the Options menu to specify a tile image.
   The Load a Tile Pattern from Disk dialog box allows you to select a tile from clipboard or disk. The selected tile displays in the color palette.
4. Select a line width.
   The line width determines the spacing between tiles, as shown in Figure 7.25.
5. Select the Straight Line tool, then draw your first line. Press the Shift key to draw a line at a 45° angle.

6. Right-click to create additional straight lines in a polygon.
   A star composed of multiple star tiles is shown in Figure 7.26.
7. Press Alt-C followed by the S key.
   Selecting a different painting mode protects the tile pattern from the Undo command. □

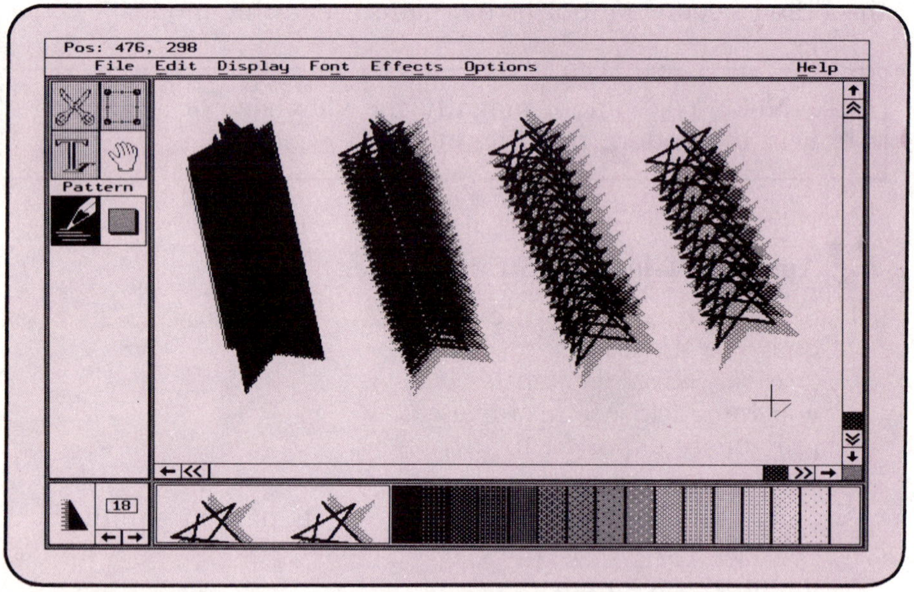

Figure 7.25 Four strings of tiles created with line widths of 1, 6, 12, and 18 pixels.

Applying a Repeating Pattern of Tiles

1. Select and copy the tile image to the clipboard or to disk. Skip this step if you intend to use an image previously exported to disk.
2. Select the Tile Pattern command from the Effects menu by pressing Alt-C followed by the P key.
   Selects pattern painting mode.

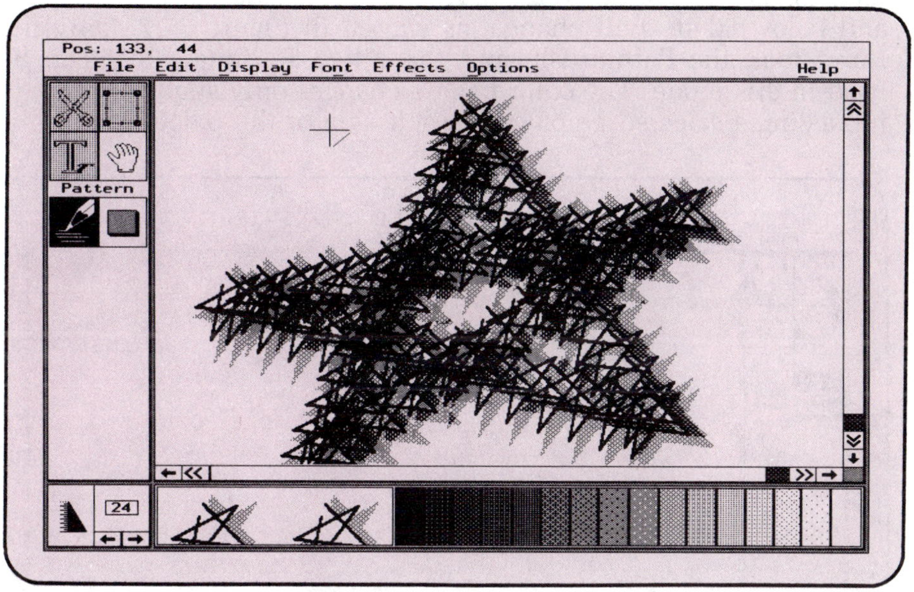

Figure 7.26 A polygon of tiles.

3. Use the Set Tile Pattern... command from the Options menu to specify a tile.

   The Load a Tile Pattern from Disk dialog box allows you to select a tile from clipboard or disk. The selected tile displays in the color palette.

4. Select the Filled Rectangle tool, then draw your shape.

   The rectangle will be filled with a pattern of repeating tiles. The rectangle will not have an outline.

5. Press Alt-C followed by the S key.

   Selecting a different painting mode protects the tile pattern from the Undo command. □

Tinting Images

Choose the Tint command from the Effects menu to enter the tint painting mode. The Tint command is only available when your monitor is configured to display 4 or more colors. Your toolbox and color palette will change, as shown in Figure 7.27. Only the Hand tool, the Paintbrush, and the Filled Rectangle tool can be used in this mode. The color palette changes only slightly, displaying a single selected color on the left side of the palette.

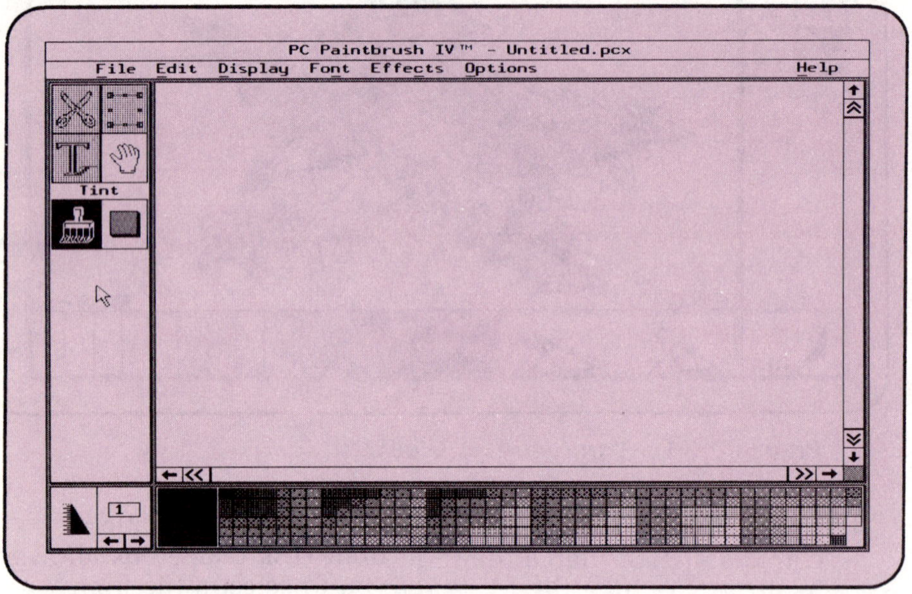

Figure 7.27 The tint painting mode.

In the tint mode, painting in the drawing window will mix the hue of existing pixels with the hue of the selected color. For example, If you select blue from the palette and paint over a yellow area in the drawing area, the area will change to green.

+ Unfortunately, the tint mode requires a large palette to produce decent results. If you drag over a yellow area of the painting with a blue tint, but the palette doesn't contain the correct shade of green, Paintbrush will leave the yellow pixels unaltered. Generally, the tint mode requires that your monitor be configured to display 256 colors; the Tint command is therefore useful almost exclusively to owners of Paintbrush Plus. Also, tint mode only works with highly saturated colors; it will not produce results if you use a palette of gray values.

The Paintbrush and Filled Rectangle tool function dissimilarly in the tint mode. Drawing with the Paintbrush tints an area uniformly. If you draw over an area more than once, you will not increase the tint unless you reselect the tool or select a new color. Repeated applications of the Filled Rectangle tool, however, will tint colors additionally, whether or not you reselected the tool.

The Quick Steps, *Tinting a Small Area*, describe how to use the Paintbrush tool in the tint mode; *Tinting a Large Area* explains how to use the Filled Rectangle tool in the tint mode.

Q Tinting a Small Area

1. Select the Tint command from the Effects menu by pressing Alt-C followed by the T key.	Selects tint painting mode.
2. Select a color in the palette.	
3. Select a line width.	Thick line widths tint larger areas, thin line weights allow finer control.
4. Select the Paintbrush tool, then paint over the area you want to tint.	As you drag, the hue of the area changes depending on the selected color.
5. Select a different value or reselect the Paintbrush. Skip this step if you want to tint the area uniformly.	Allows you to tint the area additionally.
6. Press Alt-C followed by the S key.	Selecting a different painting mode protects the old colors from being restored by the Undo command. □

Q Tinting a Large Area

1. Select the Tint command from the Effects menu by pressing Alt-C followed by the T key.	Selects tint painting mode.
2. Select a color in the palette.	

3. Select the Filled Rectangle tool, then draw a rectangle around the area you want to tint.	After you release, the hue of the area changes depending on the selected color.
4. Continue drawing with the Filled Rectangle tool.	Repeated applications of the tool tint the painting additionally.
5. Press Alt-C followed by the S key.	Selecting a different painting mode protects the old colors from being restored by the Undo command. □

Summary

In this chapter, you've learned:

- You can blend colors, smear brush strokes, and tint images using different painting modes. You access painting modes by choosing commands from the Effects menu.
- The Hand tool is available in all painting modes. The Scissors, Gadget Box, and Text tool are only available in the standard painting mode.
- The Filled Rectangle tool is the only drawing tool available in all painting modes. This tool is most useful for applying a special effect to a large portion of the painting.
- Thick line weights work best in most painting modes because they allow you to cover the largest area in the fewest strokes.
- Your palette must offer 256 true colors or 16 gray values for the brightness and contrast painting modes to produce predictable results.
- The Set Gradient... command from the Options menu allows you to determine the direction of a gradient fill.
- To specify a tile image, you first choose the Set Tile Pattern... command from the Options menu. You can then either select an exported image from the Tiles directory or select the Load from Clipboard button.

- The tint mode requires a palette of 256 true colors. Drawing with a gray value in this mode produces no effect.
- You can return to the standard mode at any time by pressing Alt-C followed by the S key.
- Each painting mode is described in a separate section in this chapter. Quick Steps describe how to use the drawing tools available in each painting mode to create interesting special effects.

Chapter 8

Printing a Painting

What You Will Learn

- *What to do with your finished painting*
- *Printing documents created in Paintbrush*
- *Advanced color-printing capabilities in Paintbrush Plus*
- *Compensating for non-square screen or printer pixels*

Your Finished Painting

By now, you have undoubtedly grasped the ease with which images can be created in Paintbrush—whether elegant black and white images or captivating full-color paintings. But what can you do with your paintings after you finish them?

You basically have two possibilities: You can import the painting into a different program, where it can be integrated with text and other graphics and then printed as a finished document, or you can print the painting directly from Paintbrush.

Importing Paintings

Many different kinds of software accept Paintbrush files—either in the Paintbrush TIF or PCX format or in a converted format. The most popular categories of software importing Paintbrush files include the following:

- *Drawing software*, such as Micrografx Designer or Adobe Illustrator. These programs allow you to enhance sketches created in Paintbrush into smooth-line illustrations.
- *Page-layout software*, such as Aldus PageMaker or Ventura Publisher. These programs allow you to integrate text and graphics into printed documents, such as newsletters, flyers, and catalogs.
- *Presentation software*, such as Harvard Graphics or Autodesk Animator. These programs allow you to use full-color paintings in slide shows, animated presentations, and self-running demonstrations.

To import a painting into a different program, first save it to disk as either a PCX or TIF file, as recommended in the *Saving a Painting in PCX or TIF Format* section in Chapter 2. Then quit Paintbrush, start the other program, and import the PCX or TIF file. Unfortunately, the method for importing paintings varies from software to software. Some programs even require that you convert the file to a different format before importing it. Consult your drawing, page-layout, or presentation program's documentation for specific information on importing files.

Printing from PC Paintbrush

You can print a painting directly from Paintbrush if you selected a printer during the installation procedure, and if your printing device is connected or networked correctly with your computer. The remainder of this chapter explains how to use the Print command and its options to print a painting.

The Print Command

To initiate the printing process after creating a painting or loading an existing painting, choose the Print... command from the File menu. The Enter Print Options dialog box, shown in Figure 8.1, will appear. If you are using Paintbrush Plus, choosing Print... displays the Print the Picture dialog box, which provides a few more options, as shown in Figure 8.2.

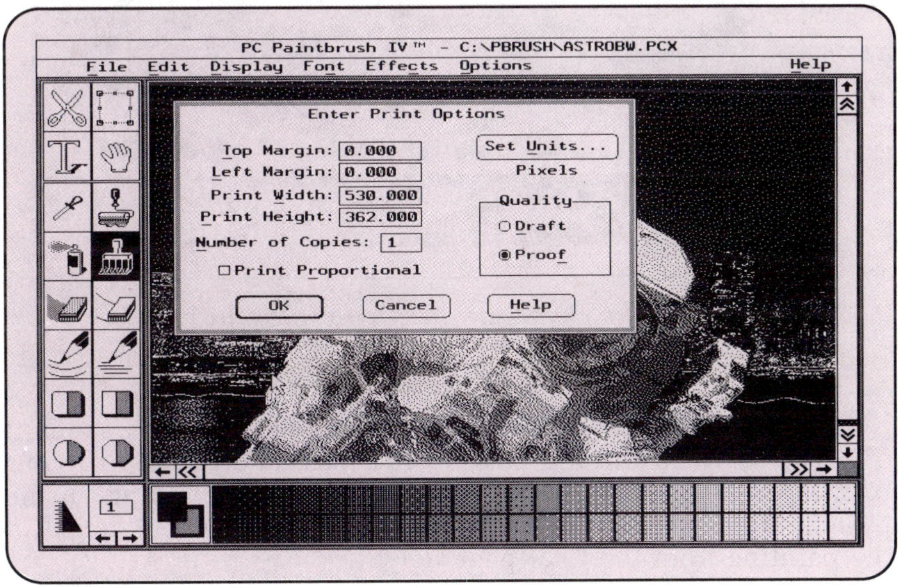

Figure 8.1 The Enter Print Options dialog box in PC Paintbrush.

The Enter Print Options and Print the Picture dialog boxes contain printing options which allow you to control the size of margins, the size of the painting, the number of copies, as well as other basic printing attributes.

Controlling Margins

You can specify the amount of white space between the edges of the printed page and the boundaries of your painting. This area of white space is known as the *margin*.

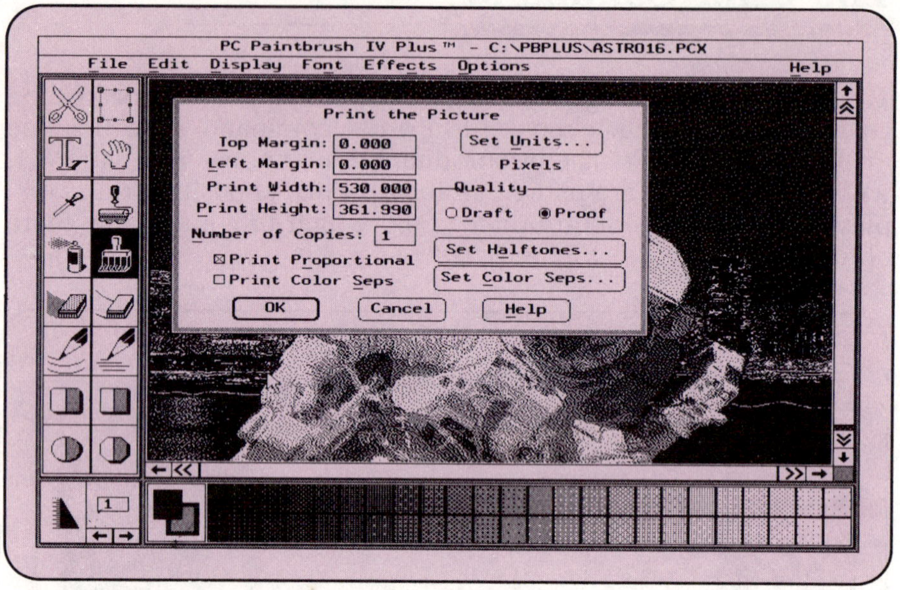

Figure 8.2 The Print the Picture dialog box in PC Paintbrush Plus.

The value in the *Top Margin* option determines the amount of space between the top edge of the page and the top of your painting. The bottom margin will be the area remaining on the page after Paintbrush subtracts the top margin and the height of the painting from the total page height.

The value in the *Left Margin* option determines the amount of space between the left edge of the page and the left side of your painting. The right margin will be the area remaining on the page after Paintbrush subtracts the left margin and the width of the painting from the total page width.

> **Note:** Paintbrush assumes you want to specify your margins in pixels. To change this unit of measure, select the Set Units... button.

Most printers require a margin of at least one-half inch (150 pixels for a standard 300-dots-per-inch laser printer) for all four margins—top, bottom, left, and right.

Painting Size

After setting the margins, you can determine the print size of your painting using the *Print Height* and *Print Width* options and the *Print Proportional* check box.

The value in the Print Width option determines the width of the painting in pixels or in another unit of measure. The value in the Print Height option determines the height of the painting in pixels or in another unit of measure.

When selected, the Print Proportional check box protects the relative dimensions of your painting. Changing the value in either the Print Width or Print Height option will automatically change the value of the other option so that the proportions of your painting stay the same. Be careful: If you deselect the Print Proportional check box, you may stretch or squash your painting during the printing process.

The default values for these options represent the size of your painting in printer pixels. Since screen pixels are larger than printer pixels, your painting will appear smaller when printed at a one-to-one ratio—that is, one printer pixel for every on-screen pixel. For example, if you are printing to a standard 300-dots-per-inch laser printer, your painting will shrink to less than one-quarter of its on-screen size. To avoid shrinkage, enter a larger value in either the Print Width or Print Height option box while the Print Proportional box is checked. For example, if your painting is 640 pixels wide and you enter 1280 in the Print Width option, each screen pixel will print 2 printer pixels wide.

> ▶ **Tip:** When entering a new value for the Print Width or Print Height option, multiply the default value by a whole number, such as 2, 3, or 4.

Number of Copies

One of the greatest advantages of electronic art is that it can be printed often and in quantity without wear or tear on the original. The *Number of Copies* option allows you to print several copies of a painting or just one. Select this option then enter a value between 1 and 99 to determine how many copies of the current painting will print.

> **Tip:** If you are planning to distribute over ten copies of a painting, you may find it more cost-effective to print a single copy and photocopy duplicates.

Print Quality

Speed and quality have an inverse relationship in many areas of life—so too in the dot-matrix printing process. When printing to a dot-matrix printer, you can opt for either speed of printing or quality of printed output. In Paintbrush, you specify speed or quality by selecting one of two Quality options: *Draft* and *Proof*.

If you select the Draft option, you sacrifice print quality for speed of printing. The printer head will make only one pass over the page per printer pixel; consequently, printed output will have a grainier appearance. If you select the Proof option, your printed output will be higher quality but the printing process will take longer. The printer head will make several slightly overlapping passes to create smoother text and graphics.

The Quality options only apply to dot-matrix printers, such as an IBM ProPrinter or NEC Pinwriter. If you are printing to a laser printer or a comparable high-resolution device, your output will look the same and print at the same speed whether the Draft or Proof option is selected.

Advanced Printing Options

The color printing options offered by Paintbrush are limited. Since the Enter Print Options dialog box provides no color-handling controls, your use of color will be dictated by your printer's capabilities. If your printer only prints in black and white, you must paint in black and white. If you own a color output device, like the Okimate 20 or the Tektronix Inkjet, then you can paint and print in color.

+ Paintbrush Plus offers more color-handling possibilities. You have the capability to print color paintings to black and white printers in either of two ways: You can *halftone* your paintings, instructing your printer to mimic colors using patterns of pixels, or you can print *color separations*, which are suitable for commercial color process printing.

Halftoning

+ The Print the Picture dialog box in Paintbrush Plus offers a Set Halftones... button, shown in Figure 8.2. Click this button to display the Halftone Options dialog box, shown in Figure 8.3; then select the halftone pattern that will be used to print your color painting.

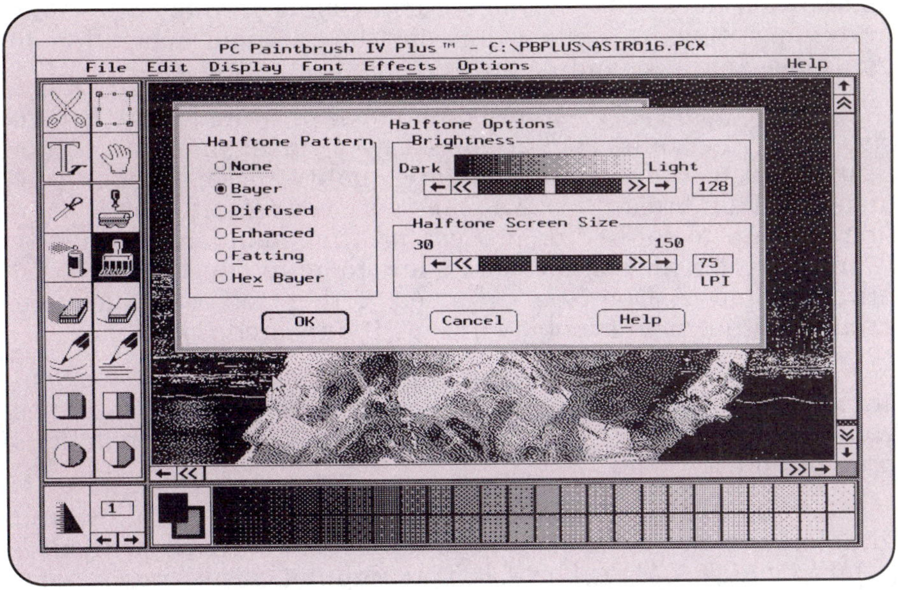

Figure 8.3 The Halftone Options dialog box.

If you have read the sections on halftones in Chapters 2 and 7, you probably know how these options work by now. If you want an idea of how a typical piece of colored artwork will print using each Halftone Pattern option, refer to Figures 2.7 through 2.12 in Chapter 2. Figures 2.13 and 2.14 show the effect of adjusting the Brightness scroll bar. Figures 2.15 and 2.16 show the effect of changing the Halftone Screen Size value.

The options in the Halftone Options dialog box are designed specifically for adjusting the output of gray-scale paintings. They also dictate how individual color separations print.

Color Separations

In the *Coloring with Pigments* section of Chapter 4, we described how the hues cyan, magenta, yellow, and black can be mixed to print any color on a white sheet of paper. If the Print Color Seps check box is selected in the Print the Picture dialog box, Paintbrush Plus will break down each color in your painting to its cyan, magenta, yellow, and black components. Each of the four hues will be printed on a separate piece of paper, known as a *separation*. If you're printing to a black and white printer, each separation will appear black but will bear the name of its hue. This instructs a commercial printer to use the cyan separation to apply cyan ink, the magenta separation to apply magenta ink, and so on.

Unfortunately, full-color commercial printing is very expensive, and you could end up spending a lot of money for poor results because of the rudimentary quality of separations produced by Paintbrush Plus. To make sure your Paintbrush separations are up to four-color process printing standards, you may want to print some samples and show them to a few commercial printing houses. Don't be surprised if they tell you that your printed output won't look as nice as it appeared on screen.

Select the Set Color Seps... button to display the Color Separations dialog box shown in Figure 8.4. This dialog box allows you to control the number of separations and the notations printed on each page.

Two mutually exclusive Number of Seps options allow you to determine the number of separations that will be printed: *4 (CMYK)* and *3 (CMY)*. The 4 (CMYK) option prints four separations, one each for the hues cyan, magenta, yellow, and black. This is the standard setting. The 3 (CMY) option prints three separations, one each for the hues cyan, magenta, and yellow. No separation is printed for black.

Generally, you will want to select the 4 (CMYK) option. However, if you find that your paintings come back from the commercial printer looking substantially darker than they appear on screen, select the 3 (CMY) option to lighten a painting and give it a more "washed-out" appearance.

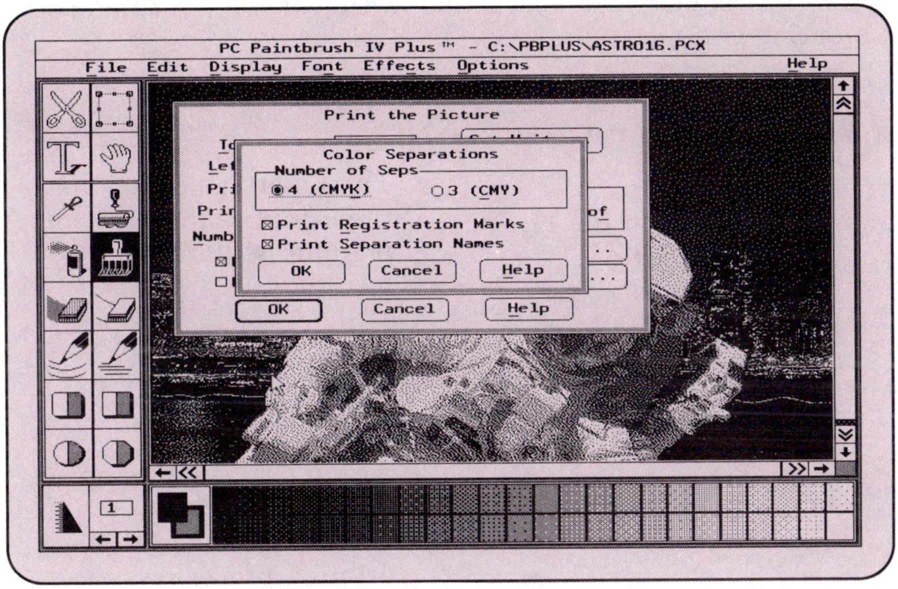

Figure 8.4 The Color Separations dialog box.

Two check box options allow you to specify the page markings: *Print Registration Marks* and *Print Separation Names*. The Print Registration Marks option prints the marks used to line up each separation, termed *registration marks*. If you turn this option off, your printed painting may end up looking like an oddly colored comic strip in a Sunday newspaper. The Print Separation Names option prints the name of the hue associated with each separation. If you turn this option off, your commercial printer may use yellow where they should have used cyan or vice versa, in which case an orange painting would come out purple. Unless your painting is so large that it consumes an entire page, both check box options should always be selected.

The printing options discussed so far in this chapter provide the means to print any document created in Paintbrush. The three Quick Steps which follow summarize the use of these options. Read *Printing Basic Paintings* if you are printing a black and white painting to a black and white printer or a color painting to a color printer.

+ The last two Quick Steps apply only to Paintbrush Plus. If you are printing a gray scale painting to a black and white printer, read *Printing Halftoned Paintings*. If you are printing color separations to a black and white printer, read *Printing Color Separations.*

Printing Basic Paintings

1. Choose the Print... command from the File menu or press Alt-F followed by the P key.
   The Enter Print Options or the Print the Picture (Paintbrush Plus) dialog box displays.
2. Adjust the print options as necessary. At least change the Top Margin and Left Margin to 0.5 inch.
3. Press Enter or click OK.
   A status statement appears in the caption bar, indicating how close the printing process is to completion. □

Printing Halftoned Paintings

1. Choose the Print... command from the File menu or press Alt-F followed by the P key.
   The Print the Picture dialog box displays.
2. Adjust the print options as necessary. At least change the Top Margin and Left Margin to 0.5 inch.
3. Select the Set Halftones... button.
   The Halftone Options dialog box displays.
4. Select options.
5. Press Enter or click OK twice to begin printing.
   A status statement appears in the caption bar, indicating how close the printing process is to completion. □

Q Printing Color Separations

1. Choose the Print... command from the File menu or press Alt-F followed by the P key.	The Print the Picture dialog box displays.
2. Adjust the print options as necessary. At least change the Top Margin and Left Margin to 0.5 inch.	
3. Select the Set Halftones... button.	The Halftone Options dialog box displays.
4. Select options and press Enter or click OK.	
5. Press Alt-S or click Print Color Seps.	Selects the Print Color Seps option.
6. Select the Set Color Seps... button.	The Color Separations dialog box displays.
7. Select options and press Enter or click OK twice to begin printing.	A status statement appears in the caption bar, indicating how close the printing process is to completion. □

Aspect Ratio

Depending on the models of your monitor and printer, you may have read as far as you need to in this chapter. You will need to read the next sections about aspect ratio only if you are using one of the monitors *or* printers listed in Appendix A. If you are using one of the monitors listed in Appendix A but at a different resolution than is given—such as 640 x 480, 800 x 600, or 1024 x 768—you can skip the next sections, if your printer is not included in Appendix A.

Aspect Ratio Theory

Paintbrush assumes that your screen and printer have square pixels. However, the monitors and printers listed in Appendix A have slightly to extremely rectangular pixels. A monitor set to a standard resolution of 640 by 480 pixels displays square pixels, but a monitor set to a resolution of 640 by 200 pixels displays rectangular pixels that are almost two-and-a-half times as tall as they are wide.

This can present a problem when Paintbrush displays images on screen or prints images. For example, when you press the Shift key while drawing with the Ellipse tool, Paintbrush normally produces a circle; that is, an equal number of pixels radiate horizontally and vertically from the center point. But if your screen displays rectangular pixels, the circle will display as an elongated ellipse. Likewise, if your printer has rectangular pixels, the circle will print as an ellipse.

The current aspect ratio, a user-defined or Paintbrush default value, tells Paintbrush how to compensate mathematically for non-square pixels. If, for example, your printer has a resolution of 240 by 144 pixels per inch, its pixels are over one-and-a-half times as tall as they are wide and the aspect ratio needed to compensate for this is 1.667. (Don't worry, Paintbrush automatically calculates the aspect ratios of both the monitor and printer for you.) If you direct Paintbrush to use this aspect ratio for your printer, a circle which appears 167% wider than it is tall on screen will print correctly.

Compensating for non-square pixels becomes additionally complicated if both your monitor and printer use rectangular pixels. For example, if your monitor displays disproportionately tall pixels and your printer creates disproportionately wide pixels, there is no single aspect ratio that can compensate for both extremes. You'll have to choose between tall, thin screen images or short, wide printed images.

For this reason, you must decide your painting medium before beginning to paint. Do you intend to display your painting on screen or import it into a presentation program? Then you should select an aspect ratio that compensates for the screen display. Or do you want to print your painting? In this case, you should select an aspect ratio that compensates for the printer resolution.

> **Tip:** Always adjust the aspect ratio before creating a painting because the aspect ratio should be consistent throughout a painting.

The Set Aspect Command

To specify an aspect ratio, choose the Set Aspect... command from the Options menu. The Adjust the Aspect Ratio dialog box shown in Figure 8.5 will appear. Paintbrush displays the aspect ratio that is currently in effect near the top of the box.

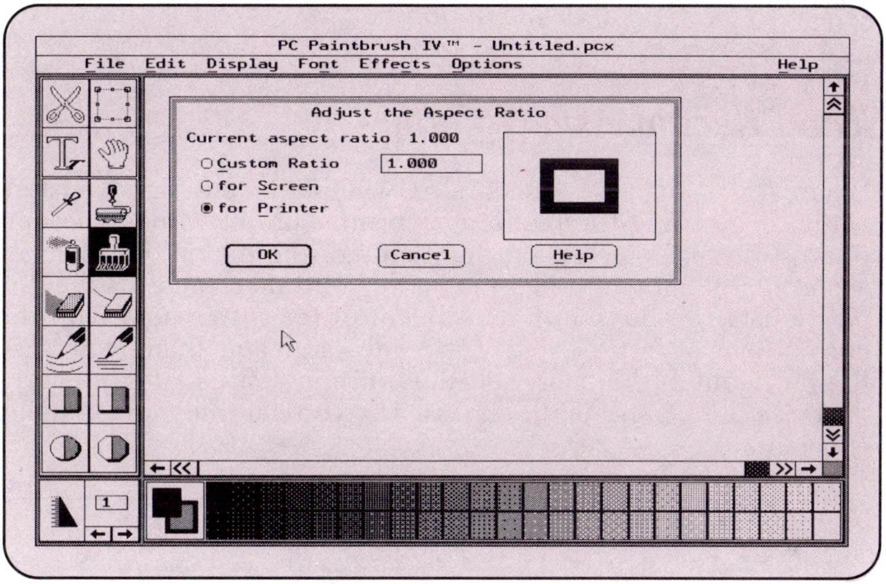

Figure 8.5 The Adjust Aspect Ratio dialog box.

You can select one of three options in the Adjust Aspect Ratio dialog box: *Custom Ratio*, *For Screen*, and *For Printer*.

Select the Custom Ratio option and enter a value into the option box on the right if you want to specify your own aspect ratio. The value in the option box takes effect only if the Custom Ratio option is selected. The For Screen option adjusts the aspect ratio to compensate for rectangular screen pixels. The aspect ratio for the monitor you selected using the PbSetup program will appear near the top of the dialog box. The For Printer option adjusts the aspect ratio to compensate for rectangular printer pixels. The aspect ratio for the printer you selected using the PbSetup installation program will appear near the top of the dialog box.

Since Paintbrush assumes you normally print your paintings and therefore want to correct for disproportionate printer pixels, the For Printer option is selected by default. If you intend to print your paintings, always using the same printer, you won't need to change this default. However, should you want to print an image to a different printer, you can use the Custom Ratio option. Simply select the option, then enter the appropriate aspect ratio value for the secondary printer from Appendix A. If your secondary printer isn't listed in Appendix A, enter an aspect ratio of 1.000 in the option box.

The Effect of Aspect Ratio

When you change the aspect ratio, whether by entering a custom value or by using the monitor or printer preset values, the outline of the rectangle on the right side of the dialog box changes accordingly. Shown in Figure 8.6, this outline represents the disparity between the width and height of images created with the current aspect ratio. Aspect ratio values greater than 1 increase the horizontal thickness of the outline; values less than 1 decrease the horizontal thickness. The vertical thickness remains constant.

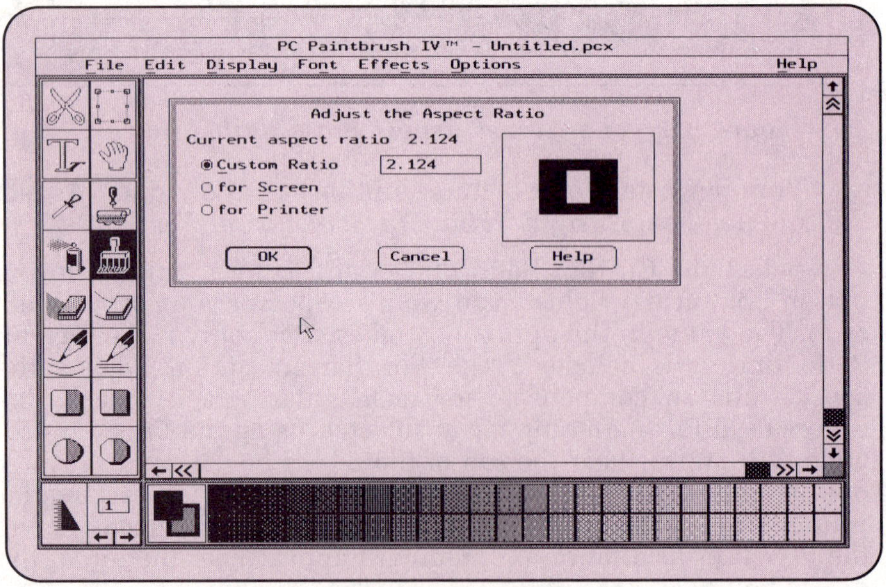

Figure 8.6 The Adjust Aspect Ratio dialog box.

Aspect ratio affects the appearance of squares, circles, and line widths. Figure 8.7 shows a squiggly line and a square created with an 8-pixel line width when the aspect ratio is set to 2.124.

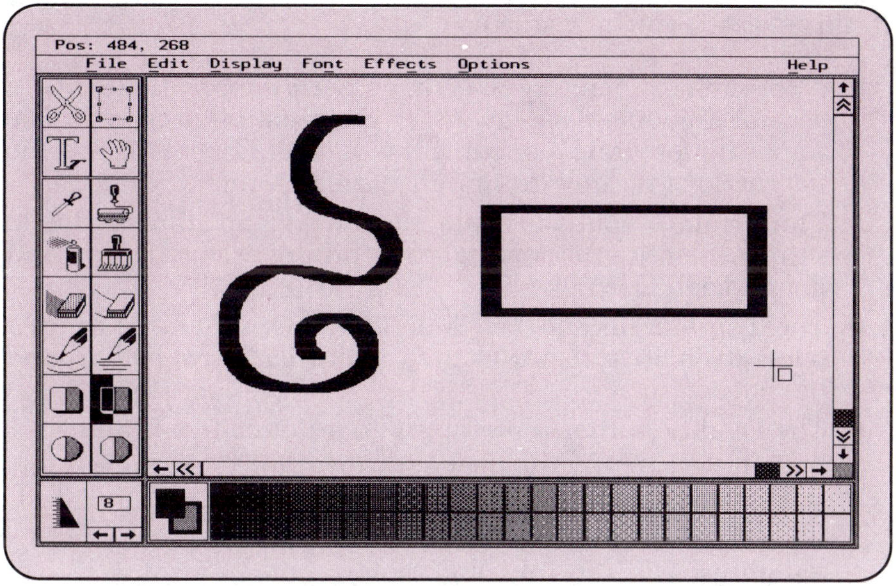

Figure 8.7 The effect of aspect ratio on a free-form line and a square.

Aspect ratio is a seldom used option. If you are importing your paintings into a page-layout program, you can ignore it entirely. You can also avoid using the Set Aspect... command by reconfiguring Paintbrush whenever you use a different printer; simply run the PbSetup program and select the printer from the list of printers. However, you will find aspect ratios useful if you are creating images to be displayed on a specific monitor which has rectangular pixels, or if you are switching back and forth regularly between printers with differently sized pixels. You will also want to consider aspect ratio if you are importing your paintings into a presentation program.

Summary

In this chapter, you've learned:

- After saving a painting to disk, you can import it into any of several drawing, page-layout, or presentation programs. The importing program's documentation should contain specific instructions on how to import the Paintbrush file.
- The Print... command from the File menu allows you to print a painting, assuming your printer is configured and networked correctly.
- The Top Margin and Left Margin values should be at least one-half inch so that a printed image isn't cropped around the edges.
- The Quality options only apply to a dot-matrix printer.
- In Paintbrush Plus, you can specify how a color or gray scale painting is printed to a monochrome printer by selecting the Set Halftones... button.
- Paintbrush Plus prints four color separations for use in commercial color process printing. A page is printed for each of the subtractive primary hues: cyan, magenta, yellow, and black.
- If your monitor or printer is listed in Appendix A, you may have to adjust the aspect ratio before creating a new painting to compensate for non-square pixels.
- Paintbrush adjusts the aspect ratio automatically so that the current printer operates as if it uses square pixels. You can ignore the Set Aspect... command unless your painting will be displayed on a monitor with a different aspect ratio or your painting will be printed on a different printer than Paintbrush is configured for.

Chapter 9

Capturing Computer Screens

What You Will Learn

- *The function of the Frieze utility*
- *Using Frieze within Paintbrush*
- *Capturing images created in other programs*
- *Loading Frieze into computer memory and unloading it*

What is Frieze?

The Frieze program is a screen-capture utility included with Paintbrush. Frieze is a simple program to use, yet it provides a wide range of screen-capture possibilities. But before we explain Frieze in detail and how to put it to good use in Paintbrush or in another program, we'll talk in general about screen-capture programs.

Whys and Hows of Screen Capture

One of the problems commonly associated with personal computers, especially MS-DOS-based personal computers, is the proliferation of incompatible file formats. There are probably more different file formats than programs! As a result, a document created in one program often cannot be used in a different program—unless a third program first converts the document's file format.

For example, suppose you created an image in a different painting program, such as Dr. Halo or Mouse Systems' PC Paint. Both programs offer a few features not available in Paintbrush although, in general, Paintbrush is a more sophisticated program. Now that you own Paintbrush, you can use its capabilities to enhance your image created in either of these programs. However, Paintbrush only recognizes the PCX and TIF formats, which are not used by Dr. Halo or PC Paint. Without a conversion program, you'd have to redraw your image from scratch.

Nor can Paintbrush recognize images stored in the CompuServe GIF format, graphs created in Lotus or Harvard Graphics, or text screens from Microsoft Word or WordPerfect. Some of the programs just referred to import Paintbrush images, but they do not export images that can be edited in Paintbrush.

A screen-capture utility is like a spy satellite that hides in your computer's memory while you're running Paintbrush or a different program. When instructed to do so, it takes a picture of the current screen and stores it in a specific format, such as PCX, regardless of the format(s) used by the current program. By automatically converting images from one format to another, a screen-capture utility gets around the problem of incompatible file formats.

The Frieze Utility

The Frieze utility is loaded into your computer's memory every time you start Paintbrush. This means that you can have Paintbrush spy on itself, storing screen shots of the current file to disk so that they can be retrieved for later use. Frieze stores all screen shots as PCX documents to the file name and location that you specify. This storage technique is especially useful for creating backups of a painting, always nice to have in case you make a big mistake, or for saving a painting in different stages of development.

When you quit Paintbrush, Frieze is automatically removed from memory. Therefore, you cannot take pictures at the DOS prompt.

To use Frieze with a program other than Paintbrush, you will need to load Frieze into memory from the DOS prompt and then start the other program. The specifics of using Frieze in a different program are discussed in the *Using Frieze with a Program Other than PC Paintbrush* section later in this chapter.

Using Frieze inside Paintbrush

To use the Frieze program inside Paintbrush, first start Paintbrush as usual. Open the painting that you want to *shoot*, or capture, then press the Shift key simultaneously with the PrintScreen (PrtSc) key, usually located near the top of your keyboard. The Frieze menu, shown in Figure 9.1, will appear across the top of the screen.

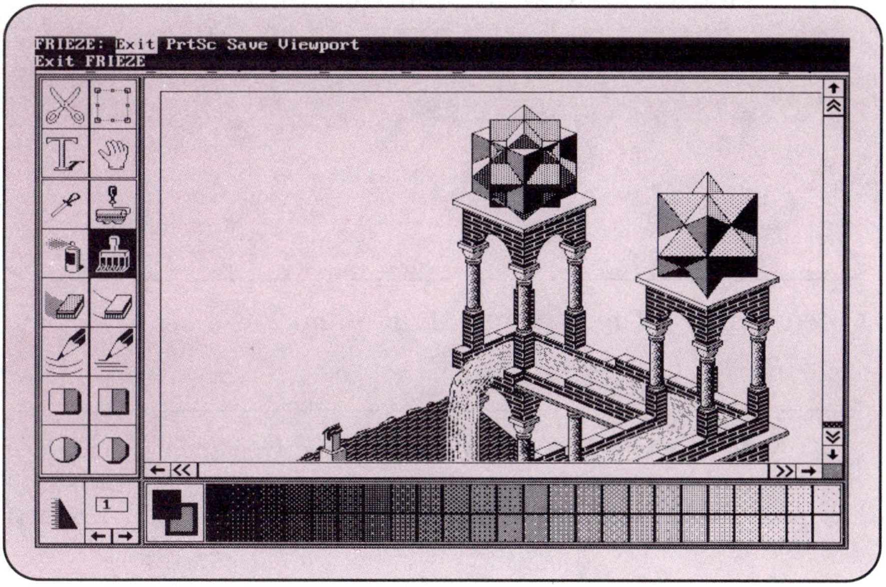

Figure 9.1 The Frieze menu.

If the Frieze menu does not appear or you simply hear a beep, this indicates that Frieze has not been loaded into memory. If you configured Paintbrush not to use a printer, the program does not load Frieze but loads a lesser utility instead, called "TinyFrieze." TinyFrieze saves memory but does not capture screens. To load Frieze, quit Paintbrush and enter pbsetup at the DOS prompt. Follow the instructions until you arrive at the PbSetup Main Menu shown in Figure 9.2. Press the R key followed by the C key to enter the printer selection menu, select a printer other than None, and follow the directions to return to the DOS prompt. Restart Paintbrush, then try again to run the Frieze utility by pressing Shift-PrintScreen.

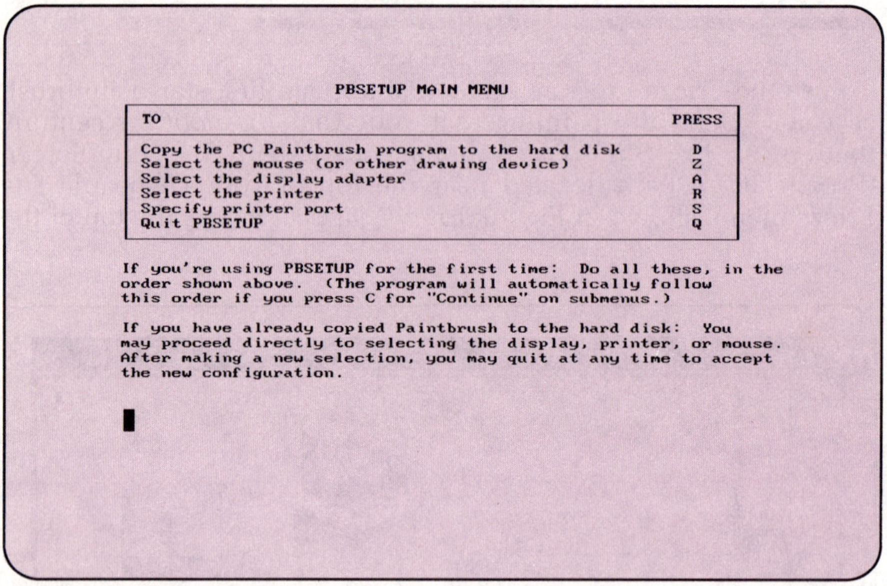

Figure 9.2 The PbSetup Main Menu.

> **Note:** To use Frieze, you must specify a printer selection other than None when you configure Paintbrush.

The Frieze Menu

Once the Frieze menu appears, the cursor is locked on screen and the mouse is inoperable. Use the Left and Right Arrow keys instead of the mouse to navigate from one option to the next in the Frieze menu. The current menu option will appear highlighted. Press Enter to execute the highlighted option or, to execute an option that is not highlighted, press the first letter in the option name.

The Frieze menu offers the following four options:

- Select the *Exit* option or press the E key to quit the Frieze utility and return to Paintbrush.
- Select the *PrtSc* option or press the P key to invoke the standard DOS print screen function and send the current screen to the printer. For more information on this function, refer to the DOS documentation included with your computer.
- Select the *Save* option or press the S key to save the current screen to disk as a PCX file. A prompt requests you to enter the path and file name of the current screen.
- Select the *Viewport* option or press the V key to determine the portion of the screen that you want to capture. The next section, *Capturing the Screen*, explains how to use this option.

Capturing the Screen

To capture the current screen in Paintbrush and save it to disk, select the Save option from the Frieze menu. The Save to: prompt will then display, as shown in Figure 9.3, requesting you to enter a path (drive and/or directory) and a file name for the current screen. For example, if you type <u>c:\pbrush\screen01.pcx</u> and press Enter, you will save the current screen to a file called SCREEN01.PCX in the Pbrush directory of your C drive. Be sure to add a .PCX extension to the file name so that Paintbrush can recognize it as a picture. If you don't use a .PCX extension, Paintbrush won't display the file in the scrolling field in the Load a Picture dialog box when you try to open the file.

> **Caution:** Frieze does not warn you when you overwrite an existing file, so choose your screen-capture file name carefully.

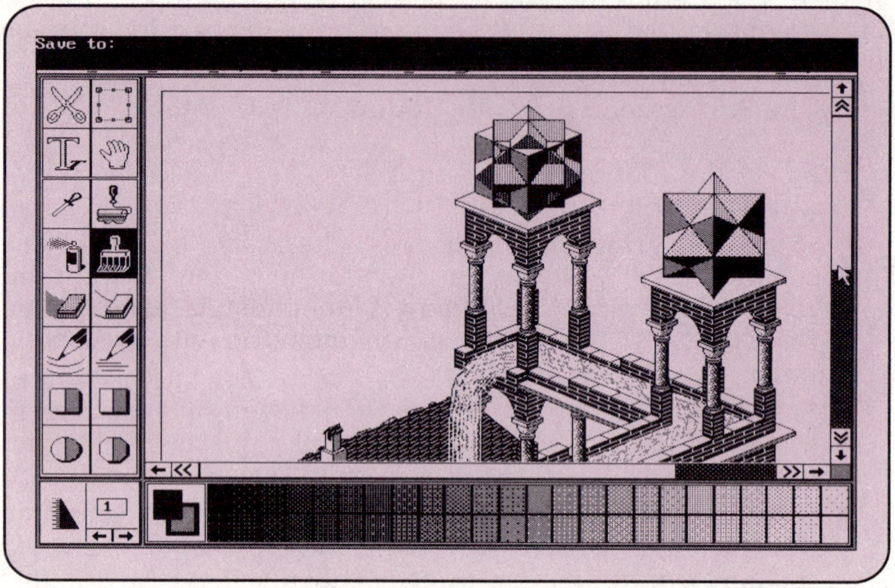

Figure 9.3 Selecting the Save option displays the Save to: prompt which requests a path and file name for the captured screen.

To capture only a portion of the current screen, press Shift-PrintScreen to display the Frieze menu, then select the Viewport option before you select the Save option. A list of instructions will appear, as shown in Figure 9.4. Press any key to hide the instructions and display only the Paintbrush desktop. If you look carefully, you'll notice the entire desktop is surrounded by a thin rectangular outline. This outline is the *viewport* itself. You can adjust either the top, left corner or the bottom, right corner of the viewport using the arrow keys and other keys listed in Table 9.1. The corner being adjusted is termed the *current corner*. Pressing the Spacebar allows you to alternate between the two corners.

Table 9.1 Keys Used to Adjust the Size of the Viewport

Key	Function
Left Arrow	Moves the current corner to the left
Right Arrow	Moves the current corner to the right

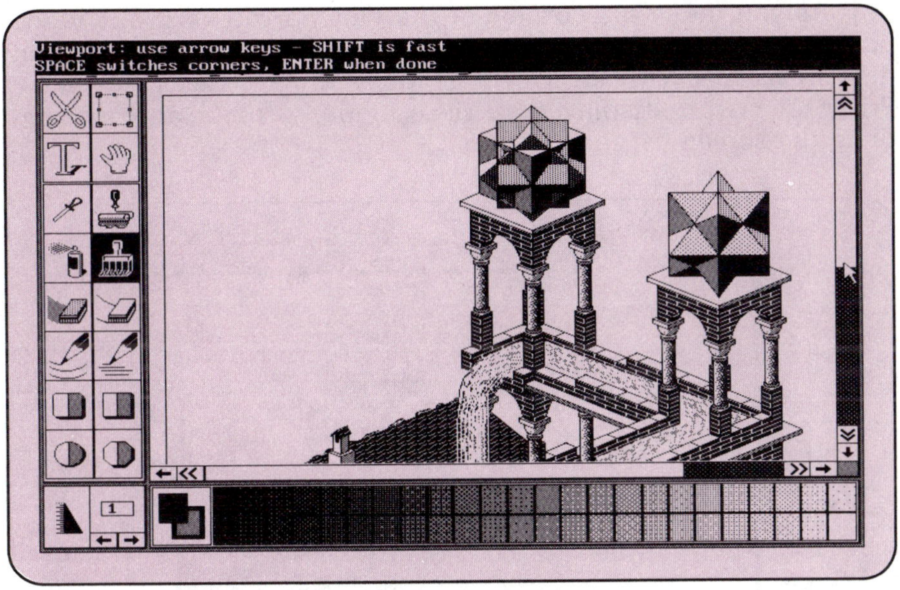

Figure 9.4 Selecting the Viewport option displays instructions in the caption bar.

Key	Function
Up Arrow	Moves the current corner upward
Down Arrow	Moves the current corner downward
Home	Moves the current corner up and to the left
PageUp	Moves the current corner up and to the right
End	Moves the current corner down and to the left
PageDown	Moves the current corner down and to the right
Shift	This key in combination with any of the preceding keys moves the current corner more quickly
Spacebar	Toggles the current corner from the top, left corner to the bottom, right corner or vice versa
Enter	Accepts the current viewport
Escape	Cancels the Viewport option and redisplays the Frieze menu

As you move the corners of the viewport inward, the viewport becomes smaller, as shown in Figure 9.5. After you delimit the screen area with the viewport, press Enter. Then press Shift-PrintScreen to redisplay the Frieze menu so that you can complete the screen capture.

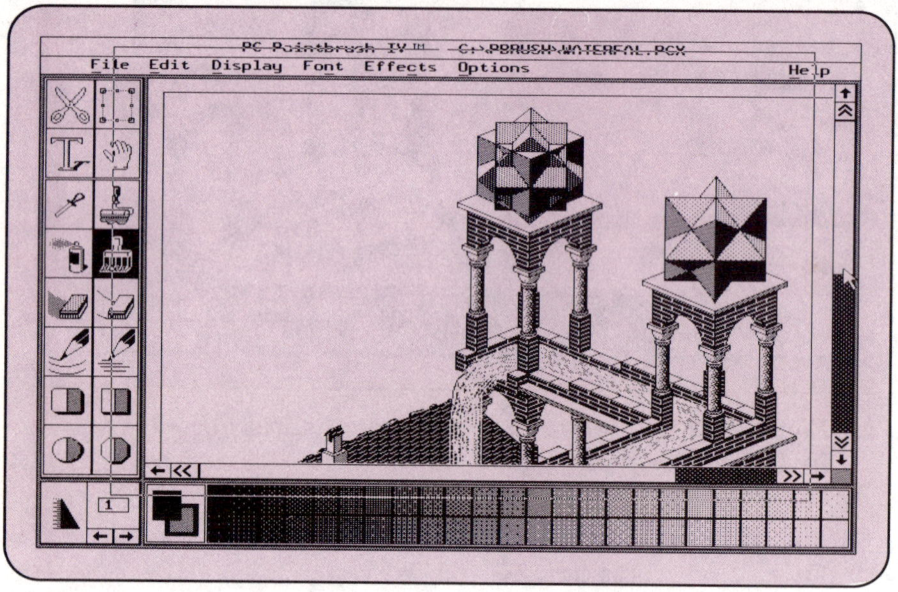

Figure 9.5 Adjusting the corners of the viewport.

If you do not select the Viewport option immediately before you select Save, the Frieze utility will take a picture of the area last specified with the Viewport option. If you have not used Viewport since loading Frieze, the utility will take a picture of the entire screen.

> **Tip:** Press Alt-D followed by the S key to hide everything but the current painting before you take a screen shot.

If you want to capture only the painting, you can hide the menu bar, toolbox, cursor, and other desktop elements by choosing the Show Screen... command from the Display menu or by double-clicking the Gadget Box icon in the toolbox. Then press

Shift-PrintScreen to proceed with the capture. Figure 9.6 shows the result of selecting the Show Screen command prior to pressing Shift-PrintScreen.

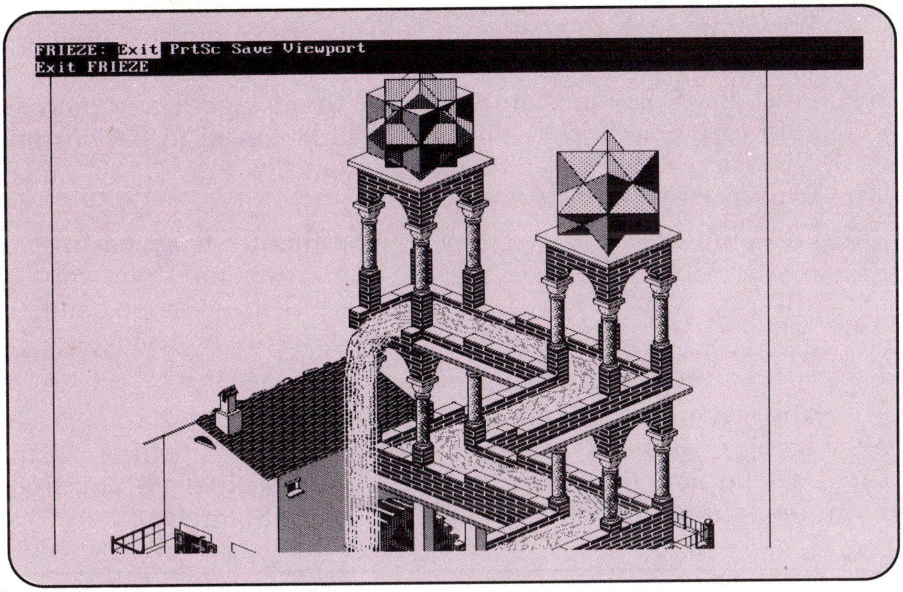

Figure 9.6 Capturing a painting in the full-screen display mode.

Capturing a Screen in PC Paintbrush

1. Type `paint` at the DOS prompt and press Enter.	Starts Paintbrush, which loads the Frieze utility automatically.
2. Open a painting.	
3. Position the cursor at the position desired.	Unless you first choose the Show Screen... command, Frieze includes the cursor in the screen shot.
4. Press Shift-PrintScreen.	The Frieze menu displays. The cursor locks and the mouse becomes inoperative.
5. Press the V key.	Selects the Viewport option. If you want to capture the entire screen, skip to step 8.

6. Use the Arrow keys and Spacebar to adjust opposite corners of the viewport and press Enter.	Arrow keys move the current corner, the Spacebar toggles the current corner.
7. Press Shift-PrintScreen.	The Frieze menu displays again.
8. Press the S key and enter a path (drive and/or directory) and a file name with a .PCX extension.	Without a path, the picture will be saved to the current directory.
9. Press Enter.	The picture is saved to disk. After the save, you can move the cursor and operate the mouse again. □

Any screen shot can be loaded into Paintbrush immediately after being captured with the Frieze utility. By opening a captured screen and shooting it again, you can achieve a painting-within-a-painting effect, as demonstrated in Figure 9.7.

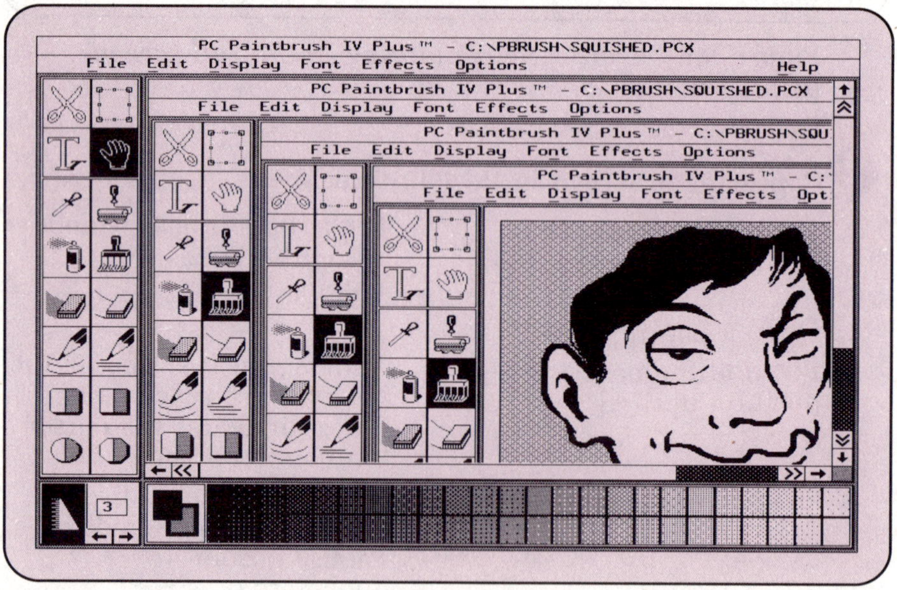

Figure 9.7 The result of too many screen shots in succession.

Using Frieze with a Program other than PC Paintbrush

To use Frieze with a program other than Paintbrush, you must load the Frieze program into memory using the Frieze command. The Frieze command file, named FRIEZE.COM, is located in your Paintbrush directory Pbrush, unless you specified another directory name during the installation procedure. To use the Frieze command, you type `frieze` at the DOS prompt, then enter values for seven different *parameters*, or variables, and press Enter. To see examples of the Frieze parameters, enter `type paint.bat` at the DOS prompt. This will display the contents of the PAINT.BAT file used to start Paintbrush. Three lines of text similar to the following text will appear on screen:


```
FRIEZE PSCRIPT S1 0000 ACNQ 640 480 4
pbrush m acnq 640 480 4
frieze
```

When you enter `paint` to start Paintbrush, your computer carries out the instructions in the PAINT.BAT file one line at a time. The first line instructs your computer to load the Frieze utility using the parameters listed, the second line starts Paintbrush itself, and the last line removes Frieze from memory when you quit Paintbrush.

Loading Frieze into Memory

To load Frieze into memory, you must enter values for each of the seven parameters following the Frieze command, as in the first line in the PAINT.BAT file. These parameters tell Frieze the model of printer you are using, the current printer port, if the current palette will be captured with the screen, the type of monitor you are using, the resolution of the monitor, and the number of colors. Your parameter values probably won't match ours in the PAINT.BAT file exactly since your version of Paintbrush is configured differently than ours.

The last four parameters are the most important. Together, they describe the *video mode*. You must configure Frieze to run in the same video mode as the software whose screen you want to capture. For example, the presentation program Autodesk Animator will run only when your monitor is configured to display 320 by 200 pixels and 256 colors; therefore, you must set Frieze to run in the same video mode. If, for example, you set Frieze to run in 16-color mode and then try to capture a screen in Animator, your computer will lock up.

Table 9.2 displays the actual entry you should make at the DOS prompt to run Frieze in the most popular video modes. Locate your video card, monitor resolution, and number of colors in the table, then type the corresponding Frieze command and parameters at the DOS prompt. In place of [prn], enter your printer as it appears when you display the contents of your PAINT.BAT file. In place of [port], enter `p1` for LPT1, `p2` for LPT2, `p3` for LPT3, `s1` for com1, or `s2` for com2. In our PAINT.BAT file, the [prn] value is `PSCRIPT` and the [port] value is `SI`.

Table 9.2 Parameters Used with the Frieze Command in Different Video Modes

Video Card	Resolution	Colors	DOS Prompt Entry
CGA	320 x 200	4	`frieze [prn] [port] 0000 atwo 320 200 1`
CGA	640 x 200	2	`frieze [prn] [port] 0000 aibm 640 200 1`
EGA	320 x 200	4	`frieze [prn] [port] 0000 atwo 640 200 2`
EGA	320 x 200	16	`frieze [prn] [port] 0004 aega 640 200 4`
EGA	640 x 200	2	`frieze [prn] [port] 0000 aega 640 200 1`
EGA	640 x 200	16	`frieze [prn] [port] 0004 aega 640 200 4`
EGA	640 x 350	2	`frieze [prn] [port] 0000 aega 640 350 1`
EGA	640 x 350	4	`frieze [prn] [port] 0000 aega 640 350 2`
EGA	640 x 350	8	`frieze [prn] [port] 0004 aega 640 350 3`
EGA	640 x 350	16	`frieze [prn] [port] 0004 aega 640 350 4`

Video Card	Resolution	Colors	DOS Prompt Entry
VGA	320 x 200	4	frieze [prn] [port] 0000 atwo 320 200 2
VGA	320 x 200	256	frieze [prn] [port] 0004 acn8 320 200 1
VGA	640 x 480	2	frieze [prn] [port] 0000 acn1 640 480 1
VGA	640 x 480	4	frieze [prn] [port] 0000 acnq 640 480 2
VGA	640 x 480	8	frieze [prn] [port] 0004 acnq 640 480 3
VGA	640 x 480	16	frieze [prn] [port] 0004 acnq 640 480 4
PCjr	320 x 200	4	frieze [prn] [port] 0000 atwo 320 200 5
PCjr	320 x 200	16	frieze [prn] [port] 0004 afor 320 200 1
PCjr	640 x 200	2	frieze [prn] [port] 0000 aibm 640 200 2

▶ **Note:** Frieze cannot capture a screen in super VGA mode: 640 by 480 pixels and 256 colors, 800 by 600 pixels and 16 colors, or higher.

If none of the Frieze command parameters in Table 9.2 work with your software, try configuring Paintbrush to a display mode matching that of the software using the PbSetup program. Then redisplay the contents of the PAINT.BAT file and type the first line of the file exactly as it now appears. For example, to configure Paintbrush to run in the same display mode as Autodesk Animator, you might change your monitor configuration to the IBM PS/2 VGA/MCGA option offered by the PbSetup program. After you quit PbSetup, display PAINT.BAT, then enter the new first line at the DOS prompt.

If you want to capture the palette along with the screen to ensure correct color matching, use 0004 rather than 0000 for the third Frieze parameter. Notice that all the video modes in Table 9.2 using 4 or more colors use 0004 for the third parameter.

Starting the Program that Will Use Frieze

After you load Frieze into memory, start the program whose screens you want to capture. Then press Shift-PrintScreen. If the Frieze menu appears at the top of the screen, Frieze is configured correctly. If your computer locks up (no longer responds to keyboard or mouse instructions) or if the options in the Frieze menu do not display correctly, you have configured Frieze for the wrong resolution or the wrong number of colors. You must quit the current program, remove Frieze from memory, and reload it using different parameters.

Note that Frieze cannot capture text screens. Therefore, if you are running a text-based program, such as a word processor, you must display your text in graphics mode in order to capture it. Figure 9.8, for example, shows a Microsoft Word screen being captured; the Word graphics mode is 640 by 480 pixels and 2 colors. Not all word processors can display text in graphics mode.

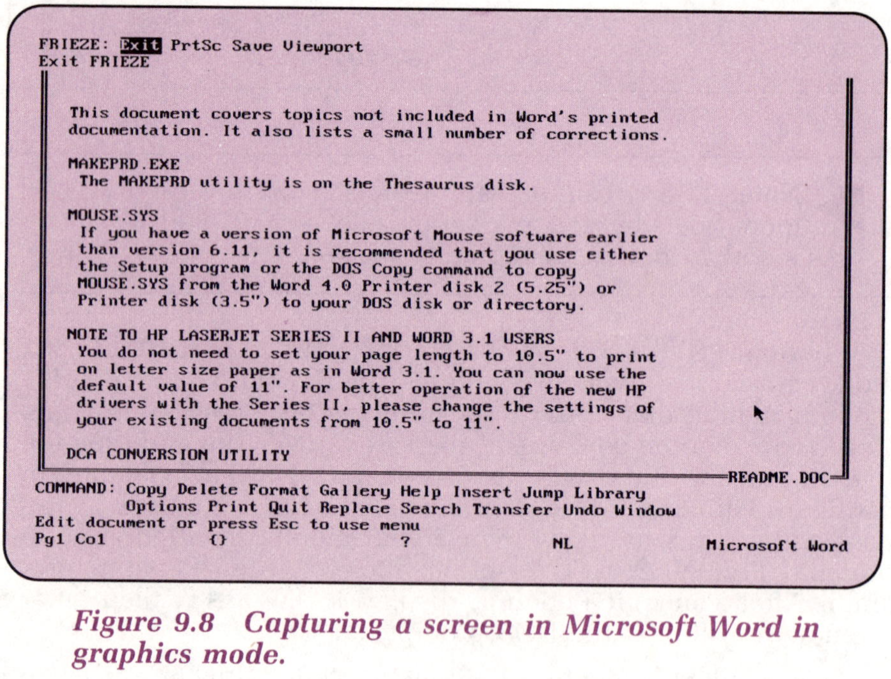

Figure 9.8 Capturing a screen in Microsoft Word in graphics mode.

Removing Frieze from Memory

After you have captured the screen pictures and quit the program, you should remove Frieze from memory to make the memory it used available for other programs. Otherwise, you may get out-of-memory errors when trying to run other programs. There are two ways to remove Frieze from memory. First, you can type `frieze` at the DOS prompt then press Enter. The message `Removing FRIEZE from memory at users request` will display on screen as Frieze is unloaded from memory. Alternatively, you can reboot your computer by pressing Control-Alt-Delete. Rebooting or turning off your computer clears all information in memory, including the Frieze utility.

The following Quick Steps summarize the procedure for using Frieze with a program other than Paintbrush.

Q Using Frieze with a Program other than PC Paintbrush

1. At the DOS prompt in the Pbrush directory, run the PbSetup program, select the correct monitor, then quit PbSetup.	Configures Paintbrush to match the video mode of the program whose screens you want to capture.
2. Type `type paint.bat` and press Enter.	The contents of the PAINT.BAT file display.
3. Type the Frieze command line as it appears in the first line of PAINT.BAT and press Enter.	A message displays telling you that the Frieze utility has been loaded.
4. Start the program whose screens you want to capture. If necessary, change directories first.	
5. Press Shift-PrintScreen, then proceed with screen capture.	Displays Frieze menu, then saves screen captures to file specified.
6. Quit the program whose screen you just captured.	
7. In Pbrush directory, type `frieze` and press Enter.	Removes Frieze from memory.

Frieze Batch Files

If you intend to use Frieze with a specific program frequently, you should create a batch file similar to PAINT.BAT that will complete all three steps for you automatically: load Frieze, start the other program, and remove Frieze when the program quits. This will save you time and effort in the long run because you won't have to look up Frieze parameters or experiment with them over and over again.

The following Quick Steps describe how to create a Frieze batch file in the DOS directory. The DOS directory is generally the best location for batch files because it is almost always included in the PATH statement in the AUTOEXEC.BAT file. You will then be able to run the Frieze batch file from any directory. Use a short name for the batch file so that you have fewer keystrokes to type when you start the batch file.

Q Creating a Frieze Batch File

1. Type `cd\dos` and press Enter. — Makes the DOS directory the current directory.
2. Type `edlin [name].bat` and press Enter. In place of [name], type the name you want to use for this batch file. — Edlin, the DOS line editor, creates a new file, and an asterisk (*) prompt appears.
3. Type `1i` and press Enter. — Allows you to insert text into the batch file starting at line 1. The prompt displays as `1:*`.
4. Type `cd\pbrush` and press Enter. — This line instructs DOS to change to the Pbrush directory, which contains the Frieze utility. The line editor advances to the next line.
5. Type `frieze` followed by the correct parameters for the program's video mode and press Enter. — This line loads Frieze into memory. The line editor advances to the next line.

6. Type a line to change to the directory containing the program and press Enter. Type a second line to start the program and press Enter.	For example, enter `cd\word` and `word`. The line editor advances two lines.
7. Type `cd\pbrush` and press Enter; then type `frieze` and press Enter.	These lines instruct DOS to change to the Pbrush directory and remove Frieze from memory. The line editor advances two lines.
8. Press Control-C.	The asterisk prompt reappears without a line number preceding it.
9. Type `e` and press Enter.	The line editor saves your file to disk under the name specified and returns you to the DOS prompt. ☐

Figure 9.9 shows the process of creating a batch file to capture screens in Microsoft Word. After we created the batch file, named WD.BAT, we listed it (by typing `l` and pressing Enter from within the line editor) to check for errors.

Using the Frieze Batch File

To verify that your new batch file works, type the name of the batch file (minus the .BAT extension) at the DOS prompt and press Enter. If the batch file operates correctly, Frieze will load into memory, then your program will start automatically. You can then capture screen pictures following the instructions in the *Capturing a Screen in PC Paintbrush* Quick Steps section.

When you quit the program, Frieze will be removed from memory. You can then start Paintbrush and edit the picture. The video mode used by Paintbrush does *not* have to be the same mode Frieze used to take the picture. If you use a different number of colors, however, Paintbrush will have to convert the file during the opening operation, as discussed in the *Converting Paintings* section of Chapter 2. Figure 9.10 shows a picture captured in Autodesk Animator. Although it was captured in a

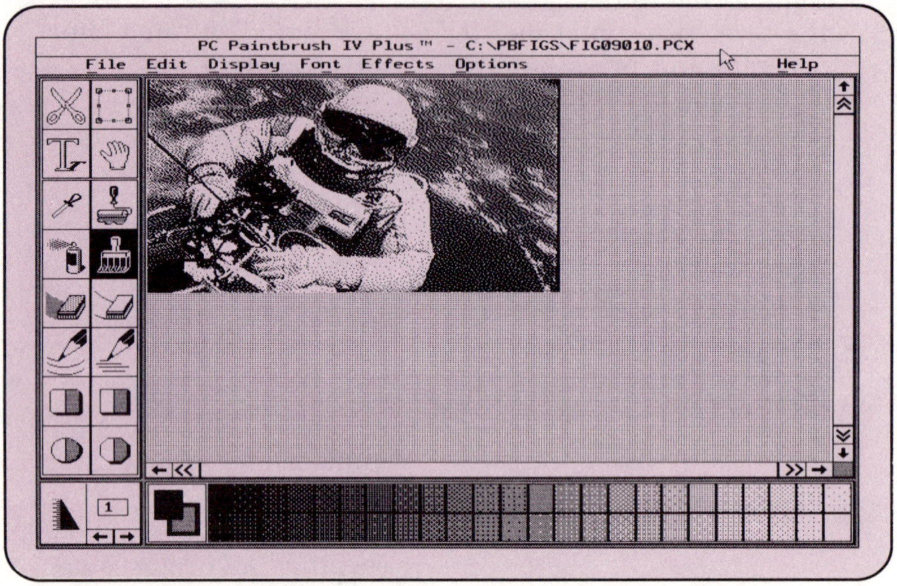

Figure 9.9 Using Edlin, the DOS line editor, to create a batch file.

video mode of 320 by 200 pixels and 256 colors, we opened it in Paintbrush in a video mode of 640 by 480 pixels and 2 colors by using the conversion options.

Summary

In this chapter, you've learned:

- The Frieze utility can be used to capture screens inside Paintbrush or in almost any other program.
- By capturing screens, Frieze provides you with the means to convert an image from a foreign format to the Paintbrush PCX format.
- If you configure Paintbrush to run without a selected printer, you will save memory but you will not be able to use Frieze inside Paintbrush.
- Pressing Shift-PrintScreen displays the Frieze menu.

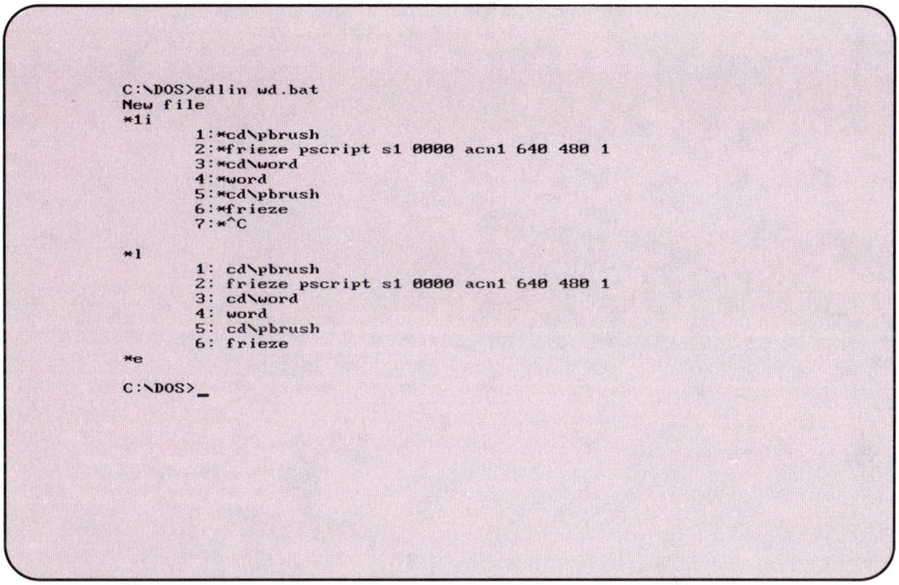

Figure 9.10 An image captured in Autodesk Animator and converted to a different video mode.

- The Frieze Viewport option allows you to specify the portion of the screen that you want to capture. You adjust the size of the viewport using the keys shown in Table 9.1.
- To save a captured screen to disk, select the Save option, then enter a path and file name.
- Table 9.2 lists the most popular video modes and their corresponding Frieze command parameters. You enter the Frieze command and correct parameters at the DOS prompt to load the Frieze utility into memory.
- You can remove the Frieze utility from memory by entering `frieze` at the DOS prompt.
- If you use Frieze regularly with a specific program other than Paintbrush, create a batch file to load Frieze, start the program, and remove Frieze when the program quits.

Appendix A

Monitors and Printers Requiring Aspect Ratio Adjustments

This appendix lists the monitors and printers which do not have an aspect ratio of 1.000 and which therefore may require you to adjust the aspect ratio prior to printing. Monitors and printers are listed separately. Refer to the *Aspect Ratio* section in Chapter 8 for instructions on how to use the Set Aspect... command to adjust the current aspect ratio.

Monitors Requiring Aspect Ratio Adjustments

If you use one of the monitor brands listed but at a different resolution—such as 640 x 480, 800 x 600, or 1024 x 768—the monitor's aspect ratio will be 1.000. You therefore do not need to adjust the aspect ratio for the monitor.

Monitor Model	Resolution	Aspect Ratio
AT&T Display Enhancement Board	640 x 400	1.200
ATI EGA Wonder800+	752 x 410	1.376
ATI EGA Wonder800+	800 x 560	1.071
ATI VIP	800 x 560	1.071
ATI VGA Wonder	640 x 400	1.200
COMPAQ Standard	640 x 200	2.400
Everex Viewpoint VGA	640 x 400	1.200
Everex Viewpoint VGA	512 x 480	0.800
Genoa SuperEGA HiRes+	640 x 528	0.909
Genoa SuperEGA HiRes+	752 x 410	1.376
Genoa SuperEGA HiRes+	912 x 480	1.425
Genoa SuperVGA	720 x 512	1.055
Genoa SuperVGA	640 x 350	1.371
Hercules Incolor	720 x 348	1.552
Hercules Graphics Card	720 x 348	1.552
IBM CGA	320 x 200	1.200
IBM CGA	640 x 200	2.400
IBM EGA	640 x 200	2.400
IBM EGA	640 x 350	1.371
IBM PCjr	320 x 200	1.200
IBM PCjr	640 x 200	2.400
IBM PS/2 VGA/MCGA	320 x 200	1.200
IBM PS/2 VGA/MCGA	640 x 200	2.400
Matrox VGO-AT	720 x 480	1.125
Number Nine Pro 1280	1280 x 1024	0.938
Number Nine Revolution	512 x 480	0.800
Olivetti M24 Standard	640 x 400	1.200
Paradise VGA 16-bit Plus	640 x 400	1.200
Paradise VGA Professional	640 x 400	1.200
Quadram Quadcolor I	640 x 200	2.400
Quadram Quadcolor I	320 x 200	1.200
Quadram Quadcolor II	640 x 200	2.400

Monitor Model	Resolution	Aspect Ratio
Quadram QuadVGA Spectra	640 x 350	1.371
Sigma Color 400	640 x 200	2.400
Sigma Color 400	320 x 200	1.200
Sigma EGA 480	752 x 420	1.343
Sigma L-View	1664 x 1200	1.040
Sigma L-View	1024 x 780	0.985
Sigma VGA/H	800 x 560	1.071
STB Grahix Plus II	640 x 200	2.400
STB MultiRes	752 x 410	1.376
STB MultiRes II	704 x 519	1.017
STB SuperRes 400	640 x 400	1.200
STB SuperRes 400	320 x 200	1.200
Tandy 1000	320 x 200	1.200
Tandy 1000	640 x 200	2.400
Tandy 1200	320 x 200	1.200
Tandy 1200	640 x 200	2.400
Tandy 1200	640 x 400	1.200
Tandy 3000	320 x 200	1.200
Tandy 3000	640 x 200	2.400
Tandy 3000	640 x 400	1.200
Tecmar Graphics Master	640 x 200	2.400
Tecmar Graphics Master	640 x 400	1.200
Tecmar Graphics Master	720 x 200	2.700
Tecmar Graphics Master	720 x 352	1.534
Tecmar Graphics Master	720 x 400	1.35
Tecmar Graphics Master	720 x 704	0.767
Tecmar VGA/AD	640 x 350	1.371
Tecmar VGA/AD	640 x 400	1.200
Tecmar VGA/AD	800 x 440	1.364
Toshiba T3100	640 x 400	1.200
Tseng Labs Monochrome	720 x 348	1.552
Venetek PS2000	1280 x 1024	0.938

Continued

Monitor Model	Resolution	Aspect Ratio
Video Seven FastWrite	752 x 410	1.376
Video Seven FastWrite	640 x 400	1.200
Video Seven FastWrite	640 x 488	0.984
Video Seven Vega Deluxe	752 x 410	1.376
Video Seven V-RAM VGA	640 x 400	1.200
Video Seven V-RAM VGA	756 x 410	1.383
Wyse 700 Display	1280 x 800	1.200
Wyse 700 Display	640 x 800	0.600
Wyse 700 Display	640 x 400	1.200
Xerox 6065 HighRes	640 x 400	1.200
Xerox 6065 with EGC	640 x 400	1.200

Printers Requiring Aspect Ratio Adjustments

Printer Model	Resolution per Inch	Aspect Ratio
Brother	120 x 144	0.833
Calcomp ColorMaster	200 x 197	1.015
Canon BJ-80	120 x 144	0.833
Canon BJ-80	240 x 144	1.667
Citizen 120D	120 x 144	0.833
Diconix C150 Inkjet	80 x 48	1.667
Diconix C150 Inkjet	160 x 96	1.667
Diconix 300X Inkjet	60 x 36	1.667
Diconix 300X Inkjet	120 x 72	1.667
Epson FX	240 x 144	1.667
Epson JX	120 x 144	0.833
Epson LX	120 x 144	0.833
Epson MX	120 x 144	0.833

Printer Model	Resolution per Inch	Aspect Ratio
Epson RX	120 x 144	0.833
Gemini X	120 x 144	0.833
Hewlett Packard Thinkjet	96 x 48	2.000
Hewlett Packard Thinkjet	192 x 96	2.000
IBM Color Impact	144 x 168	0.857
IBM Color Inkjet	100 x 96	1.042
IBM Graphics Printer	120 x 144	0.833
IBM Graphics Printer	240 x 144	1.667
IBM ProPrinter	120 x 144	0.833
IBM ProPrinter X	180 x 195	0.923
IDS Prism	84 x 112	0.750
LaserMaster DDPI	300 x 150	2.000
LaserMaster DDPI	600 x 300	2.000
Okidata 84, Series B	103 x 154	0.669
Okidata 92	72 x 144	0.500
Okidata 93	72 x 144	0.500
Okidata 192	120 x 144	0.833
Okidata 193	120 x 144	0.833
Okidata 292	120 x 72	0.833
Okidata 293	120 x 72	0.833
Okimate 20	72 x 144	0.500
Panasonic KX-P1080	120 x 144	0.833
Panasonic KX-P1080	240 x 144	1.667
Panasonic KX-P1090	120 x 144	0.833
Panasonic KX-P1090	240 x 144	1.667
Panasonic KX-P1592	120 x 144	0.833
Panasonic KX-P1592	240 x 144	1.667
Panasonic KX-P1595	240 x 144	1.667
Tandy DMP	120 x 144	0.833

Index

D

G

H

I

Q

R

U

V

W

X-Y-Z

Quick Guide to Quick Steps

Look for this symbol to find your quick guide to these common procedures.

Continues

Reader Feedback Card

Thank you for purchasing this book from Howard W. Sams & Company's FIRST BOOK series. Our intent with this series is to bring you timely, authoritative information that you can reference quickly and easily. You can help us by taking a minute to complete and return this card. We appreciate your comments and will use the information to better serve your needs.

1. Where did you purchase this book?

- ☐ Chain bookstore (Walden, B. Dalton)
- ☐ Independent bookstore
- ☐ Computer/Software store
- ☐ Other ______________________________
- ☐ Direct mail
- ☐ Book club
- ☐ School bookstore

2. Why did you choose this book? (Check as many as apply.)

- ☐ Price
- ☐ Author's reputation
- ☐ Quick and easy treatment of subject
- ☐ Appearance of book
- ☐ Howard W. Sam's reputation
- ☐ Only book available on subject

3. How do you use this book? (Check as many as apply.)

- ☐ As a supplement to the product manual
- ☐ In place of the product manual
- ☐ For self-instruction
- ☐ As a reference
- ☐ At home
- ☐ At work

4. Please rate this book in the categories below. G = Good; N = Needs improvement; U = Category is unimportant.

- ☐ Price
- ☐ Amount of information
- ☐ Examples
- ☐ Inside cover reference
- ☐ Table of contents
- ☐ Tips and cautions
- ☐ Length of book
- ☐ How can we improve this book? ______________________________
- ☐ Appearance
- ☐ Accuracy
- ☐ Quick Steps
- ☐ Second color
- ☐ Index
- ☐ Illustrations

5. How many computer books do you normally buy in a year?

- ☐ 1–5 ☐ 5–10 ☐ More than 10
- ☐ I rarely purchase more than one book on a subject.
- ☐ I may purchase a beginning and an advanced book on the same subject.
- ☐ I may purchase several books on particular subjects.
  (such as ______________________________)

6. Have you purchased other Howard W. Sams or Hayden books in the past year? ____
   If yes, how many? ______________________________

7. Would you purchase another book in the FIRST BOOK series? ______________

8. What are your primary areas of interest in business software?
- ☐ Word processing (particularly ______________)
- ☐ Spreadsheet (particularly ______________)
- ☐ Database (particularly ______________)
- ☐ Graphics (particularly ______________)
- ☐ Personal finance/accounting (particularly ______________)
- ☐ Other (please specify ______________)

Other comments on this book or the Howard W. Sams book line: ______________

____

Name ______________
Company ______________
Address ______________
City ______________ State ______________ Zip ______________
Daytime telephone number ______________
Title of this book ______________

Fold here

NO POSTAGE NECESSARY IF MAILED IN THE UNITED STATES

BUSINESS REPLY MAIL
FIRST CLASS PERMIT NO. 336 CARMEL, IN

POSTAGE WILL BE PAID BY ADDRESSEE

SAMS
11711 N. College Ave.
Suite 140
Carmel, IN 46032–9839